D1256615

SEESAW:
A DUAL BIOGRAPHY OF
ANNE BANCROFT AND MEL BROOKS

SEESAW:
A DUAL BIOGRAPHY OF
ANNE BANCROFT
AND
MEL BROOKS

William Holtzman

DOUBLEDAY & COMPANY, INC.
GARDEN CITY, NEW YORK
1979

Library of Congress Cataloging in Publication Data

Holtzman, Will.
    Seesaw, a dual biography of Anne Bancroft and Mel
Brooks.

    Includes index.
    1. Brooks, Mel. 2. Bancroft, Anne, 1931-
3. Actors—United States—Biography. 4. Moving-
picture producers and directors—United States—
Biography. I. Title.
        PN2287.B695H6   791'.092'2 [B]
            ISBN: 0-385-13076-7
Library of Congress Catalog Card Number 78-22616

Copyright © 1979 by William Holtzman
ALL RIGHTS RESERVED
PRINTED IN THE UNITED STATES OF AMERICA

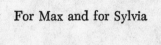

For Max and for Sylvia

SEESAW:
A DUAL BIOGRAPHY OF
ANNE BANCROFT AND MEL BROOKS

New York City, 1961

The first week of February brought a cold snap. The Manhattan sky was blue and cloudless, the air unsmudged by smog. Coffee sales were up at Schrafft's and Chock Full O'Nuts. Midtown manhole covers sighed steady jets of steam.

At four o'clock on February 5, two men in overcoats turned the corner at Sixth Avenue and Fifty-fourth Street, entered the lobby of the Ziegfeld, and stepped into the darkened theatre just as rehearsal was drawing to a close. Onstage a woman stood and sang the final few bars of "Married I Can Always Get." Her voice was full and sure, her white gown favored her dark hair and eyes.

The last chord had scarcely sounded when one of the latecomers, the shorter man, jumped to his feet for an ovation, shouting bravos and huzzas as he hurried down the half-lit aisle. The woman no sooner conjured a vision that was equal parts Clark Gable and Robert Taylor than the actual admirer climbed the stage, stepped into the light, and said, "Hey, Anne Bancroft, I'm Mel Brooks."

1

Henry Greenberg stepped out of his Prospect Place walk-up, squinted into the mid-morning sun, and poked down the block for a pack of Camels. It was a June day like any other in Brooklyn's Brownsville section, loud, crowded, muggy. Greenberg came to Saratoga Avenue, crossed, and noticed Cecil and Milton Welsh standing at the opposite corner. *Shvartzer!* By 1926, Brownsville, slung in a dingy swerve of the elevated Long Island Rail Road tracks, had begun a grudging integration between poor Jews and even poorer blacks.

Greenberg and the Welshes had words. When they ran short of insults they fought, tumbling into the street and clotting the dense Monday traffic. Brownsville was a ghetto like most. Violence was contagious and cathartic, almost recreational, and a private scuffle was never far from a public brawl. That day, beat cop Conrad Pope rounded the corner onto Prospect Place just in time to see hell break loose. Pope waded into the sprawling free-for-all and was quickly the worse by a bruised chin and a gnawed ankle. His fill of valor, Pope called the station house for reserves.

Whistles, shouts, and sirens mingled and washed over the tenement at 515 Powell Street, a raucous chorus behind Kitty Ka-

minsky's first signs of labor. The commotion had not long subsided when Kitty was moved to the kitchen of the Kaminsky flat
where within hours she gave birth to a son. Already there was
Irving, the oldest, then Lenny and Bernie. Now Melvin, born
June 28, on the far edge of a near-riot.

That was the summer the Brooklyn Robins became the
Dodgers. Four bits bought a bleacher seat at Ebbets Field and a
lively afternoon with Babe Herman, Burleigh Grimes ("Boily" in
local parlance), Rabbit Maranville, and assorted motleys known
affectionately as "Dem Bums." For those who preferred their
divertissement indoors and silent, fifteen cents meant The Metro-
politan moviehouse where Pola Negri's *Good and Naughty*
vamped its way through shopworn Hollywood exotica. A larger
outlay of time and money brought a jostling ride on the IRT and
a balcony seat on Broadway where the choices included the prim
Helen Hayes in J. M. Barrie's *What Every Woman Knows*, the
bawdy Mae West in *Sex*, and the perennial *Abie's Irish Rose*.

On balance, Brownsville was its own best show. The open-air
pushcart market on Belmont Avenue was a free-fire zone of price
haggling and incidental gossip, a daily surge of Yiddish. Hud-
dled conversations over on Pitkin Avenue were as likely to
berate the Dodgers' dismal record as to celebrate the tenth anniversary of Margaret Sanger's prototypal birth control clinic down
on Amboy Street. Sundays, socialist-tinged debates flared among
tradesmen congregating at the corner of Stone and Pitkin, and
tamer *landsmanschaften* meetings gathered kindred townsmen of
the Old World. Saturdays, the shops were closed, the pushcarts
parked, and Yiddish replaced with Hebrew in over seventy or-
thodox synagogues. If Brownsville had its ethnic diversity—
Moors, Italians, Syrians, Blacks—it was unmistakably Jewish in
character and custom. But then Brooklyn Jewishness was its own
diversity, an odd melding of Old World tradition and New
World ethos, a kind of cultural seesaw with the family as ful-
crum.

The Kaminsky household was the neighborhood in miniature.
Kitty Kaminsky, born Kate Brookman in Kiev, was a warm,
good-natured woman and an indefatigable wife and mother who
had a Circean way with a matzoh ball. Maximilian Kaminsky

emigrated from Danzig as a boy, met and married Kitty in Brooklyn, and earned a living as a process server.

Tenement life was by force social and shared, privacy was an abstraction that lived in town and uptown. The Powell Street flat was regularly alive with friends and relatives. Kitty would cook, Max would sing, Grandma would tell jokes with Yiddish puns and punch lines, and Uncle Joe would dispense cryptic advice: "Don't buy a cardboard belt" . . . "Never eat chocolate after chicken" . . . "Marry a fat girl, don't marry a face." Irving, Lenny, and Bernie would shuttle in and out. And little blue-eyed Melvin would be adored endlessly by neighbors, by family, above all by Kitty. It was a poor but happy Brooklyn-Jewish family, and Melvin was its centerpiece.

In 1928, amid the frenzied optimism of the Jazz Age, the Kaminsky household was shaken when Max fell ill with what was later diagnosed as tuberculosis of the kidney. There was no known cure and his condition rapidly deteriorated. By the New Year it was touch and go, and on the numbingly cold morning of January 14, 1929, Max Kaminsky died. The death certificate put his age at thirty-four.

Kitty buried her husband, then busied herself sustaining the living. A saintly Aunt Sadie helped the family through the grim times until Kitty found work in Brooklyn's garment district. Now the lone breadwinner, the four-foot-eleven-inch mother of four worked a ten-hour day and trundled home piecework at night, sewing bathing-suit sashes by lamplight often till dawn. At the age of twelve, Irving found part-time work, and was joined in order by Lenny and Bernie, bringing the combined family income to roughly thirty-five dollars a week.

The Kaminskys muddled through misfortune, and just as the gray drudgery of the sweatshops was Kitty's accepted fate, little Melvin became her one luxury. Where work was wretched and tedious, he was all innocence and wonder. With Max's death, this was not just her youngest son, this was her last. The nurturance and affection that is the province of any child was Melvin's in full. With the other sons forced into premature adulthood, it was almost as if Melvin had become an only child.

The Kaminskys were nothing if not resilient. They weathered

severity and change, and claimed a hard-won stability. The flat slowly came back to life, and Uncle Joe resumed his pose as family oracle, often as not with his longstanding fiscal watchword: never invest money, bank it! Max wasn't one year in the grave when the bottom dropped out of the stock market, taking with it the Brownsville branch of the Bank of the United States as well as a good part of the community. The Depression probably took the Kaminskys less by surprise than most. They had already withstood privation and understood that hardship did not arrive by headline, it was a simple fact of life. Besides, those who had less to begin with had less to lose with the crash. Throughout, Kitty, possessed of a great sense of pride and dignity, would sooner have perished than have gone on relief.

By the early 1930s the entire family was in the employ of the Rosenthal and Slotnick knitting mills, save Melvin, who was fast preparing his debut on the street. Without the watchful supervision of a full-time mother or the distraction of his own job, Melvin was a prime candidate for Brooklyn's version of the great outdoors. On corners teeming with Mannies, Moishies, and Milties, Sollies, Shorties, and Ziggies, Speeds, Ducks, and Chicks, there soon appeared "Kaminsky."

Street-corner society is a breeding ground for the selective sentimental memory. The nostalgic over-the-shoulder glance suspends the cruelty, vandalism, and chronic boredom in a fond haze of camaraderie, style, and factual pranks that ferment their own fiction with the years. Melvin's initiation came at a tender age and was certified early when he made his mark as the 1932 ring-a-levio (a modified hide-and-seek *cum* Bastille) champion of Atlantic Avenue. That may well have been the peak of his prowess on the curbside sports circuit. Melvin had no particular gift for punchball, a kind of batless baseball. Nor did he advance much past the fundamentals of stickball, another bastardization of baseball calling for a broom handle and hard rubber ball manufactured by the Spalding company and named for reasons yet arcane a "Spaldeen." Bernie was a better pitcher, Lenny a better catcher. Irving was a worker.

Melvin was a talker (he'd begun at sixteen months) and, failing that, a runner. Neighborhoods were ethnically aligned and fiercely territorial. The price of incursion was a bloody nose or a black eye—a good thrashing might cost a favorite tooth—but only if the intruder were caught. Against superior size or numbers, running was indispensable, it was shrewd, even epic. Once Melvin accidentally hopped off the Nostrand Avenue trolley perilously deep in an Irish stronghold. One quick look around, one overheard taunt ("Hello, Yussell!") and he was off like a shot, the Brownsville Flash. Retreat rarely implied a failure of nerve, much the contrary, since a skillfully overblown retelling could even win a measure of glory. Running and talking served a common end, survival with style.

Melvin's patter better served him on the home turf where a fast mouth earned much the same deference as a good right. Melvin was not bookish but he read more than his buddies and kept his mind limber and his tongue primed. While he acquired a certain flair for the insult, mimicry was his early forte, a talent he discovered one summer at the Sussex Camp for Underprivileged Jewish Children and smuggled back to the neighborhood to the delight of his friends and the dismay of his teachers at P.S. 19.

Irving, Lenny, and Bernie were the family scholars and despite precious hours spent at the mills, each was college bound. But for their baby brother, school was a pastime, hanging out was a life science. None was better at it than Melvin, who chummed with the older boys and narrowed the gap in age and height by sheer drive and verbal derring-do. He became a fixture at Feingold's Candy Store and a dedicated knight-errant with Georgie Mandel, Speed Vogel, and Izzie Sugarman in search of the better egg cream. The balance of street time fell to girl watching, caterwauling, and corner *shtick*, which was a kind of rudimentary stand-up comedy, an unruly verbal slapstick.

At shtick, Melvin was the maven. His style was essentially exaggeration, whether in topic or tone, pantomimed burlesque or plain cartoon noises. Images seemed to bounce around in his imagination like reflections in a carnival house of mirrors. Garbled perspective was the key, the rest was just caption. And in city life, where scale and proportion were the enemies, hyperbole and mockery made up the heavy artillery. For Melvin, a head shorter than many of his friends, humor was power.

What passed on the street was taboo at the Kaminsky flat. The gentlest barb or mildest expletive brought a firm swat from Irving, now titular head of the family. Either unwilling or unable to contain a rising comic energy, Melvin merely saw to it that his homeside clowning wore a genial mask. He learned to blunt the cutting edge of his humor with an effortless winsomeness. He was a charmer, an *enfant terrible* with an uncanny personal magnetism. Among family as among friends, entertaining offered a snug role that was well in keeping with Kitty's optimism, her "joy of living."

Melvin was not without his personal Sabbath, the one day of the week in which the entertainer was content to be entertained —Saturdays at the Marcy Theatre. Given the demands of work in a larger gentile world, the Jewish Sabbath gradually secularized and for many first-generation Americans, the daylong ritual of *shul* was supplanted by the Saturday matinee. Melvin was no stranger to movies. Irving had done a fair share of moviegoing with his kid brother faithfully in tow. Melvin was only six when he saw Hitchcock's *The Lodger*, eight when he saw *Frankenstein*. But movies with Irving seemed somehow fettered, movies alone meant freedom.

The doors of the Marcy opened at ten in the morning and Melvin was there without fail, eleven cents admission in one hand, a ration of Oh Henry! bars in the other. For working parents, the matinee was a tireless babysitter. The children would wreak their havoc, sprinting up and down the aisles, raining debris on the forward rows, but that was the management's headache. This was arguably the first generation of American youth weaned wholly on serials, cartoons, newsreels, and the stock generic movie types: chalky vampires, nobly stammering cowboys, hard-boiled gangsters. More than once, Kitty Kaminsky made her way through a darkened, deserted theatre to fetch a blissfully slumbering Melvin.

By street degrees Melvin had long since worked his way up from the rank and file, but that did not preclude a more traditional ceremony of manhood. With all the rote Hebrew necessary to recite, Melvin was bar-mitzvahed in 1939. Shortly after, the Kaminsky family took up residence at Brighton Beach bordering Brooklyn's Coney Island. Ordinarily if anything could take the sting out of moving for a young adolescent boy, it might have been to deposit him at the back door of the world's most famous amusement park. But 1939 found New York hosting the World's Fair and the fairgrounds—which easily dwarfed the best Coney Island had to offer—were a full borough away in Queens on the site of the old Corona Dump. There was, at least, some solace in the silent movies shown for free in the lunchrooms along the Coney Island boardwalk.

Brighton Beach might have seemed an unkind exile but then all a seasoned city kid really needed was a street corner and willing company. The new neighborhood had that and more. The Kaminskys by chance had settled only a few doors away from the Rich family (formerly Vaudeville's "Wilson and Rich") whose son Bernard (better known as Buddy) had just gone to work playing drums for Artie Shaw's big band following a successful tour with Bunny Berrigan. Here within shouting distance was a bona fide member of show business. For a veteran of streetside burlesque, it was an opportunity that couldn't go unexplored. Accompanied by a new friend, Billy, Melvin finagled informal drum lessons from Buddy, and the would-be protégés became just bad enough to fantasize their own plunge into the entertainment world. After all, to the uninitiated drumming was just enthusiasm in four-four time, the perfect place to hide an enthusiastic but untrained musician (the bandstand's answer to sandlot's right fielder). With luck, drumming might be just the foot in the door of show business Melvin was then looking for.

Rim shot. That was the way the drummer helped rehabilitate a hobbled joke at the Catskill Mountains resorts that made up the borscht belt. After a set in the evening show the band would take five and the drummer stay behind as some brash, overbearing comic took the stage, thanked the bandleader, and then dusted off the inevitable museum piece: "Good evening ladies and gentlemen, I just flew in from Chicago and, boy, are my arms tired." The drummer would wind up and rap the rim of his snare with the shaft of his drumstick—rim shot, bingo! The audience laughs by conditioned response, a gag is resurrected.

In 1940, at age fourteen, Melvin took to the mountains, though not as a drummer. For room, board, and eight dollars a week, Melvin played menial, which was not without certain rewards. Resort owners were legendary for what might politely be referred to as thrift. They were never averse to maximizing the sundry talents of their staff, and in the Catskills' formative years this often translated to double duty as day-worker and entertainer. Even the lower-echelon summer boys were put to good use, and when Melvin wasn't toiling in the kitchen or the boathouse, he was, by turns, permitted to play pool *tummler*. Like most Yiddish expressions, tummler is more a category of experience than a concise definition. He might be a social director, organizing dances and bridge tournaments, supervising outings, matchmaking, and in general seeing to it that the most ill-spent member of the International Ladies' Garment Workers Union was treated royally. Then again, he might be an entertainment director, emceeing the nightly stage show or even producing original revues with an after-hours stock company. At this level, a good tummler was a treasure, a curious composite of cheerleader, cupid, and impresario. The pool tummler was on the other hand a buffoon, a good-time Charlie purveying bad impressions and heavy pratfalls, ribbing customers and begging laughs. A pool tummler was a busboy in baggy pants.

When Melvin wasn't ferrying dishes or renting boats, he was poolside, clowning. He even devised a new twist to a stock routine. Clad in an outsized derby and a billowing alpaca overcoat, Melvin would stagger up to the swimming pool, a battered suitcase in each hand. He would then climb the high board, clamber to the edge, announce: "Business is terrible, I can't go on," and jump. Pratfall overkill. The lifeguard would then fish him out, and, on good days, the sunbathers noticed.

Successive resort summers were less aquatic, certainly less amateurish. By the early forties the Catskills were in full flower. The borscht belt had matured from modest rural hostels and *kuchulanes* (austere roadside colonies, literally "cook yourself") into paradisiacal resorts that were virtually small, self-sustaining hamlets. The quality of entertainment kept stride and what was once the domain of small-time tummlers and part-time kitchen help soon fell to full-time professionals. Long after words had been read over Vaudeville, a new variety circuit materialized in the mountain retreats and acts that had once played split weeks for the Orpheum and Pantages were now padding shows at The Concord and Grossinger's. The Catskills became the most arable new ground for show business and none of this was wasted on a young man of imagination and ambition. Melvin's time in the mountains was a tuition-free crash course in the field of entertainment.

Part and parcel of this fascination, formal education continued to pale by comparison and did not improve with a change of address. After two years in Brighton Beach, Kitty moved to Williamsburg and took an apartment in a five-story brick building at 111 Lee Avenue, just north of Hooper. The larger community spread in a rough circle beneath the eastern span of the Williamsburg Bridge and was predominantly Jewish, though by sheer proximity to Manhattan, somewhat less insular than outlying Brooklyn sections.

Williamsburg had its street life, and Melvin kept to the corners which, in turn, raised serious questions as he approached high school age. A generalized secondary education was by no means automatic and Kitty, reasoning that three scholars out of four was already a blessing, considered enrolling her youngest son in a trade school. Melvin would become an aviation mechanic but only, as it turned out, over Irving's dead body. Kitty's plan was scrapped and Melvin entered Eastern District High School where he lived up to all expectations—Kaminsky was the funniest kid in the class. Beyond simple powers of "declamation," the reputation for hilarity was even taking on a patina of renown. There were schoolmates who knew him, many more who knew of him, and the burgeoning antic image was more choice than chance. While a number of the other kids took after-school jobs, Melvin was still hanging out, honing his comedy to a careful edge.

Summers belonged to the mountains, and each fall Melvin returned to Brooklyn with a better grasp of show business funda-

mentals and a renewed sense of mission. It was something of a
clockwork apprenticeship, slow but steady, that is, until the summer of '42. Earlier, Lenny Kaminsky had introduced his kid
brother to Don Appell, then an actor and later a producer, director, and playwright. Appell in turn referred the would-be showman to the social director of Ellenville's Butler Lodge. Comedy
was certainly Melvin's most identifiable talent, but he had yet to
undergo the baptism of fire of a paying audience, and the job he
eventually nailed down was not as a stand-up but as a drummer
and, needless to add, tummler. Drumming had its advantages.
Melvin sat in on the act of the Butler's house comic, peppering
the routine with rim shots, studying the verbal pitfalls and pratfalls. The act was vintage borscht belt—mother-in-law jokes,
second- and third-hand gags the audiences had long since committed to memory and accepted with liturgical compliance:

> Good evening ladies and germs. A bum stopped me on the
> street the other day and told me he hadn't had a bite in
> three weeks . . . so I bit him. (Rim shot, laugh)

> Talk about small. My hotel room's so small I had to go into
> the hall to change my mind. (Rim shot, laugh)

> Skinny? My girl friend's so skinny, we went to a restaurant
> the other day and the waiter said, "Check your umbrella?"
> (Rim shot, cymbal, big laugh)

> But seriously, folks, you've been a beautiful audience. I wish
> I could take you home with me. (Tag, off)

The one-liners would fall like summer rain, ceaseless and sweaty.
Gag, drum, giggle; gag, drum, guffaw; big finish, exit, encore,
exit—the awful prose of jaded jokes that Melvin would punctuate
like a dog-eared manuscript. The worse the material, the more
important the drumwork. Given nothing better, audiences will
laugh at sheer rhythm. Melvin was a quick study and soon knew
timing inside out. He knew how long to wait a laugh, when to
hit the silk, and how to work an audience for maximum result.
That is, he knew it theoretically, once removed from the spot-

light and the flop sweat. Inevitably, the student became understudy.

In a scenario that was as true as it was trite, the house comic took ill and the manager, Pincus Cantor, selected Melvin as alternate. Faced with the hard reality of going on solo, Melvin chose the path of least resistance and simply parroted the act he had punched up in the past. The audience played its part agreeably, laughing at the preordained junctures and applauding with friendly complacency. The audience was satisfied. The management was satisfied. Melvin was not. There was something repellent in the stale jokes. It was too automatic, too ritualistic. There was none of the do-or-die danger of the comedy Melvin had cut his teeth on. It was too safe, and safety had never been his style.

The regular comic was slow to recover and the erstwhile rhythm section was conscripted to go on again the next night. Melvin knew full well that he could never repeat the threadbare bits of the night before. He weighed the alternatives and in the interest of originality decided just to take the stage and wing it. By late afternoon he was working on a good case of stage fright when a series of screams suddenly coursed through the lodge. The staff traced the voice to a linen closet and found the chambermaid, Molly, who had accidentally locked herself in and had been pleading in Yiddish, *"Los mir arois!"* ("Let me out!"). The staff and guests had a good laugh, and the incident was soon forgotten by all but Melvin, for whom a locked closet might have seemed an enviable refuge.

Showtime arrived. The orchestra struck up entrance music, and Melvin walked on hoping his knees wouldn't buckle. He greeted the audience: "Good evening, ladies and gentlemen," paused a full, unerring beat, and shouted: "LOS MIR AROIS!" The crowd went to pieces. Mel continued to ad-lib, mining the absurdity with which a Catskill resort is rich, and finished to hearty applause. It was the street corner all over again, and Melvin stayed the season as the house comic, with varying results.

Street-corner society has never been noted for rabid political colloquy. Melvin's crowd was far more likely to be found talking Dodgers or gawking at Sheila Rabinowitz. But the events of the middle and late thirties proved emphatically that politics could not exist in a vacuum, that there was such a thing as global conscience. And Jews understood conscience, since the institutional failure of conscience fosters persecution and persecution was precisely what brought Jews to America. That and the fact that Jewish immigrants were inextricably tied to the world Jewish community brought the growing atrocities of Hitler's Europe closer to home. Melvin's politics were passionate and moral. He hated Nazis.

Melvin completed high school against the backdrop of World War. And though by the midpoint of his senior year the tide of battle had effectively turned to the Allies, for all the patriotic fervor at Eastern District the Wehrmacht might have been massing for an attack on Ebbets Field. Melvin was highly susceptible to the continuing call to arms and while still in school he enlisted in the Army. With some difficulty, his family persuaded him to await induction upon graduation. That June, Melvin Kaminsky officially outlasted Eastern District High School and numbered among his few official accomplishments: a seat on the Senior Council, a stretch as Dean's Assistant, and a phantom membership on the Fencing Team. Beside his yearbook picture, where classmates pronounced life goals ranging from motherhood to neurosurgery, Melvin added his own: "To be President of the U.S."

Melvin Kaminsky went off to war with little more than a studied sense of preposterousness and a stage name (the most palpable by-product of his Butler stint). Aware that "Kaminsky" was unwieldy at best, Melvin had experimented with Kitty's family name. Brookman became Brooks. "Brooks." It rolled nicely off the tongue and just cleared the teeth with a click. It was its own punctuation, not unlike a rim shot. It had even been enshrined in song:

> Here I am, I'm Melvin Brooks
> I've come to stop the show.
> Just a ham who's minus looks
> But in your heart I'll grow.

I'll tell you gags, I'll sing you songs,
Just happy little snappy songs that roll along.
Out of my mind
Won't you be kind?
And please love Melvin Brooks.

2

There was a WPA ditch at the corner of Seddon and Maclay in the Bronx. Shorty, shirtless but hatted, swung a pick. Whitey, taller and blond, leaned on a shovel. There was no particular hurry, not in the WPA, not in 1935. Shorty sighed and found a fresh grip on his pick when Whitey motioned him still. There at the edge of the excavation stood a moonfaced little girl, her hair pulled to the side in a ribbon bow, her mouth drawn to a tentative smile. She toed the curb, then spoke: "Hey you! Wanna hear me sing?" Whitey winked, half expecting a shy, off-key warble. The little girl squared off and in a voice more Sophie Tucker than Shirley Temple sang:

> Snap your fingers,
> Turn around a bit,
> Shake your shoulders,
> Go to town with it . . .

. . . fingers popping, shoulders shimmying to the last lusty note. She came back often after that, volunteering the soon familiar showstopper, sometimes adding an encore of "College Rhythm."

Her name was Anne and she lived around the corner on St. Raymond Street.

She was born Anna Maria Louisa on September 17, 1931, the second daughter of Mildred (née DiNapoli) and Michael Italiano. It was a nuclear, matriarchal, lower-middle-class Italian family. Michael worked as a cutter in Manhattan's garment district, and came home to a modest flat in the Westchester Square section on the eastern edge of Parkchester. The neighborhood, bordered on the north by the tracks of the New Haven line, on the east by Westchester Creek, was compact but residential whereas much of the Middle and West Bronx was cramped and congested. The area had its share of five- and six-story apartment buildings, but these were spaced by clusters of brick duplexes that passed clotheslines across tidy alleyways and tended patches of manicured lawn with high symmetrical hedges that often cloistered plaster religious statuary.

The Bronx Zoo was an accessible dozen blocks to the west and the IRT brought Yankee Stadium within easy reach. The neighborhood was predominantly and proudly Italian, the sort where the local children would teasingly remind each other that: "Five cents will get you a ride on the bus, garlic will get you a seat."

Anne grew up *una buona ragazza di famiglia,* "a good girl from a good family." Family was the keynote. The Italianos were firmly embedded in the extended family orbit, which at one point numbered close to eighty. Short of hiring a hall, the only practical gathering place for the family was out of doors, which usually meant summer picnics upstate. The outings were a special joy for Anne. While the other kids frolicked and fought and diligently worked the crease out of their Sunday best, Anne hovered near the main picnic table; not to eat, but to sing. It was a familiar sight—an uncle strumming a guitar and Anne perched next to the potato salad singing her heart out. At two, she could manage "Under a Blanket of Blue." Four brought the peppy "Snap Your Fingers" and "College Rhythm," and the repertoire quickly widened to include "Sleepytime Gal," "It Had to Be You," plus whatever tune was making the rounds or gracing the Hit Parade. Joanne, the Italianos' first-born, was a better singer, but Anne was the irrepressible performer, the "personality kid."

The family was the most appreciative audience, but family members were not always available. Weekdays, with Millie keeping house and Joanne dressing dolls or scuttling underfoot in the kitchen, Anne took her show on the road to the corner deli, the WPA work site, wherever she found a willing public. On at least one occasion she stayed for one too many curtain calls and came home to a remedial spanking. Such were the perils of street-corner showmanship.

The Depression was two years old when Anne was born. The Italianos were more fortunate than many in that Michael worked steadily throughout the early thirties. When Anne was six, Millie gave birth to a third child, another daughter, Phyllis, and the family led a life that was unadorned, but seemingly secure. The baby was barely one year old when the aftershocks of the Depression reached the garment district and Michael was laid off. Millie, never one to sit idly by in crisis, packed her daughters off to their grandmother's house, and undaunted by the fact that employment was still a rare commodity, began job hunting. A still-sagging economy was no match for Millie's mettle. She found work as a switchboard operator at the main branch of Macy's Department Store in Manhattan's Herald Square, where she stayed on long after Michael returned to work, even after he was promoted to patternmaker.

Life as the daughter of working parents did not dampen Anne's vitality. Grammar school did. The adult recognition that had been so intrinsic to her pleasure in performance was in short supply at P.S. 12. The classroom was in effect a strange and competitive family, and where other adults proved a soft touch for Anne's exuberance, teachers, frankly, frightened her. School loomed as a potential enemy, but no less an enemy to be won over. Anne quietly excelled at her study exercises, and even surfaced as the lead in a kindergarten pageant about the American republics. To all reports, a finer "District of Columbia" never trod the boards. Anne returned to the P.S. 12 stage the following year and starred as Mama Bear in the school's rendition of *The Three Little Bears*. But although she was again a critical success, her makeshift costume—a paper bag perforated and plunked over the head—no doubt took something away from the nuance of the role.

The plays alerted the teachers to Anne's gift for performance. Between official productions, she was escorted from classroom to classroom and encouraged by the teachers to serve up samples of her precocious song and dance. Aside from singing, shimmying, and snapping, Anne learned to roll her eyes with an agility that rivaled Eddie Cantor's.

If Anne's impulse for performance was nothing more than a little girl's playful miniaturization of glamour, an innocent inversion of what was essentially a shy personality, Millie was willing to nourish that impulse. Although money was still tight, Anne was permitted tap-dancing lessons which she attended with such thorough concentration that she lost her appetite and started losing weight. Budding talent was one thing, but in an Italian household not eating was tantamount to sin. Anne's lessons were terminated, leaving her skinnier if not significantly wiser about her potential for stagecraft. That would simply have to await some other litmus.

The episode said less about Anne than Millie, whose venture into the working world, far from eroding her maternal hold, consolidated it. Where other working mothers were often of necessity permissive, Millie was unblinkingly protective. Weekdays, the girls were restricted to the neighborhood where the principal outdoor amusement was "hangoseek," which was local vernacular for hide and seek. Moviegoing was reserved for Sundays, and then only after services at Santa Maria Roman Catholic Church.

As the girls came of social age, dating was closely monitored pending parental approval, which was anything but automatic in coming. The rule was tested only once, when Joanne engineered a sneak date, was caught, and had the hell beaten out of her by Millie as a deterrent to both the culprit and any other daughter within earshot who might have entertained similar thoughts.

If such watchfulness did nothing to relieve Anne's undercurrent of shyness, it did leave her more energy to apply to performing. She became a regular at block parties and church picnics, leading Michael to confide to another relative that maybe one day Anne would become an actress, an admittedly slender possibility which brought only a laugh and skepticism: "Some dreams, some pipe dreams, Mike." Anne overheard the exchange but it only rallied her vague fantasies of fame behind the equally vague label, "actress." She even went so far as to scribble her new objective on the back of the apartment building: "I want to be an actress." For Anne, the decision required no great leap of faith, just an exercise of imagination, like the time she went to the circus and was so enthralled with the jugglers that she turned to Millie and said, "Hey, Ma, I can do that." Other children were content to be entertained. Anne identified with the entertainer. There was no doubt in her mind then that she could be a juggler, just as there was no doubt now that she could be an actress . . . if she only knew what an actress was.

School was as good a place as any to start finding out. Anne entered Christopher Columbus High and shortly joined the Drama Society where she caught the attention of her classmates and her teachers. The consensus was that there was something special if still unformed in the girl's feel for drama. But despite her early foothold in the theatre clique, and classwork that consistently fell within the upper percentiles, Anne had yet to overcome her shyness. Outwardly, she gave the impression of confidence and sophistication, and she earned the affection and admiration of the other students some of whom looked upon her as a sort of demi-celebrity. Her appearance had become quite striking. Her face, framed in thick, black, shoulder-length hair, had gone from a girlish roundedness to a soft pear shape that left the cheekbones in fine relief and tapered down to a wide smile that could light a room. Besides which, her figure was showing the first lines of young womanhood. She was constantly asked out on dates, but Millie's dating ban held sway through Anne's sophomore year. However well liked she was, popularity, the brass ring of late adolescence, was not fully its own reward—Anne considered herself phony.

Theatre was not only a creative outlet, it provided a certain protective shell. Anne participated regularly in school productions and kept an eye out for other extramural thespian activities which, as it turned out, were not long in coming. A neighbor and friend of the Italianos worked as an announcer for a small

radio station in Peekskill, a small upstate town some forty miles
north of the Bronx. Anne learned that he was puzzling over a
fifteen-minute programming gap on Saturday mornings, and she
quickly conspired to fill the time with a troupe of amateur actors
presenting capsule dramatizations. The neighbor presented the
plan to his station manager who promptly approved it. Anne became the driving force behind a collection of friends who
adopted the rather high-toned name of "The Radcliffe Radio
Players." Less commercials and credits, their quarter hour
dwindled to between nine and eleven minutes in which to render
the likes of Shakespeare, Poe, and Hardy, working from scripts
furnished by a service that streamlined the classics for just such
occasions.

Each Saturday morning, the troupe packed off to Peekskill for
another abbreviated *coup de théâtre,* but the name of Anne Italiano was not to be found within the Who's Who of the cast.
Given the classical repertoire and the dignified "Radcliffe" aegis,
Anne felt obliged to respond in kind with a more imposing stage
name. At length, she turned to the corner street sign for inspiration, thus transforming herself into the stately Anne St. Raymond, Saturdays only.

Michael's "pipe dream" was taking on an edge of credibility.
Some of the relatives were beginning to keep closer tabs on
Anne's theatrical comings and goings, but that could be a mixed
blessing, as when Aunt Kate went to see her niece in an amateur
production of *Night Must Fall.* The role required Anne to smoke
a cigarette and though she didn't normally smoke, she did for the
performance. Kate, seated at the rear of the performance hall,
knew that Millie had strictly forbidden her daughters from
smoking, and spotting the smoldering cigarette, impulsively
shouted: "I'm going to tell your mother." If the outburst was testimony to Anne's ability to finesse a stage prop, it was no less
mortifying for the fact.

While Millie might have been strict she wasn't unreasonable,
and when prom time neared during Anne's junior year, the middle daughter was at last pronounced of dating age. Anne's social
life not only normalized but nearly overshadowed her acting,

which, with the inevitable curricular limits of a large public high school, was still rudimentary. Much of what stage work Christopher Columbus had to offer was on the order of the melodramatic *Curse You, Jack Dalton* in which Anne also appeared.

Whether out of boredom or some simple desire for variety, Anne's passion for drama started to flag during her senior year, to be replaced by another interest. Anne had always excelled scholastically, nowhere more so than in the sciences. Since achievement-minded high school students tend naturally to play to their academic strength (aptitude is often mistaken for attitude) Anne became infatuated with science. Performance may have had its special intoxication, but perhaps for that very allure was not entirely to be trusted. Acting was hardly without objective standards—even at the amateur level, it required a certain mastery of technique, an appreciation of a basic emotive vocabulary. Still, the bottom line of performance was audience reaction, a strictly subjective variable that stood in sharp contrast to the quantifiable methods of science. In its way, theatre was no less a laboratory than science, the key distinction being that where the scientist stands outside the experiment, the actress stands within the crucible of performance. Anne had come to suspect that her zest for playwork was more an expression of a general need for notice than it was an indication of a specific desire to become an actress. As far as she was concerned, a career as a laboratory technician might just as easily satisfy any yearnings for fame. If Anne had allowed herself any thoughts of becoming the next Bernhardt, those were easily exchanged for thoughts of becoming the next Salk.

Millie did not warm to the news. Both she and Michael had long supported their daughter's acting aspirations, and neither was especially disposed to change. Besides, any quick inventory of the respective fields showed a hundred actresses of note for every Marie Curie. None of which deflected Anne from her recent plans for a career in science. What did, finally, was considerably less logical or high-minded.

Jay Okin was one of Christopher Columbus High's most sought-after young men. He was tall, good-looking, and he was showing an interest in Anne. The two of them had worked together on a few plays, and one day found themselves sitting alone in the school auditorium. They were caught up in the musing typical of high school seniors, and the conversation turned to future plans. Jay took Anne's hand, then explained that he had given the matter careful thought and had decided to enroll at the American Academy of Dramatic Arts. Unlike some of the city's more specialized acting studios, the Academy provided a broad curriculum that might open any number of doors into the entertainment world. Located on Fifty-second Street, it was accessible, more or less affordable, and it was a good way to extend and explore the relatively unrefined acting impulses of high school amateurism. Anne agreed that the Academy had a good deal to offer, not least of which was Jay.

Science's loss would be theatre's gain. Anne announced to her family that the following fall would find her in the American Academy of Dramatic Arts, provided she could meet costs. Her parents applauded the decision, and Millie all but sealed it by offering to finance the five-hundred-dollar tuition fee from her Macy's pay check.

Anne graduated from Christopher Columbus in just three and a half years. She had compiled a more than respectable B-plus academic average, had been elected to the student honor society, Arista, and, as the year-end senior awards ceremony approached, was considered the odds-on favorite for the school drama medal. If Anne was looking for one last sanction for her recent career choice, the ceremony was a surprising setback—another student walked away with the medal. The drama teacher later took Anne aside and apologetically explained that while she was the most deserving candidate, the actual recipient showed potential and needed encouragement of a formal sort. The rationale did little to soften the disappointment which, as it turned out, was only the first of a pair of unwelcome surprises. The second came when Anne later reported for classes to the Academy and Jay Okin was nowhere to be found.

Anne had little in common with most of her new classmates. For one thing, at sixteen she was younger than they were. For another, Millie's sacrifice to meet tuition costs and Anne's own supplemental part-time work had a certain sobering effect on her approach to study. Where many of the students could afford a disinterested approach, Anne was more purposeful. She attended classes, moonlighted for carfare as a receptionist at the Girl Scout headquarters, and during lunch hours, when the other students checked out for a quick sandwich, she stayed behind and rehearsed scenes on an empty stage.

The AADA worked from the outside in, soft-pedaling sophisticated dramatic theory in favor of courses in voice and speech, dancing and fencing. The training was more technical than motivational, which was appropriate for students who first had to familiarize themselves with the physical tools of performance before tackling anything so recondite as Stanislavski. The program suited Anne who, although she subscribed to the catchword of "actress," did not rule out the possibility of becoming a pop singer.

Meanwhile, Anne continued to contribute to her education, taking jobs at local drugstores and, at one point, giving English lessons to Peruvian singer Yma Sumac. But the seriousness with which Anne faced her studies was no guarantee of redemption, and as she neared completion of her program the first traces of panic were beginning to show. Anne of course knew that she was a standout in most of her classes, just as she knew that there was a world of difference between learning to act and earning a living at it. The approaching graduation forced it all into sharp focus—Anne had invested her time and Millie's money and the expectation was that the promising young actress would become a working young actress. The hard reality of the long-awaited transition scared Anne to death. The gotta-dance girl would finally have to come up with the goods.

As graduation neared, Anne's daily routine was unchanged, if tinged with a new intensity and urgency. She continued her lunch-hour rehearsal regimen, and the extra work finally paid off in wholly unexpected fashion. It was just two weeks shy of the end of term. Anne stood alone on the stage of the Academy's rehearsal hall, going over a scene from *Fly Away Home* in which she played a Mexican girl. Frances Fuller, a fine actress and teacher at the Academy, by chance stopped by the hall and stayed to watch Anne work. Whether it was the accumulated polish of two years of study, the simple maturation of innate talent, or the collected fright of the pending graduation, Anne was superb that noon. Afterward Frances talked with Anne and ended by recommending she audition for television's "Studio One," a popular and prestigious dramatic series. The suggestion was something more than whimsy. Frances Fuller was married to Worthington Miner, the creator and producer of "Studio One."

"Studio One" originally operated out of jerry-built studios situated above the Vanderbilt Avenue side of Grand Central Station. The modest setting belied the program's cachet. "Studio One," conceived by Miner in his role as manager of program development for William Paley of CBS, was the bellwether of live television drama which it turned out at the all-but-impossible rate of one production per week. The series was inaugurated auspiciously with a mystery, *The Storm*, which starred the distinguished Broadway actress Margaret Sullavan. But early success was not allowed to settle into complacency. Under Miner, "Studio One" was constantly evolving, experimenting with both old and new material, proven and untested talent, while at the same time battling the breakneck production schedule and a rather crude soundstage. Unlike film, where a performance could be synthesized, or theatre, where a performance could accrue over time, live television was evanescent—one night, one shot, all or nothing. The pressure, spontaneity, and sheer danger could excite and animate an entire production, making the occasional mistakes and miscalculations endurable.

Anne could not have asked a better opportunity. She contacted the production office and was assigned a time to read for the casting director, Robert Fryer. Anne arrived at the office to discover she was one of six actresses auditioning for the part. Her turn came, she read satisfactorily, and she even imagined she noticed a glimmer of approval in the casting director's eyes. When all had read, Fryer came out to the waiting room, swept the room with a quick glance, and said: "I'm sorry, girls, Miss Italiano has the part."

As it turned out, Anne had read well, in fact, too well for that week's production (*Walk the Dark Streets*). She was sent to read for Worthington Miner who assigned her a larger role in the next week's production of Turgenev's *The Torrents of Spring*. That left the newcomer more time to consider her dramatic debut, not to mention time to reconsider her last name. Not that she considered "Italiano" déclassé, just that a stage name seemed somehow *de rigueur*. If a career was being born, it deserved to be christened. Anne discarded "St. Raymond" as a silly pretension of the past, and with her family proceeded to try on names. It was Joanne who finally came up with one, neither English nor strictly Italian, but with just a hint of dark-eyed mystery. Anne would make her professional debut as "Anne Marno."

"Studio One" was unassailably reputable, but in early tight-budget television, pay was not always commensurate with reputation. For one week of rehearsal and one hour of performance, Anne earned $125, not a princely sum, but then again not bad for a young woman of eighteen. Rehearsals went smoothly as the air date arrived—Monday, April 17, 1950. The competition was stiff that night. Over on WABD, Tarzan Hewitt was grappling with Sammy Berg at Sunnyside Garden. WPIX had Sonny Parisi and Keen Simon trading punches by live remote from Eastern Parkway Arena. But the real competition was on WNBT, where "Robert Montgomery Presents" was featuring a rendition of *Our Town* starring Burgess Meredith. All WCBS had to offer was Louise Albritton, John Baragrey, and some ingenue named Marno. Although television had not yet become the ratings swamp of its later life, chances are there were enough Italianos, immediate, extended, and unofficial, to budge the most stubborn Nielsens up a point or two.

The Torrents of Spring went off well and without mishap, pausing only to let Betty Furness plug a kitchen full of appliances and remind viewers: "You can be sure if it's Westinghouse." Anne, playing the young, forsaken "Gemma," showed no sign of jitters and delivered her part fluidly. At 11:00 P.M. it was all over, ending as abruptly as it had started. Anne gathered her things and made the slow trip back up to the Bronx, bracing herself for her toughest critics. She arrived at the front door of the Italiano apartment when something caught her eye—a simple sign that read: WELCOME HOME STAR!

Anne opened the door to find the apartment filled to overflowing with family, relatives, and friends, all of whom applauded as she entered. Anne was deeply moved. The party resumed with wine and coffee, and little Italian cakes Millie had made for the occasion. It was as touching an opening-night reception as Anne would ever know.

3

There was nothing in Mel Kaminsky's past to anticipate 1950. Nothing that would logically find him on the writing staff of television's most successful, professional, and sophisticated variety show. Nothing that would realistically find him among the literate and elite prodigies of "Your Show of Shows." Nothing, and everything.

In June 1944, Mel's army enlistment became active upon his graduation from high school, and the seventeen-year-old recruit reported to Virginia Military Institute, where, among other things, he was inexplicably taught the basics of riding and saber-rattling. If the training was outmoded, the war also, it seemed, was soon to be a thing of the past. Mel had scarcely donned his fatigues when the Allied D-Day assault was launched and a beachhead won on French soil. Mel was next transferred to Fort Sill, Oklahoma, and by the time he completed basic training (in the course of which he shed both weight and his regimental fervor) Paris had been liberated. By mid-September, the Allies were preparing a final push into Germany, and it wasn't at all clear that there would be much war left to fight by the time Mel reported to the front.

He was finally shipped to the European Theater of Opera-

tions, landing at Le Havre in February 1945. Mel first saw duty
as a forward observer for the artillery. Unfortunately his tactical
vocabulary tended to desert him under fire, and instead of relay-
ing logistical map co-ordinates, he lapsed into broken Brooklyn-
ese: "No, no! You're going over, dummy! Aim for the big tree by
the church!" Mel was soon an ex-forward observer and was reas-
signed to the 1104th Combat Engineers Group and stationed in
Belgium near the Ardennes Forest.

Mel's arrival followed by a week and a half the Pyrrhic victory
of the Battle of the Bulge, and with the German line of resistance withering fast, the combat engineers shifted into overdrive,
constructing bridges in advance of the onrushing infantry. The
Allies crossed the Rhine on March 7 and two months and a day
later Germany surrendered. Pfc. Kaminsky spent the whole of
V-E Day holed up in a village wine cellar near Wiesbaden, up to
his ears in May wine.

Mel was promoted to corporal and continued to serve with the
Occupation Forces in Germany under the official military desig-
nation of Noncom in Charge of Special Services. A free translation would have been: "GI Tummler." Mel, already a celebrated
barracks cut-up, entertained at officers clubs and camp shows for
four months and then finished his hitch at Fort Dix, New Jersey,
where with two other friends he wowed the troops with a
raunchy rendition of the Andrews Sisters—Patti, LaVerne, and
Maxine—in army drab and five o'clock shadow.

The war seemed to affect most veterans in one of several ways.
There were those who wanted to put the caprices of combat
quickly behind them. They sought secure jobs or started modest
little businesses. Others, with the help of the GI Bill, decided to
improve themselves through higher education. Still others for
whom the war opened up new vistas and dislodged old values,
were eager to pursue some course that would allow them greater
personal and creative expression. Mel would do some of each:
employment (the Abilene Blouse and Dress Company which he
would use as a stopgap when money was tight), education
(Brooklyn College, although enrollment was virtually the extent
of his formal higher education), and show business (summer
stock and later again the Catskills). If the service had done noth-

ing else, it instilled in Mel an appreciation of the bold frontal assault, with an eye to the flank and rear.

The Red Bank Players was a third-rate summer stock company
based in the town of Red Bank on the North Jersey Shore. From
the start it was never more than a shoestring operation, working
out of the local high school auditorium and straining against a
meagre production budget. The only vestige of theatrical legitimacy was the fact that this was an Equity company, which
seemed to give it a leg up on the other companies proliferating
during the summer of 1947. Unfortunately, the manager of the
Red Bank Players was only able to pay lip service to the Equity
pay stipulations. Scale, already stingy at forty-six dollars per
week, was more than the coffers could withstand and rather than
sacrifice the chance to perform, the cast refunded all but six dollars of its weekly wage. Acting in Red Bank was its own reward:
it had to be.

Mel learned that the company was forming and arrived just in
time to nail down a position as stagehand. He became fast
friends with Red Bank's Barrymore, John Roney, and John's
cousin, Will Jordan. The three shared modest quarters and for a
spell even berths, sleeping three-abreast crosswise on a pair of
cots. Overcrowding notwithstanding, there was an initial personality partition between John and Will, and Mel, which had nothing to do with the fact that they were cast and he was crew. Mel,
for all his boisterous humor and good-natured extroversion, projected an air of defeatism. He seemed to think of himself as a
loser, which was peculiar, considering that he was every bit as
intelligent, affable, and funny as his companions. Part of the
problem was physical. Mel, like many people, had just read
Budd Schulberg's bestseller *What Makes Sammy Run?* Unlike
most, he identified with the central character, the superaggres-
sive hustler, Sammy Glick, whom the author described as "a little ferret." John, Will, and Mel, city boys all, wouldn't have
known a ferret if one had scampered in the door, but it still tied
into Mel's self-image. Self-doubt was done no favor by the fact
that John was something of a ladies' man, that Will was not far
behind, and that Mel was having virtually no luck at all (with

women he was flirtatious and grabby, but awkward and almost
adolescent). When the three of them sat up nights jogging the
machismo with tales of conquests, Mel was usually forced to
pick over adventures abroad, a favorite being the time he was
approached by a comely French hooker with the businesslike
query: "Fuck, no?"

If Mel was the victim of many jokes, he was the perpetrator of
many more. He and Will were constantly throwing lines, slipping into characterizations, or playing off each other's lunacy, as
when they would flounce into a cast party as two homosexual
lovers and coyly kiss each other on the cheek. Mel's humor was
spontaneous, bizarre, and original, although his least original
weakness was an abiding passion for Al Jolson. The movie *The
Jolson Story* had come out the year before and by 1947 it was
harder to find a Brooklyn kid who didn't do "Mammy" than one
who did. Mel was typical of the vogue. He would talk about Jolson incessantly and at the drop of a hat would take a knee and
croon, citing chapter and verse from the movie as if to prove that
he was not merely a fan but an aficionado.

For all Mel's apparent insecurity, he still came across as a
tough little guy. There was a masculine quality about him which
he was inclined to talk about, but it was no less there for the
self-consciousness. And despite the fact that he took more than
his share of kidding, he had a prickly defensiveness. One time
the company's director was picking on Mel and ultimately
pushed him too far. Mel stood firm and declared: "I will not be
the scapegoat," and then loosed a barrage of literate insults that
sent most of the players to their Websters. The director tolerated
the attack for the simple reason that the abuse was entirely
justified.

His name was Percy Montague, which was something between
pretense and folly in light of the fact that he was utterly Russian.
That, in turn, was his salvation, since Russia was held to be syn-
onymous with serious theatre and none of the company was
eager to challenge the assumption, including the proprietor, Mr.
Kutcher. But Montague's shortcomings were not long in becoming obvious. He showed scant understanding of theatre dynamics, a fault accentuated by the rather frothy repertory. And

his frame of reference was manifestly unschooled, as when he tried to guide Will through a tricky butler role with the peculiar direction: "More Arthur Treacher." Montague's days at Red Bank were numbered, which was as much as could be said of the company itself.

By midsummer, Kutcher sent Montague packing and then announced that he too was pulling out. The players were welcome to do as they saw fit, which included keeping the company afloat for the remainder of the season by whatever means possible. With that, John, Will, and Mel jumped into the breach. John added production to his chores as leading man and Will helped out with managerial responsibilities, which left the position of director unfilled. Mel heartily volunteered and that completed the takeover of the asylum by the lunatics. From that juncture on, Mel blossomed. Authority seemed to come to him naturally, and while his duties were no more than organizational at the outset, he gradually stumbled upon the rudiments of a directing sensibility, with a discriminating eye for mise-en-scène and characterization. If Mel's directorial style had few niceties (he once corrected Will's interpretation of a British character: "Too much swish.") neither did he have any pretensions. Above all, they were all having fun, they were experimenting and learning.

There were inevitable lapses in professionalism. Miscues, technical blunders, and late curtains. One night a performance was slow in starting and rather than risk the audience's wrath, John stepped onstage in his dressing gown, apologized for the inadvertent delay, and announced that there would be some preliminary entertainment. Will and Mel entered from the wings and regaled the house with close to sixty minutes of mimicry, Will with an admirable Charles Laughton, Mel with a regrettable Jolson. But nobody seemed to mind, least of all the mimics. That was the beauty of bargain-basement summer stock. The stakes were low and the expectations few. Anything short of disaster was a moral victory, anything long of adequate blocking and remembered lines, a tour de force.

The freedom of Red Bank nurtured other impulses. Onstage and off, Will was becoming aware of a knack for stand-up comedy and an uncanny gift for mimicry. John was increasingly aware of his decreasing hair and the limits that placed on his future as a leading man. Mel, meanwhile, in his meteoric rise from stagehand to director (and at least one turn as an actor), was learning to corset his energy within the demands of form, which is not to say that he was becoming conventional, rather that he was starting to meet convention halfway.

While at Red Bank, Mel tapped yet another pool of expression, writing. The step was greater than might be imagined. From the street corners of Brooklyn to the supper shows of the Catskills to the camp shows of Fort Dix, Mel had been his own palette and canvas, his own *objet de farce*. Writing required a sense of craft and an objective concession to craftmanship that was removed from, if not wholly foreign to, the rigorous formlessness of shtick. Turning a written phrase might have been no more difficult than chewing the available scenery for comic effect, but it did enforce a discipline of form. Admittedly, Mel's first work was no magnum opus. It was a short story, an allegory really, about two cats at opposite ends of the social ladder, one patrician, the other plebeian. When they finally come to words, the alley cat lectures the fat cat: "You may have this beautiful home, but I have my freedom of being able to go from trash can to trash can." It was a curious moral, certainly short of trenchant social commentary. But for the uninitiated writer, the first fling, while rarely the best, at least surmounts the worst of it.

The Red Bank Players lasted the summer and then disbanded. John Roney started giving serious thought to a career in business. Will Jordan scrambled back to Manhattan, built a sturdy comedy act, and soon was a regular on the highbrow chichi club circuit. Mel Kaminsky tested the waters at Brooklyn College, thought better of it, and waited out the winter.

By summer he was back in the mountains. Red Bank might have been show, but the Catskills was show business, and the comic adrenalin there was tonic, the street corner gone pastoral.

Mel took the measure of his drumming and decided that his future was in comedy. He worked as a house comic and began to shore up his act with original material, but while originality was refreshing, it was hardly necessary. In the mountains, change was strictly relative. Last week's jokes were always new to this week's guests. But Mel insisted on improvising; somehow the risk of it seemed like shelter. He got the old theme song out of mothballs and went to work.

An average show: The orchestra hits an uptempo vamp and Mel does his standard singing walk-on: "Here I am I'm Melvin Brooks . . ." which he intones in a nasal Jolsonesque flat palate and winds up on one knee, arms outstretched. He then goes to the comic stuff—not jokes per se, but simple satire, broad characterizations, impressions—kidding the audience, the management, himself. A finish, a bow, an exit.

The average response: middling. Most audiences didn't want to be challenged comedically. If they had wanted something truly different they wouldn't have come to the mountains in the first place. Nor, for that matter, was it at all clear that different was better.

Mel took his critical lumps and set about reshaping and refining his act, determined to find the middle ground between conservative audience tastes and his own rampaging comic imagination. One-liners were a straitjacket; aggressive insult comedy, "the shpritz," not his forte; storytelling, "shmoozing," not his style. He would just have to create his own comic category. The drive to entertain and to do it well was a goal just short of obsession. But there was no other way to go about it. Stand-up comedy is as much nurture as nature. A painter can paint, a writer write, but a comic needs an audience. And Mel fought for the right to be bad, knowing it was the only way to become good. Ambition was his mainstay, also his nemesis. Mel Brooks was talented, twenty-two, and impatient to succeed.

Will Jordan had taken a different tack and had found considerable success of his own. Will was gaining a reputation as an impressionist prodigy whose repertoire was not just prodigious but highly literate. Where other impressionists were technicians, carbon copies with calculated quirks, Will used the impression not as an end in itself but as a point of departure. He took his knack for mimicry, a second-class comedy in the eyes of some, and made it the cornerstone of a sophisticated act. The result was bookings in some of Manhattan's better clubs, the Blue Angel and the Ruban Bleu.

Mel was impressed, more so than if Will had landed a part in
a Broadway show. Not only did class club dates have an air of
legitimacy, but the work was year-round in contrast to the sea-
sonal employment of the Catskills. Even if the resort circuit was
a proving ground for young talent, it was no less a potential rut.
The audiences were essentially homogeneous, the acts often
standardized, the response more or less predetermined. It was an
environment that could encourage an inexperienced entertainer
to grow, just as it could stunt his growth with formulation. Today's promising young comic could become tomorrow's hack.
Success in the mountains was something to be both coveted and
held at arm's length. It was a unique work experience and not
strictly transferrable to other reaches of show business. Will's
success in the city seemed inviolable and respectable to Mel who
was mildly awed and maybe a little envious. Despite Mel's quick
ascendance in the Catskills (at one point he was employed by
Grossinger's, the jewel of the borscht belt) there was a lingering
sense of failure about him. As far as Will could tell, Mel still considered himself a loser.

What Mel might have lacked in confidence, he more than
made up for in chutzpah. The same aggressive outsider mental-
ity that proved his passport with the older toughs in Brooklyn,
seemed to serve him on the periphery of show business. Alienation, imagined or real, was incentive. Mel seemed to operate best
from a one-down position, as if it forced him to get a running
jump on others. He was taking life at full stride, and the momentum alone carried him into situations that a more measured step
might have missed, into the company of winners: Sid Caesar, for
instance.

Mel first met Sid before the war. He was Sidney then, burly
and handsome, fresh out of Yonkers High School, with a touch
on the tenor saxophone that took him through some of the better
big bands of the day, Charlie Spivak, Claude Thornhill, Shep
Fields. While Sidney was decidedly serious about his music he
also had a delightfully unserious side. His father, Max Caesar, an
Austrian immigrant who died in 1945, was the proprietor of a
small Yonkers diner, the St. Clair Lunch. A choice blue-collar
greasy spoon, it attracted a full complement of foreign-born local

workers. The St. Clair swam with dialect and broken English, Italian, Russian, Polish, German, Lithuanian, and some tongues as yet unclassified. Sidney was a shy kid and a good listener, and whether by design or sheer osmosis, the time spent at the diner trained his ear for dialect. Years later, between sets with the big bands, he would entertain the other sidemen by imitating the old voices in a kind of linguistic double-talk, though dialect was only one side of his mimicry which ranged over any number of subjects, animate and inanimate. The more laughs, the better he liked it.

By the time Sidney came to the Catskills to play sax at the Avon Hotel in Woodridge, New York, he was working the audience for laughs and loving it. Owner Meyer Arkin took an interest in the budding young comic and let him divide his time between the bandstand and stand-up. Sidney meanwhile took an interest in the boss's niece, Florence Levy, whom he later married in July 1943. By then, the transition from musician to comedian was complete. In the best of show business traditions, he shortened his name from Sidney to Sid, and after he had completed a triumphant run as staff comic at Kutsher's Country Club, the mountains came to Caesar.

In November 1942, Sid enlisted in the Coast Guard. But whereas Mel's service mostly articulated his aspirations, Sid's enlistment actually accelerated his career. While pulling pier duty in Brooklyn, Sid was approached by his senior officer, Lieutenant Vernon Duke (an outstanding composer-lyricist with a raft of Broadway credits) and was asked to tend the comic duties in a revue-recruiting show he was preparing for the Coast Guard, *Tars and Spars*, which would star Victor Mature. Sid, who had already contributed material to another Coast Guard revue, "Six On, Twelve Off," eagerly accepted the offer and was dispatched to Palm Beach where the new show was to rehearse and open before touring the country. Duke, meantime, hoping to insure the show's success, contacted one of the best variety producers in the business—Max Liebman. Max was not just a producer, although he was tastefully and flawlessly that. He was a consummate showman who had worked as a mountain tummler and a Broadway producer and virtually everything else in between,

finding time along the way to mold and launch the career of
Danny Kaye as well as doctor a passel of Broadway musicals.
Max agreed to serve as civilian director and producer on *Tars
and Spars*, caught a train to Palm Beach, and promptly met
Duke's comic whiz kid, Sid Caesar.

Not since Danny Kaye had Max come across a young comic
better equipped to succeed. Sid's virtuosity was perhaps less immediately visible than Danny's, his technique less polished, his
presence less charismatic. But the raw material was awesomely
there. Max, shrewdly stingy with praise, considered Danny the
only true comic genius he had ever known. But this new kid was
not far off the mark. Sid's comedy seemed largely instinctive, an
advantage in that it provided him with an a priori comic vocabulary, a disadvantage in that it made that vocabulary less accessible, harder to portion and professionalize.

Max and Sid worked closely, expanding and strengthening the
existing material and even adding some of their own, including
an airplane bit that was to become seminal Caesar. *Tars and
Spars* received glowing reviews, was trimmed to sixty minutes,
and picked up steam as it toured the country. Before it was over,
Columbia Pictures purchased the rights, gave the lead to Alfred
Drake, and retained Sid as the only holdover from the original
cast. Sid was discharged from the Coast Guard in December
1945; the picture was released the following February. He
stayed on at Columbia at five hundred dollars a week, but despite good notices on his motion-picture debut, and except for a
minor part in a minor movie, *The Guilt of Janet Ames*, his career
was becalmed. By the end of the year, Sid had had his fill of
Hollywood foot-dragging, and hurried back to New York to accept a booking at the Copacabana, as good a comic's showcase
as the city had to offer. With the opening drawing near, Sid
breezed into Max Liebman's midtown office. Max asked him
what he planned for the Copa, Sid shrugged, said he'd do what
he'd always done, the dialect, the mimicry, a sketch or two, bits
and pieces. Max was dumbfounded. Headlining the Copa was
not like mugging in the house band at the Avon. The theatrical
requirements were of another order entirely, the audience more
exacting, the critics often unforgiving.

Max and Sid picked over Sid's comic compendium and pulled together an act. There was the airplane bit, an imitation of a haywire slot machine, and a nice spoof contrasting English and Russian styles of acting. Sharing the bill with Sid was the Michael Durso Orchestra and the Fernando Alverez Samba Orchestra with its rendition of "One Brazilian in a Million." The opening came and went. Sid was a hit. One night during the run, Sid was paid a visit by a good friend, Don Appell, who had with him a young man calling himself Mel Brooks. Mel, who had once casually met Sid the saxophonist, now formally met Sid the comedy headliner.

After closing at the Copa, Sid and Max toured the nightclub circuit for six months, and in 1947 returned for a banner engagement at the Roxy Theatre. None of Sid's progress escaped Mel's notice, least of all the Roxy date. When Sid settled in for another successful run, Mel again showed up to "renew the acquaintanceship." The reunion went well and the two of them seemed to sense a certain comic kinship. Mel's unruly creative imagination dovetailed nicely with Sid's unorthodox repertoire, and though the two of them were different in many respects (Sid was tall, imposing, and powerful, Mel short, pulsating, and feisty), they became friends and the friendship became Mel's license to suggest bits and characterizations which Sid welcomed and gladly paid for.

The first time Max Liebman laid eyes on Mel Brooks was in 1948 backstage at the Broadhurst Theatre. At Max's suggestion, Sid was appearing in Jo Hyman's revue *Make Mine Manhattan* and taking Broadway by storm. Max had had a hand in the show's writing and production which facilitated his ongoing grooming of Sid. One day Max stopped by to say hello to his protégé, when he noticed "this kid" whom Sid introduced as Mel Brooks. Before they could even exchange pleasantries or platitudes, Sid urged Mel: "Do for Max what you just did for me." With no more encouragement than that, Mel spun onstage so that he faced the empty house, and launched into his Catskills theme song, from socko start to one-knee finish. After more than a score of years in show business Max thought he had seen it all, but he had never seen anything quite like this. If this peculiar introduction made any impression on him, he diplomatically kept it to himself.

And yet, if Max Leibman thought he had seen the last of this kid, he was sadly mistaken. Mel was already caught up in the slipstream of Sid's success. Later that year when Max approached Sid to join him and some hand-picked associates in a television venture, Sid accepted and invited along Mel. When the show premièred in January 1949 as "The Admiral Broadway Revue," it did so without the formal services of Mel. Nonetheless, throughout the show's nineteen-week run, Mel stalked the corridors, excluded from the staff writing sessions, but no less willing to throw a line or gag whenever Sid emerged from behind closed doors. For his troubles, Mel was paid fifty dollars a week out-of-pocket by Sid.

Even after the show was dropped by Admiral only to resurface the following February in full flower as "Your Show of Shows," Mel was still without official recognition, seemingly the inveterate outsider. Sid kept him close by, ever a corridor away, and continued to turn to him in a pinch for material, but Mel declined further Caesar handouts, hoping instead to become an accredited contributor. Some were beginning to admit that Mel might be able to make a positive contribution to the show. Others just passed him off as some kind of mascot, Sid's sidekick. But whatever the reigning policy, Mel's material kept creeping into the show.

"Your Show of Shows" was an instant critical success, and its popular following swelled by the week. It was soon obvious to all involved that the program would be settling in for several seasons. That would mean more material, and there was this miniature tummler decorating the hall. Mel's siege was weakening the battlements. By the seventh show, Max granted a dispensation and permitted onscreen credit on the post-performance credit crawl: "Additional Dialogue by Mel Brooks." Mel had his foot in the door, and wouldn't budge until he was a fully recognized insider. By the next season the crawl read: "Written by: Max Liebman, Sid Caesar, Lucille Kallen, Mel Tolkin and Mel

Brooks." He had all but browbeat his way into the inner circle, but the point was he had made it. The self-pronounced loser was at last securely among winners. That, at least, made him a winner by association. Mel was determined to become a winner in his own right.

4

Ten thirty-eight East Tremont, Apartment 4B, Bronx, New York. Molly, Jake, Rosalie, Sammy, and Uncle David—they would have been within virtual shouting distance of Anne Italiano's old neighborhood had they, in fact, existed. But they were fictional characters, the widely known regulars of Gertrude Berg's, "The Goldbergs." In 1950 any connection between Anne and the family was strictly professional.

Gertrude Berg invented the Goldbergs for radio, with their NBC radio debut in November 1929 as "The Rise of the Goldbergs." The program's popularity quickly snowballed and even came to rival "Amos 'n' Andy" for audience size and loyalty. Molly Goldberg's trademark opening, "Yoo-hoo! Mrs. Bloom!" was second in familiarity only to "Holy mack'l, Andy" (which probably says less about the quaintness of radio's Golden Age than it does about the then condescending naïveté of the country's ethnic awareness). To her credit, Berg did not dwell on urban Jewish stereotypes so much as personalize them into slice-of-life miniature dramas and warmly humorous, if often maudlin, morality playlets. To her further credit, the series, which she authored, produced, and starred in, was astonishingly durable. "The

Goldbergs" remained on NBC through 1934, vanished for a year, then reappeared on CBS radio where it stayed for the better part of the next fifteen years.

When Worthington Miner was made manager of program development for CBS Television in 1948, one of his priorities was to produce a half-hour situation comedy. Rather than experiment with some untested property ("Studio One" provided all the conceptual originality one producer could hope for or want) he turned to the radio for inspiration and singled out "The Goldbergs" for adaptation to television. While many of television's early favorites had been spirited away from radio, success in one medium was no guarantee of success in the other. The visible cast did not always suit the audience's mental picture of a radio character and that disparity alone could doom a series. Besides, hallowed radio stars were not necessarily eager to test the uncharted shallows of this new medium.

Miner's choice was vindicated when radio's Goldbergs won immediate television acceptance. Gertrude Berg was to all appearances Molly Goldberg incarnate, motherly, mild-mannered, mildly overweight, and benevolently manipulative. Philip Loeb was fittingly irascible as her husband "Jake," Larry Robinson made an innocuous son "Sammy," Arlene McQuade a forthright daughter "Rosie," and Eli Minitz a sage "Uncle David." The show also provided a steady stream of featured players, among them a young actress calling herself Anne Marno.

Anne's able showing on "Studio One" became her ticket to other Worthington Miner productions. Fresh-faced, gifted, and with a manner and speech that clearly carried the stamp of her Bronx upbringing, Anne was a natural for "The Goldbergs." Portraying a neighborhood kid, she appeared with some regularity and braced herself for the show's unrelenting production schedule.

"The Goldbergs" aired Monday nights between nine-thirty and ten. Rehearsal began the previous Tuesday, running from three to seven at the Nolo Studios on West Fifty-seventh. Friday morning the cast moved to Caravan Hall on East Fifty-ninth for a brief run-through, broke for lunch, and then gathered at the CBS building on Madison Avenue to brush up on the preceding week's script which was presented with minor changes on radio each Friday evening from eight to eight-thirty. Saturdays were off days, Sundays another run-through. Monday, the cast collected at Leiderkranz Hall on East Fifty-eighth and rehearsed from noon until air time. At nine-thirty, Molly Goldberg would casually greet the viewing public from the open window of her simulated Tremont Avenue tenement, shmooze liberally, cause and solve a small family crisis, and find time in between plot detours to extol the virtues of Sanka coffee. It was a hectic pace and Anne's limited duty was a blessing since it left her time to try her luck elsewhere.

Anne was working but being typecast. Her dark hair and soft features could be made to suggest any number of ethnic types, and with live television drama spreading in the wake of "Studio One" Anne was seldom without a job. Beginning with *Torrents of Spring* in April 1950, Anne worked forty-nine of the next sixty-nine weeks. Many of the roles were incidental, but several were leads.

After a featured turn with Robert Sterling that May in a "Studio One" production of *The Man Who Had Influence,* Anne landed her first starring role opposite Charlton Heston, also on "Studio One." "Letter From Cairo" was aired Monday, December 4, and it told the story of a young man, Mitch Henderson, combing the political underworld of postwar iron curtain Europe in search of a missing friend. Henderson meets a Czechoslovakian girl who becomes a pawn in underground intrigue. Anne of course played the Czech girl and the network press releases pointed to her proudly as a "Studio One" "find."

Just how much of a find was indicated by the coded casting card kept by Franklin Schaffner, who directed Anne in *Torrents of Spring,* and later again in *The Man Who Had Influence.* Anne Marno's index card read: "CDXX," which, decoded, meant that in Schaffner's opinion she could play comedy or drama, and that she was an excellent actress. It was a high compliment, especially in view of the superb actors who graced so many "Studio One" productions (Jessica Tandy, Margaret Sullavan, Hume Cronyn, Mildred Natwick, Jack Lemmon, E. G. Marshall, Kevin McCarthy, to name only a few).

But Anne's acknowledged versatility and acceptance in a highly competitive medium left her no illusions. She was a realist, the first to admit she had everything to learn about acting and plenty of time in which to learn it. On only her third television show, she was talking to a young actor, Rod Steiger, who asked her what she thought about the Method's patriarch, Stanislavski. Anne's unassuming reply was, "Who's he?" Steiger loaned her a volume of *An Actor Prepares* but she didn't read it, preferring instead to learn from experience and the comments of those around her.

Anne's native talents were being refined by an acting technique that was more than adequate and improving with each job. She took direction well and had the luxury of learning her art via on-the-job trial and error. The simple yardstick of her nascent artistry was the fact that she was making precious few errors.

If there was any cause for concern, it was the recurrent typecasting. Not so much that she was playing ingenues—that is the passing fate of most young actresses—but that she was playing "ethnic" ingenues. Such pigeonholing led to many opportunities, but it also carried certain restrictions. Television dramatists were for the most part white and male, and their ethnic female characters were often stereotyped. Anne could particularize a given type but she could also be trapped by a kind of categorical writing. Still, she was working, and for the present the benefits of employment outweighed the dangers of typecasting.

Anne returned to "Studio One" in April of 1951, this time as a Latvian girl, in Robert Anderson's adaptation of Jan Valtin's love story *Wintertime*. The story told of a romance between a German merchant marine officer who returns home after two years in an American prisoner-of-war camp and meets Lisa, the Latvian girl. John Forsythe played the officer and Anne, Lisa. The show was well received and it figured in an offer to Anne from another CBS dramatic series "Danger." She took the job and with it the chance to work with one of television's most promising young directors, Sidney Lumet.

The Killer Scarf, from a script by Walter Bernstein, was the story of a young circus acrobat, Heidi, who must choose between her guardian, Fernandez, and an animal trainer, Carlos. What distinguished the show was its setting. Bernstein and Lumet arranged for their circus drama to coincide with the coming to town of the genuine article, and they abandoned the safety of the CBS Studio for New York's Madison Square Garden. It was an ambitious undertaking, especially in live television, where an average soundstage gave a director all the headaches he could handle. But then, if wrestling and boxing could be captured on live remote, why not drama? On Tuesday, May 1, *The Killer Scarf* was broadcast from backstage at the Garden with the King Brothers and Barnum and Bailey Circus noisily in progress on the main arena floor. Aside from the featured players, the production dripped with authentic circus color. Caged animals roared on and off camera, circus performers acted as extras, and a vendor (played by Stanley Prager) shuttled back and forth hawking hot dogs. There was ambiance galore and even something of plot, with Greg Morton as Fernandez, Ray Danton as Carlos the animal trainer, and Anne as the shapely Heidi. It was a three-ring thirty minutes and it gave Anne her first taste of location work (not even Stanislavski could help when a snarling leopard stepped on your lines).

For Anne there was typecasting, and then there was imaginative typecasting. Where others had seen a guileless, vulnerable allure in her large brown eyes and velvety voice, producer Robert Stevens saw the potential for a shadowy and mystical, even diabolical, side. Stevens signed Anne for a week's "Suspense Theatre," yet another CBS live thirty-minute drama, and handed her the role of a young woman said to have psychic powers. *A Vision of Death*, with Henry Hull and Jerome Cowan, was a preternatural murder mystery ("pulse-quickening" according to press releases) in which the very psychic powers intended for a chosen victim become the young woman's undoing.

For marginally more upbeat fare, Anne returned to Sidney Lumet and "Danger," and promptly became a gangster's consort in a drama called *A Murderer's Face*. The show, aired in August 1951, was an old chestnut about an ex-con who has his face altered by plastic surgery (it was the plot that could have used the face-lift). Anne played opposite Robert Pastene in what was to be one of her last appearances as Anne Marno.

Although live television drama was widely held in high regard, few of those actors working in the medium regarded it as an end in itself. Television was in many ways a hybrid of theatre and film, but it lacked its own autonomous identity. Moreover, dramatic acting on television was the worse for commercial constraints—interruption, brevity, and censorship—all of which worked against performance.

Consequently television was as much a staging area as a stage, a place where credentials could be collected and reputations made for work elsewhere. The legitimate theatre was only a matter of city blocks away and network hookups brought Hollywood within reach (in fact, shrewd movie scouts were already in the habit of poaching in the television preserves for bright young talent). For Anne, exploring beyond television seemed not so much a question of whether and if but of how and when.

So far Anne's career had pretty much taken care of itself. She had been hired directly out of acting school and in little more than a year had risen from bit and supporting roles to featured and starring roles. She was working steadily and at the same time improving her craft in the company of skilled professionals. And perhaps more important, she was redeeming the faith of Michael and Millie, to say nothing of their five-hundred-dollar investment. Nineteen-year-old Anne Italiano had a burgeoning career, a generous income, independence, a stage name. She also had a boy friend.

John Ericson was an actor. His father was a successful businessman, his mother a former Shakespearean actress of some repute. After graduating from Newton High School in Elmhurst, New York, John enrolled at the AADA, where he studied for two years, acting summers at the Gateway Theatre in Gatlinburg, Tennessee, with a summer stock company directed by one of the Academy's instructors. At six feet two inches and 180 pounds, John was an athletic, all-American sort, with light brown hair, gray-green eyes, an angular jaw, and a broad, effortless smile. He appeared on "Studio One" and "Philco Playhouse," and was

about to return to Gatlinburg for a fourth summer, when he
stopped by the ANTA Theatre on West Fifty-second Street to
audition for a film role about which he had heard. Within hours
he was chosen from among three hundred actors and within two
weeks was on his way to Italy to appear in Fred Zinnemann's
Teresa.

When John returned from Italy, he and Anne started seeing
each other and soon were inseparable. Both were young, attractive, and more than getting by in a most difficult profession. John
was a few years Anne's senior but friends remember her as the
poised and confident one (if still detectably shy), him as the innocent, incurable romantic. Whatever their differences, both
soon took to calling their relationship an "engagement," although no wedding plans were immediately forthcoming. Had
there been plans, they probably would have been set aside for
John's next acting job.

Donald Bevan and Edmund Trzcinski had written a service
comedy-melodrama set in a German prisoner of war camp, a
play entitled *Stalag 17*. The show's director, Jose Ferrer, had been
casting the role of Sefton, a hard-bitten loner accused of being
a Nazi informer and left to exonerate himself by uncovering the
actual double agent. John auditioned for the part and Ferrer
hired him. The production opened on Broadway to strong reviews in May 1951. John was accorded special praise for a performance that was to win him the New York Critics Award as
the stage's most promising newcomer. However, success had its
debts and John was obliged to stay with the play through its
New York run (ultimately eighteen months) as well as a road
tour (another six).

New York must have seemed the best of all possible worlds to
Anne and John. To frustrated young actors and actresses, the
city could be a hellhole; an inhospitable place to wait tables
and save tips for carfare to auditions, praying for call-backs or
non-paying parts on off-off-Broadway let alone steady, paying
work. There might not have been, as the saying rhapsodized "a
broken heart for every light on Broadway," but there were prob-

ably twice that many hopefuls waiting tables while waiting for
the least opportunity to act.

The odds against a single novice finding regular acting work
directly out of school were astronomical. And yet both John and
Anne had managed as much with every reason to think that the
best was yet to come.

That summer Anne was approached by Frank Gregory, a
"test" director who worked out of Twentieth Century–Fox's East
Coast office. Each year Gregory put together screen tests to
showcase New York talent for the edification of the West Coast
office. This particular test was to feature a young actor named
Doug Rogers in a scene from *The Girl on the Via Flaminia*. The
scene required an actress, and Gregory asked Anne if she would
be willing to assist. There was nothing to lose and perhaps something to gain by way of experience. She agreed to help out.

In the course of rehearsal, Anne shone. Although the test was
naturally designed to favor Rogers, Gregory decided to redis-
tribute the footage equally between the two, allowing Anne a
share of camera time and close-ups. The test was shot, printed,
and sent off to the Coast for screening.

Anne continued to divide her time between television work
and John. The likelihood of marriage seemed less and less remote until on October 12 their plans were thrown a curve.

Anne was over on Fifth Avenue taking in the annual Columbus Day Parade. Meanwhile, her agent was frantically scour-
ing the crowds that lined the sidewalks. Finally he spotted her in
front of Bergdorf Goodman, pulled her aside, pressed her against
the plate glass, and told her his news—the Fox executives had
passed on Doug Rogers but were eager to sign Anne Marno. It
seemed too good to be true, certainly too good to pass up, and
Anne gladly signed.

Anne and John were not entirely unprepared for this eventu-
ality. He had been thinking of doing more filmwork at some
point and this was all the extra incentive he needed. The plan
was for Anne to go West and start work for Fox. John would
finish the run with *Stalag 17* and then join her on the Coast.
They would be married and for all anyone knew maybe become
the next Pickford and Fairbanks.

In mid-November Anne left New York escorted by Millie. For Anne, who had never seen a palm tree or a private swimming pool nor, for that matter, ever flown in an airplane, it must have all seemed the edge of some great fantasy.

5

Max fired Mel, sometimes daily, even hourly. The seasoned producer and the unschooled writer would reach an impasse over some material, a question of taste, of judgment, of comic acumen. Tempers would smolder, voices swell, until the otherwise tranquil Max would pluck the lighted cigar from his lips and dart it at Mel, whose dodging soon became second nature. Spleens backwashed, it was back to business. Of course Mel was never truly fired. Had he been that expendable he'd have never been hired in the first place.

The hallmark of "Your Show of Shows" was professionalism, and Max Liebman was its arbiter, its curator, its mainstay. Professionalism, not in the mechanical but the theatrical sense, with the producer not a one-man show but a showman sufficiently organized to accommodate creative disorganization and temperament. Much as Max demanded decorum during rehearsal and performance, he encouraged mayhem during writing and rough-outs. Max, who had worked for Sam Goldwyn during a stint with M-G-M, was fond of a particular Goldwynism: "From a polite story conference comes a polite script." The show's creative process was always professional, but polite? —never. Under Max's unerring eye, "Your Show of Shows" was the ideal climate for writers and performers alike to learn, to improve, and in some cases, to perfect their craft. Mel liked to call it "Max Liebman University." And, in truth, the show was a kind of clearinghouse for Max's own cumulative show business knowledge. But while "Your Show of Shows" could be said to bear his stylistic imprint, it never did so to the diminishment of its stars. Max knew how to spot talent, how to distill and present it, when to protect, when to probe it, but most of all he knew when to leave talent to its own devices. Like the best of producers, Max knew exactly his own worth.

He was born in Vienna and brought up in Brooklyn. The son of a furrier, he attended Boys' High School, where he was a prominent member of the drama club, the debating society, and the school magazine staff, where he served as a humor columnist and eventually editor. He helped write and produce the class play, and upon graduation in 1917, he went not to Broadway, as his schoolmates expected, but to Texas to try his hand as a speculator in oil leases. His career in the oil fields was short-lived, though his speculative nature was still very much alive. He traveled to Hollywood and found work writing titles for silent pictures. Tiring of that, he teamed with a minor vaudeville monologist and toured the midwest circuits, writing and producing the act. In 1920 he returned to New York and applied his growing expertise to flash acts—miniature revues with singing, dancing, and patter that closed the bill at quality vaudeville houses.

In 1925, at the age of twenty-three, Max hired on as social director at the Log Tavern summer camp, just finishing construction near Stroudsburg, Pennsylvania. At the outset he pepped and tummled, getting a rise out of his guests at any cost, if need be by taking a dip fully clothed. But Max quickly distinguished himself from the usual dime-a-dozen tummlers when he began producing shows for the camp. The stage was primitive, the lighting crude (candles at one point), the company limited (he was emcee, comic, and occasionally stage manager, dousing the lights on his own black-out skits), but he made the best of it, and that was often damn good. Summer camps were then something of a Broadway tributary, and there was no shortage of promising young writers and performers. Max threw together his first show with the help of Yip Harburg and Morrie Ryskind and, from that auspicious start, steadily improved.

After seven summers at Log Tavern, Max took a large step forward by accepting the position of social director at Camp Tamiment in the Poconos. With its 1160-seat theatre, lavish operating budget, and ready supply of staff theatre hopefuls, Tamiment became a kind of rural off-Broadway, more studio workshop than quaint summer stock. Max assembled a first-rate stock company which included Pat Carroll, the dancing team Mata and Hari, Betty Garrett, Anita Alvarez, Imogene Coca (who had already made her Broadway debut in *New Faces of 1934*), and Danny Kaye (doubling as waiter and tummler). The production staff showed at least as much potential with the likes of its young choreographer, Jerome Robbins. Max's goal was straightforward and by all standards but his, impossible—a thoroughly new revue each Saturday night. Given the regular turnover of guests, repetition would have been forgivable. But Max would have none of it. He demanded, and got, a new show every week, complete with dancing, singing, and comedy. If the pace was torturous, the compensations were many. To begin with, the Tamiment guests, many of them professionals from New York, were a sophisticated and appreciative audience. Likewise, Unity House, a summer retreat run by the ILGWU, was only a mile down the road and whenever the union secured a block of tickets, the staff could count on a tough but attentive house. What's more, once word of Tamiment's extraordinary output reached the city, hardly a performance went by when the audience wasn't buzzing with agents and talent scouts.

For Max, off-season was the theatre's on-season, and come fall he returned to New York and an office at 240 West Forty-second Street, where he read new plays and bailed out others already in production and struggling toward opening night. He gained a reputation as a canny play doctor, as well as a writer of original nightclub acts and a healer of faltering ones. But like any doctor, he was not always his own best patient. In February 1939, his revue *Off to Buffalo!* opened on Broadway and shuffled off to oblivion before the week was out, gaining him a charter membership in the newly formed "One Week Club." After a recu-

peratory summer at Tamiment, Max was approached by the
Shuberts to prepare a musical revue for Broadway with a tiny
budget of $5,500. He mounted the show at Tamiment and that
September *The Straw Hat Revue* opened to good reviews and
became the vehicle for Danny Kaye's legitimate debut. The next
summer, Max returned to Tamiment and Kaye went into Moss
Hart's play *Lady in the Dark*. It was only a matter of time before
Kaye would receive the Hollywood call, and when he did, Max
was asked to come, which was only natural, since along with
Danny's wife, Sylvia Fine, Max had had a strong hand in writing and conceiving most of his best material. Besides, it was
practically family. Don Hartman, who had been a waiter at Log
Tavern and preceded Max as social director at Tamiment, had
been hired by M-G-M and was asked to co-produce Kaye's first
film, *Up in Arms*. Max worked on this and other Kaye films, and
stayed on to punch up other Metro projects. His option had been
renewed and he was on three-week hiatus when he received a
call from Vernon Duke asking him to help produce and direct
Tars and Spars. Max accepted on the condition that his contribution be completed within the three weeks prior to renewal at
M-G-M.

His reputation preceded him. With the wartime ban on civilian air travel, Max took to the rails. When he arrived in Palm
Beach he was met by the show's young comic discovery, Sid
Caesar. Sid was fully aware of what Max had done to propel
Danny Kaye's career, and frankly was ready to be discovered.
That same night, Duke arranged an audition for Max, who was
told that this Caesar kid clowned and made sounds, "one of the
greatest 'sounds-men' in captivity." Max, long the witness and
mentor of Kaye's stunningly original comic virtuosity, was skeptical, but when he watched Caesar work, he was "bowled over."
In the course of ensuing rehearsals, Max was struck by two
somewhat opposing sides of Sid's work: that here was a stark
brilliance softened by a certain sincerity and winsomeness, and
that Sid had "no discipline that would tie him to a script." Max
worked assiduously at bringing these characteristics into focus,
balancing spontaneity and discipline, and Sid was a model student.

Max guided *Tars and Spars* through its winning opening, left his blessings for a successful road tour, and hurried back to M-G-M. Within a year he was back in New York, explaining to friends that he "never had more than one foot in Hollywood" in the first place. Happily back in his home town, Max reappeared among the Shubert Alley regulars, and with Sid's star steadily on the ascent, was asked to write and direct several sketches for a revue that would serve as the comic's Broadway debut. *Make Mine Manhattan* opened in New Haven to tumultuous reviews, gained momentum through Philadelphia, and opened at the Broadhurst Theatre in January 1948 charming the critics and establishing Sid as the season's find.

Never one to rest on his laurels, Max persisted in what was for him an ongoing talent hunt. In that spirit, he took in a little show at Town Hall and was so impressed by what he saw that he called the show's producer to find what team of writers had been responsible for the material. The "team" turned out to be Lucille Kallen, a young, attractive, diminutive, dynamic woman from Toronto. Max approached her and invited her to join him that summer at Tamiment. That May, Lucille journeyed to the Poconos where she met another writer, a tall, somber-looking gentleman with rather more than a trace of accent, Mel Tolkin. There was an instant rapport between the two and they teamed to fill Max's inexorable new-revue-a-week quota, collaborating not only on comic sketches but on music and lyrics as well. It was exhausting, but a glorious summer for all.

This was Max's fifteenth season at Tamiment. In that span, he had prepared summer after summer of lively, original, quality entertainment. He had prevailed in Hollywood and on Broadway, had seen at least two protégés (Danny Kaye and Sid Caesar) rise to stardom. He was forty-six years old, with more than his share of success, and had every reason for complacence. Just to maintain that pace would have been difficult enough. But Max thrived on experimentation, and something had happened to place a new seed of creation in his imagination. Before returning to Tamiment in 1948, Max had taken an apartment on Ninth Street in Greenwich Village. One day he dropped in at Wanamaker's Department Store on some errands when he noticed a bulky, boxy gadget on display—Max had just seen his first television set. The broadcast was clumsy—some college glee club rendering "The Whiffenpoof Song" or something like that—but the immediate content mattered less than the form. Max made a mental note: "This is for me, this is my medium."

He carried this thought through the summer at Tamiment and so it was with more a sense of predilection than prophecy that he greeted Harry Kalcheim, an agent with William Morris, who arrived one Saturday with an advertising man, Pat Weaver. Weaver was with Young and Rubicam, and represented a client who was contemplating sponsorship in commercial television. The two men visited with Max that afternoon and evening, and after dinner as Max excused himself to tend to that night's entertainment, Kalcheim and Weaver apologized in advance for having to leave with the final curtain. Max recognized the old ruse, he had used it himself. It was a way of anticipating a bad or mediocre show and planning an escape from the dishonest small talk and perfunctory compliments that thwart a timely exit.

The revue went as usual—splendidly—and afterward Max was accosted by an ecstatic Pat Weaver. Weaver's runaway enthusiasm turned into a marathon discussion that lasted until four in the morning. He was astonished by what he had just witnessed, but there was a lingering skepticism: "Well, all right, I saw the show and it was very impressive. It is, I think, a good indication of what you could do in television. But on television you have to do it every week." Max paused, permitted himself a self-satisfied smile, and replied: "Come again next week. And come the week after. And come the week after that." He made his point.

Weaver returned a few times—his own fascination aside, his client had lost interest. Harry Kalcheim swung into action once more, this time courting Myron Kirk of the Kudner Agency, packagers of Milton Berle. Kirk took a look at Max's operation, liked what he saw, and approached Admiral to sponsor a weekly televised revue. Paradoxically, while Admiral was in the business of manufacturing televisions, it was now hesitant in the matter of commercial sponsorship. On the surface, it would have seemed symbiotic—better programming would mean better sales.

But the year before, Admiral had come up empty-handed in a television venture starring Dean Martin and Jerry Lewis, and was
content to return to technology, leaving creativity to others.

Max traveled to New York and personally pitched the president of Admiral on the show's concept. The president finally
relented, agreeing to underwrite the show to the tune of $1,500 a
week, inclusive—once burnt, twice dollar shy. Max winced at the
thrift but welcomed the opportunity. He'd worked gold from
dross too many times to be intimidated by initial budget stric-
tures. Admittedly, $1,500 spread pretty thinly over production
costs, actors' salaries, and writers' fees, but he knew this would
be a foot in the door of a new and vital medium. His faith had
been validated again and again, at Tamiment, in Hollywood, on
Broadway. Admiral was willing to bank the show with an eight-
week option. That would be more than enough time to use the
show itself as a kind of trial balloon. If it got off the ground, Max
was sure it would survive, with or without Admiral.

There remained the choice of network. Max had been in touch
with CBS and was leaning in that direction when he learned that
his earlier admirer, Pat Weaver, had signed with NBC as an executive vice-president. Weaver's faith in Max had not diminished
one iota and with that alone NBC was offered the show, which it
eagerly accepted and programmed for a January première. The
commitment made, Max now had to make good his conviction.

The Tamiment formula supplied a durable framework, but it
was not expressly transferable to television. Whereas Tamiment
could carry simply on the strength of its collected talents, television required a central star—that much was already clear even in
the medium's infancy. Max approached Sid Caesar and Sid accepted. For a supporting cast, Max turned to his good friend,
Imogene Coca, whom Max knew as an expert comedienne and
pantomimist, a seasoned performer and disciplined professional,
and as someone whose steadiness might temper Sid's sometimes
tempestuous brilliance. Mary McCarty was asked to help out
with the comic chores, and Marge and Gower Champion were
given the primary singing and dancing duties.

There was never any doubt about writers. In the course of the
summer just past, Lucille Kallen and Mel Tolkin had become an

estimable triple threat with comedy, lyrics, and music. They did the work of six writers, and considering the financial squeeze, would have to. That left the production staff, for which Max simply turned to his trusted Broadway colleagues. Charlie Sanford, Max's conductor from *Make Mine Manhattan,* was enlisted, as was scenic designer Frederick Fox (also of *Make Mine Manhattan*). James Starbuck was added as choreographer, and Paul du Pont as costumer. As for himself, Max prepared to do what he had done on all his revues—everything else.

The miserly budget had been stretched to its limit. Every cent had been accounted for when Sid suggested to Max that he hire on staff his friend Mel Brooks. Max's response was simple: "I have no money for him." It was a good reason, if incomplete. The extent of Max's exposure to Mel had been the brief encounter backstage at the Broadhurst which, while it did nothing to alienate the producer, certainly did nothing to captivate him. As far as Max could tell, Mel was little more than a Caesar camp follower who had had some personal success in the Catskills but was far from essential to the current project. There was no spite or animosity in the rejection, just the simple arithmetic of finance and creative input, neither of which accommodated Sid's sidekick.

That did nothing to shake Sid's confidence in Mel or his desire to have him around. He simply paid him a comic retainer of sorts, and Max raised no objection to the arrangement—if it made his star happy, where was the harm? The others either paid Mel no notice, humored him as they would the village idiot, or wrote him off as Sid's private court jester. They grossly underestimated Mel Brooks.

The "Admiral Broadway Revue" premièred Saturday January 28, 1949, decked its appointed hour's air time with sketches, production numbers, characterizations, and a good measure of Sid's patented double-talk, and won a more than respectable share of popular and critical acclaim. For the next several months, the pace never slackened. The following week's show was regularly in the works before the present week's show even aired. It was creative perpetual motion which in the tradition of theatre did more to exhilarate than exhaust the company.

Mel meanwhile became a fixture at the show's Eighth Avenue offices. But the atmosphere was too informal and the pace too frenzied for anyone to bother with him, let alone try to find out exactly what his designated function was. Lucille Kallen regarded him as some sort of Damon Runyon character, hovering about, cracking wise at the least provocation, and generally spilling his own ample energy into the show's creative maelstrom. Max allowed him to "stalk the corridors" but was careful to draw the line there. Mel was not admitted to closed-door sessions and, while it was increasingly clear that Sid was a willing conduit for much of his friend's material, Mel never received onscreen credit on the Admiral show. Despite his status as an official nonentity, his presence and assurance sometimes approached pretension. One time, without even stopping to think that Lucille Kallen was 50 per cent of the writing staff and not some secretarial factotum, Mel came to her self-importantly with some scribbled sheaf of material and brusquely said, "Type this up." She simply ignored him, or at least tried to. It wasn't long before a bare realization took hold from the lowliest stagehand to Max himself, who was forced to admit: "Nobody could disregard Mel Brooks."

Nevertheless salience was not experience, and whenever Sid hinted that Mel be added to the official payroll, Max insisted: "He's not ready yet, he can hang around." Hang around he did, with a vengeance. He became embedded in the show's offstage landscape. Whether as uncredited contributor or sassy courtier or some cross of the two, Mel's attendance was such that his occasional absence seldom went unremarked. His presence was not confined to the office. If a group stepped out for lunch, Mel was there on the sidewalk, hands in pocket, a half step ahead of the pack, joking and jabbering. If the male members closed a hard day's work with a *shvitz* and a rub at the Gotham Health Club, Mel was there in full kinesis. And while Max would have been loathe to say so, his resistance was weakening. In fact, Mel might well have found his way onto the crawl of the "Admiral Broadway Revue," had the show survived. It didn't.

Admiral picked up the option once, then another time, and promptly dropped the show for reasons strictly extrinsic to the show itself. The American public had been infected with the television bug, and it was all Admiral could do to keep up with manufacturing demands. By 1949, the onetime novelty gave every indication of exploding into a major industry. Television was its own best advertisement, and Admiral saw no reason for direct sponsorship on the level that the increasingly popular Broadway Revue would require.

The show outgrew its sponsor. Its conceptual sophistication, its theatrical fluency, its comedic literacy, and its uncompromising production standards had local reviewers comparing it not merely to other television variety shows, but favorably to the Broadway musical stage itself. It was clear to everyone involved that the show would need to breathe beyond the $1,500 a week fiscal straitjacket that the sponsor had agreed to. Much of the Revue's original material had been culled from the ample store of that brought from Tamiment by Max, Lucille, and Mel (Tolkin). That had been catalogued and collected behind each show's weekly theme (e.g. "Night Life in New York," "Hollywood," "Signs of Spring,") and, as the supply neared depletion, it was acknowledged that the writing staff would require at least minimal expansion. Furthermore, it was doubtful how much longer the costumes and orchestrations could be brought in on a shoestring, and Fred Fox's sets had been repainted so many times that, like a Chinese lacquer box, they were taking on an independent life of their own. The truth was, as Max put it: "Admiral was beginning to feel that it was giving a champagne party but was serving beer." While the "Admiral Broadway Revue" proper closed, its construct was not so much ended as interrupted. None of those involved with the show was worried about his future in the business.

Mel Brooks shared in the metamorphosis, if in a less certifiable fashion. He had started out as some energized, tummling gadfly, "Caesar's boy." But roughly halfway through the show's nineteen-week existence, he had begun to gain credibility. Beside the formidable versatility of Kallen and Tolkin, Mel's writing scope seemed narrow and unfocused. But he was an apt apprentice and the more time he spent in the company of the accomplished, the more accomplished he became. His strength was still the outlandish, the lopsided, and the bizarre, but that fastened him securely to a specific color of Sid's comic spectrum. As the show settled in, there was no mistaking that Mel had something of value to offer, and that was his sole salvation, otherwise he would have been out on his ear. He attained the dubious status of "member of the staff without credit," but the lack of stringent attribution guidelines (prior to the later standardization by the Writers Guild) actually worked to Mel's advantage. He could not at that point have made the grade as a fully credited writer, but the informal arrangement, sparing as it was, was giving him the chance to mature as a writer. Whatever was likely to rise from the ashes of the Revue, Mel had good reason to expect that he might be a part of it.

The Admiral show had barely been interred when Pat Weaver invited Max Liebman over to Rockefeller Center for a tête-à-tête. Max's "trial balloon" had more than dispelled any remaining doubts Weaver might have had about the feasibility of mounting an original weekly revue. In fact, assured that here was a showman's showman, Weaver now reasoned that if Max had been doing the impossible in an hourly program, he could do it in triplicate: "People go out on Saturday night for entertainment. We would like to give them what they would go out for." The proposal amounted to three hours of premium programming. Ambitiousness was one thing, recklessness quite another. Whatever else Max was, he was not a magician, and he knew at once that 180 minutes could not be filled by a single show without sacrifice of quality, to say nothing of sanity. Max ran a lightning mental inventory of his resources, swallowed slowly, and spoke softly: "The most I could do is an hour and a half." Weaver smiled; that was plenty.

Weaver's master plan took shape as "The NBC Saturday Night Revue," a banner title for what were to be two separate and distinct shows. Beginning at 8:00 P.M., the first hour would originate from Chicago and headline Jack Carter in a slapdash variety show. After sixty minutes with Carter (and Dorothy Claire, Benny Baker, and Cass Daley), the broadcast would swing to New York for ninety minutes of the Liebman touch, a kind of updated *Ziegfeld Follies*.

Max let it be known from the outset that the new show would not be a mere reprise or protraction of the "Admiral Broadway Revue." That had been a serviceable training vehicle, but its successor was going to be the real article, no false starts, no stumbles. The new show, like the old, would work from the time-honored revue formula, not just because it had worked for Admiral but because it had always been what Max did best. He would, with minor changes and additions, go with the same cast and staff. As for format, he gladly discarded the confining contrivance of a weekly theme or concept, opting instead for a succession of guest hosts who would, it was hoped, inject their own freshness, allow the regulars to play to their strengths (and vice versa), and help relieve Sid of some of those excruciating introductions and expositions that bought time for set changes backstage. Also, unlike the Admiral show, the new show would venture more into what was for television cultural esoterica, with operatic vignettes and balletic excerpts. Max was determined to make this more than just another show, it was to be a showpiece, a crystallization of all he had learned in some thirty years in the business. Taste would temper showmanship, showmanship would insure popularity, and popularity would be taken as a mandate to elevate taste. The show would silence the old H. L. Mencken dictum "Nobody ever went broke underestimating the taste of the American public" without incurring the crippling appellation of "highbrow." The show would optimistically, immodestly, and with an ironic brush of piety be called "Your Show of Shows."

Recruitment followed furiously. James Starbuck, Fred Fox, and Charlie Sanford would resume their duties from the Admiral show. The gifted Aaron Levine was added as something of a musical concierge, feeding ideas and orchestrations for production numbers. The technical staff would remain more or less intact. Sid Caesar, vital to the show's diversified concept, would, beyond the nominal guest star, be the true and pivotal star. Imogene Coca would remain his peerless co-star. Tom Avera, the Admiral show's resident straight man, would stay on for now in that capacity. In the dance department, the Champions would be replaced by Max's Tamiment stalwarts Mata and Hari, fronting Starbuck's enlarged chorus line. Singing duties fell to Bill Hayes, Jack Russell, and the Billy Williams Quartette. Opera stars Marguerite Piazza and Robert Merrill would supply the flossier musical moments, as well as share in the pop stuff. The show would be principally written by the doughty Kallen and Tolkin duo with a lift from Max and Sid and songwriting assistance from Jerry Bock and Larry Halofcenter, who were picked up late in the Admiral run.

When the dust settled, Mel Brooks's status was still maddeningly unresolved. He had, he figured, more than proved himself on the Admiral show. With its more relaxed budget and enlarged creative demands, the new show seemed virtually to cry out for his services, and credit. Neither was immediately forthcoming. Still Mel was not merely tolerated, he was welcomed as "Your Show of Shows" moved into interim offices at the Theatre Guild's ANTA building. His function was yet ill-defined, that is, by all but Max. From his days at M-G-M, Max recalled a lively, galvanizing man who regularly held forth in the studio commissary. Whenever a story conference ran dry the man was summoned and would burst into the room, blasting cigar smoke and good humor, then inquire, "What's the matter, boys? Who's screwing who?" He'd toss off a handful of ideas (few of which ever worked) and exit leaving behind a room of suddenly unblocked writers. If he did nothing else, he "goosed" the conference, and that was a job in itself. Max sensed that Mel would sooner or later matriculate as an official, credited member of the writing staff; it was only a matter of time. Meanwhile, he was useful as a facilitator, an in-house cheerleader, a conference "gooser," a tummler.

If Mel was there in part as the court prankster, it was not his way to take the charge lightly. His often impractical sense of humor was capable of intricate practical jokes, and one of his first and later most reliable victims was Howie Morris. Howie had appeared in a 1945 production of *Hamlet* and in 1948 was touring with *Call Me Mister* when he learned that the Admiral show was mustering and that its hulking star, Sid Caesar, was looking for someone he could lift by the lapels for cartoon comic effect. By the time the program entered actual production, Howie had landed a part in *Gentlemen Prefer Blondes,* just opening on Broadway. Like many others on the show who were also pulling double duty, Howie found he could discharge his stage responsibilities and still make it uptown for a turn or two on television. It was during his first visit to the show's midtown offices that Max introduced him to Mel Tolkin, Lucille Kallen, and a mysterious little Frenchman named "Monsieur Bri," who Max claimed was on hand to research American television. For two days, Monsieur Bri said almost nothing to Howie, and merely nodded or smiled. When he spoke at all, it was in halting French, laced with nuances sounding suspiciously Yiddish. On the third day, the Frenchman approached Howie, laughingly extended a hand and discarded his fractured French: "Howie, how the hell are you." Which was how he met Mel Brooks. When Howie became a regular on "Your Show of Shows," he likewise became the regular target of Mel's pranks. Like Mel, he was short, but with none of Mel's moxie, yet for all the horseplay, the two of them became close friends.

At precisely 9:00 P.M. on February 25, 1950, "Your Show of Shows" had its broadcast première. The credits rolled, the audience applauded, and Charlie Sanford cued the orchestra as the chorus sang:

> "Stars over Broadway
> See them glow.
> Get ready to take in
>   Your Show of Shows.
> Show of Shows! Show of Shows!
> Come on and step lightly
> And walk brightly,
> And join Broadway on parade.
> See that happy, fabulous throng
> Get their fill of rhythm and song. . . ."

Introductions followed, including the first guest host, Burgess Meredith. From there, the show swung to full tempo: Marguerite Piazza sang "Main Street, U.S.A." while Nelle Fisher and Jerry Ross danced; Gertrude Lawrence assisted in a Noel Coward spoof entitled "Life Versus Theatre"; Tom Avera interviewed Sid Caesar as psychologist Professor Kurt von Wolfgang; Bill Hayes sang "Sweet Betsy from Pike" with Fisher and Ross again dancing; Imogene Coca lectured on "Smorgasbord"; Sid played a sketch as Christopher Columbus; Robert Merrill did "The Whiffenpoof Song" more justice than it deserved; Coca returned as "Lillian Bustle"; Gertrude Lawrence sang "I Don't Know"; Sid followed with a brilliant comic monologue as a groom lightly treading the aisle; and the show finished breathlessly with all singing "Dangerous Dan McGrew."

By Monday the notices started appearing, none of them dissenting and most brimming with superlatives. Sid was singled out for his expert comic turns, and Max was roundly applauded for putting the show on its feet. "Your Show of Shows" was clearly here to stay.

Production soon settled into a pattern, although the atmosphere was too charged and the schedule too relentless ever to become routine. Mel was on hand showering ideas, bits, and lines on the others, but he was still frustrated by his omission on the crawl. Befitting Max's sense of order, material was to be typed and submitted to him via his secretary and was to list the name or names of those responsible for the first draft. Sid, who solely spoke his contributions, was excused from this formality, as was Max himself, whose only complete pieces were garnered from his store of vintage bits. During preproduction for the seventh show, Max received a draft of a sketch intended for "Nonentities in the News," a feature spot that was transplanted from the Admiral show and consisted of an interview with some offbeat personage, conducted ordinarily at an airport or some other public place. This particular sketch called on Sid to play a Stanislavski disciple, Ivano Ivanovich, who expounds upon Method acting and, by way of illustration, does an impression of a pinball caroming its way around a pinball machine (complete with bounds, clangs, and choreography) as well as his rendition of *Romeo and Juliet* (both parts, in alternately basso and falsetto Russian gibberish). The sketch was signed "Mel Brooks," and used.

That Saturday night, the credits were altered to read: "Written by Mel Tolkin, Lucille Kallen, Max Liebman, and Sid Caesar, with Additional Dialogue by Mel Brooks." As a writer, Mel had finally become an accredited contributor, or at least partially accredited. By midseason, he was receiving full credit and full pay.

Mel sanctioned was Mel redoubled. The certification of crawl credit was tonic, which with Mel was like nudging the frenetic toward the frantic. The milieu of the writing department was informal but rigorous. There were few rules and regulations, but what few there were Mel learned to violate. Mondays, Max arrived first, usually at nine. Lucille and Mel Tolkin (at over six feet tall and with Mel Brooks's induction, referred to as "Big Mel") would check in, and begin work. Howie and Coca were early shows, Sid generally appeared toward noon, and Mel, "Little Mel," troubled not the least by punctuality, acquired the habit of rolling in last, loosest, and loudest. Seldom did he ever simply enter the office, he made entrances—running, hopping, chugging, sliding as if into second base in the seventh game of the World Series. A rough proportion emerged—the later he was, the more extravagant his tale of inadvertent delay. He was indulged, he was tolerated, but not without a certain telltale dissension. It was whispered by some that Mel's lateness grew out of his unwillingness or inability to share in the constructionist, foundation work of sketches and satires. Mel had no fondness for the labor pains of the craft, he preferred the pyrotechnics.

If anybody harbored any grudge he was too busy to give it second thought. The production schedule was cyclic and unrelenting. The coming show was of necessity already in the works before the current show even aired. Friday afternoons, while the orchestra was rehearsing the present show, Lucille and Big Mel would begin to kick around ideas for the next week's domestic sketch (a regular feature, with Sid and Coca as the "Hickenloopers"). Sunday, and fast in the wake of the previous night's show, Max would meet briefly with choreographer James Star-buck and music co-ordinator Aaron Levine, and start mapping out production numbers for the coming Saturday. Monday, while the rest straggled in, Lucille and Big Mel completed a rough draft of the domestic sketch. Max would dispense other assignments and, after a lunch break, all would attempt to stand the new sketch "on its feet." Lucille would recite the script and if it survived, Sid and Coca would put it through a series of dry runs, dropping portions that failed for reasons ranging from not-funny-enough to too-funny-and-fragmented. They would improvise sections and the writers would start to pitch lines. This was virtually the only phase at which the show was written by committee, and the order of the day was chaos. Suggestions were shouted, changes heatedly challenged, disagreements given wide berth. Little Mel reliably rose to the occasion with a sometimes infuriating volume and obstinacy that often managed to attract Max's cigar like some taunting clown at a carnival bean-bag toss. Lucille, stationed at the typewriter to snare any fleeting brilliance, would have to stand on the desk and flag a sweater to make herself heard. Coca aside from improvisation, preferred to work from script and remained mostly mute leaving the others to fight out controversial points. Sid held an imperious power of veto conveyed in any number of shrugs, glares, and gestures (script crumpling being that least loved by the writers). Max did what he could to arbitrate disputes while retaining final say on what did and did not stay. And by day's end, Max had his "goosed" conference and "unpolite" script. With luck, they knocked off around six.

By Tuesday, Max would have consulted with Fred Fox and Paul du Pont regarding sets and costumes, and then would begin to supervise rehearsals for dancers and singers. The writers continued to sweat out separate assignments, with Little Mel running off at odd tangents with disconnected bits and lines that coalesced into usable comedy at a rate approaching, most agreed, one in fifty. It spoke more of the diffuse outpouring of his imagination than of his actual contribution. He would enact and improvise a premise at the drop of a hat. The others remember him as being "utterly without fear," willing to risk ridicule and scorn. And forgetting the average forty-nine unworkable notions, the one that panned out was usually a gem. Everyone endured considerable dross for that one solid gold nugget, but with a yawning ninety minutes of weekly show to fill, it was a small price to ask. In spite of his flamboyance, his spillover flashiness and annoyance, Little Mel was pulling his weight. After lunch on Tuesday, the guest star would venture in, and material presumably tailored for him or her would be tested for fit.

Wednesdays, the writers proceeded to shore up material, editing and restructuring segments, hurrying drafts for the secretaries to type and mimeograph. Rehearsals continued apace in the separate departments, and by evening, when everyone else had gone home, Max would confer with Aaron Levine and start to sound out ideas for musical numbers yet two Saturdays away.

Thursdays, while the singers and dancers continued rehearsing, the cast would read through the mimeographed script and the writers would "tighten up" the material, adding and subtracting paragraphs and pages as necessary.

Friday morning, after Lucille and Big Mel had begun to rough-out ideas for next week's sketch, the company would gather at eleven o'clock in the rehearsal hall for a dry run. This was the first step toward actually mounting and integrating the separate parts of the show, providing for a specific camera strategy and an overall look. It was a mark of Max's vision and precision as a producer that, aside from working out sundry kinks, the dry run resembled the initial conception of a given show with remarkable regularity. On occasion, even as late as Friday, it was necessary to condense or eliminate comedy features that for one or another reason refused to play. In that event, the writers were at the ready, standing by to salvage a foundering sketch or in many cases, arrive at an entirely new one. Meanwhile, at the International Theatre, where the live performance originated, trucks arrived with the scenery (which was built in Brooklyn) and while the sets were hung, the crew was put through its technical rehearsal.

Saturdays commenced promptly at eight o'clock with blocking and camera direction, which required the better part of the

morning and afternoon. At five o'clock there was a full dress rehearsal that ran unbroken from beginning to end, as though it
were an actual broadcast. Max would monitor the rehearsal with
a secretary at his side recording notes and adjustments. The rehearsal would end at six-thirty and Max would convene his staff
for a comparison of notes and a last list of alterations. If a musical number ran over, it could be speeded up by a matter of seconds. If the overage was too much, the comedy was reduced to
compensate, not because it was less important but because it was
more flexible. That fact did little to assuage hurt feelings, especially those of Sid, who regarded the production numbers warily
and felt the sketches were wantonly victimized. Sometimes as
late as Saturday, a comedy piece would flatly fail to jell, in
which case it was eliminated and a kinescope copy of some tried
and true piece ordered up from the vaults. Nobody was keen on
repeating secondhand material, but all agreed that good old material was preferable to bad new material. Sid and Coca were extraordinarily quick reads, and after a single review of an old
sketch or pantomime had their performance in hand.

The Saturday rehearsals had a composed professionalism tantamount to sanctity. Max liked to compare the theatre to a cathe-
dral, not fearful but respectful (Fred Allen would often stop by
to visit this "temple of comedy"). The pandemonium of the
week's creative process gave over to the calm crucible of performance. Where the midweek group sessions were veritable
shouting matches, rehearsals suffered absolutely no raised voices.
It was the way Max had conducted himself on Broadway, and he
insisted on applying the same values to television. The superior
results more than justified the method.

By eight fifty-five of Saturday evening, Max, the writers and
the staff collected in the control booth, Max installed as field
general in voice communication with his key subordinates. The
director would count down the seconds and the show would
commence, with Max giving instructions for stretching, quicken-
ing or cutting. As producer, Max brought with him two immuta-
ble stage precepts: there were no cue cards or prompting devices, and no canned laughter. As was only natural, the actors
would at turns drop lines or go up on dialogue, in which case

they would extricate themselves with an ad lib or two. But the bulk of the show, which many fans and critics alike assumed was largely improvised in view of its apparent spontaneity and freshness, was never made up as it went along. "Your Show of Shows" aired almost exactly as it was designed, the savory blend of disparate brilliance. It could just as easily have been called, "Your Showmanship of Showmanships."

Mel, like the show itself, matured under pressure. At no sacrifice of his trademark outrageousness and effusion, he was growing from sidekick to peer, from amateur to professional, from motley to writer. Max liked to call it "Mel Brooks's Bar Mitzvah."

One day, before the show was even a full season old, Max chanced upon Mel in the rehearsal hall. It was lunchtime and the others had already stepped out for a bite. Mel sat alone at the piano, picking out a tune with one finger. It struck Max that he had witnessed a change in the roughcast kid who once stalked the corridors. Max walked up to Mel and said: "You know, Mel, when I first saw you backstage at the Broadhurst Theatre, well, I would say from that moment until this very moment, you were a kid." The rest was clear.

6

Anne and Millie stood before Judge Orlando H. Rhodes. At twenty, Anne was too young to enter into a legal contract without parental consent. Judge Rhodes reviewed the particulars of the offer from Twentieth Century–Fox: $20,000 for the first year of work, with a sliding scale of up to $1,500 per week should she stay to term (seven years). With a barely suppressed smile, Anne nodded her comprehension of the contract, Millie her approval. Law required a statement of expenses, which Millie provided and which included a trousseau for Anne's upcoming marriage to John Ericson. As a final supervisory gesture, Judge Rhodes proposed that the young actress agree to invest $75 a week, or 15 per cent of her salary in government bonds. The proposal was accepted without hesitation and the contract was validated. Anne Italiano became the protégée and property of Fox.

Late November, 1951. Anne took an apartment on Sunset Boulevard between Ciro's and The Mocambo and marveled at the palm trees. Hollywood was the virtual antithesis of her native Bronx. Back home, November was a tricky month, late-autumn luster going suddenly glacial. A Bronx November was all grays and shadows, corners and edges, with the flush of the first chill.

Hollywood was sunny, pervasively, tonelessly, inexorably sunny. Sunset Boulevard ringed the foot of the Hollywood Hills, where the thick vegetation rimmed the ridges and canyons and camouflaged the scattered houses and palatial star retreats. The town below was flat, with few skyscrapers to protrude into the panorama. Residential Hollywood was a melange of pale yellows and greens and beiges, pink stucco predominating. The steady, flat sunlight seemed to rob the scenery of depth, leaving the impression of some two-dimensional set piece. The glossy palms and ubiquitous yucca plants only added to the unreality of it all. There was nothing in the Bronx viewpoint to assimilate the visual Hollywood. New York was made up of murky tones of light and dark, Hollywood of antiseptic pastels. For two weeks Anne basked in the overpowering sun and on the morning of the fifteenth day, she woke up bored.

There was less reason for boredom in her professional life. Anne's contract became active on November 21, and she was due to report for her first picture assignment on December 3. The interim was reserved for studio orientation and acclimation, and a meeting with Fox's president and production chief, a surviving member of the industry's movie moguls, Darryl F. Zanuck. The first order of business was nomenclature. Anne had found "Marno" serviceable and unimpeding throughout her brief television tenure, and was fully prepared to launch her movie career under that pseudonym. Zanuck objected. He pointed out that Anne's coloring and features were already suggestive of Mediterranean ethnicity (which was to say that she lacked the pleasant but bland, blank canvas upon which the industry preferred to work its dubious magic) and that a likewise "ethnic" name like Marno would serve as an invitation to typecasting. Anne, who had no particular attachment to the name, acquiesced and was handed a list from which to select a new one. Everything looked like a variation on existing movie star names, "Lana" this or "Joan" that, or was a "trick" name ("Candy Bar" or "Paddy Wagon," as she later teased). Anne finally settled on a name which despite its exaggerated Anglo-Saxon gravity was practically the only one that didn't remind her of some bubble dancer.

Anne Marno, née Italiano, was now Anne Bancroft, with Zanuck's blessings.

Anne soon learned that she was to make her movie debut in a suspense-thriller with the working title of *Night Without Sleep,* from a Charlotte Armstrong novel which had been serialized in *Good Housekeeping* as *Mischief.* It was a quick start, but also something of a false start as Anne subsequently learned that the film was primarily intended as a dramatic vehicle for the studio's resident "hot prospect," Marilyn Monroe. Monroe, five years Anne's senior, had signed with Fox in 1946 and since then had served as window dressing for some dozen mostly forgettable movies. Fox was now prepared to find out if its liege could do better than purr and bulge, and secured the Armstrong story toward that end.

With Richard Widmark as leading man, and a collection of seasoned character actors (Elisha Cook, Jr., Verna Felton, Don Beddoe, and Joan Blondell's sister Gloria) shooting got under way in early December and wrapped on January 10. The story told of a mentally disturbed babysitter (Monroe) who, following a mild psychotic episode, very nearly murders her charge. The action takes place at a hotel where Anne as Lyn Leslie works as a chanteuse, the "Roundup Room's High-heeled Cowgirl."

It was a comparatively minor role but it did require a good deal of singing, with three songs in view onstage and several more piped over the hotel's PA system as background music. The singing might have seemed consolation for the dramatic brevity, except that auditions revealed Anne's voice to be weak in the upper registers. Anne got the part, but each time she opened her mouth to sing, the voice of Eve Marley issued forth. It was a chastening experience, but in its way the perfect introduction to Hollywood.

What little acting Anne was given to do, she did well. As Widmark's love interest, she showed a kind of silken toughness which was just what the part called for. She neither shied from nor flirted with the camera, but let it catch her at odd angles lending a subtle intimacy. Anne's one scene with Monroe (the film's last) was very affecting with an actorly sense of "give-and-take" that was almost accidental and an on-set intimacy that was truly rare.

That moment aside, Anne's role suffered for want of camera time as the emphasis shifted to Monroe, who struggled gamely but vainly with an unmanageable role.

Fox held onto the film until August '52, when it was released as *Don't Bother to Knock* and roundly panned by critics. There was particular annoyance with Monroe whose babysitter went beyond mere paranoia and behaved as if a net were to be dropped over her any second. The more discerning critics singled out Anne's performance for praise and the opinion was seconded when she later received the "Golden Key Award" as one of Hollywood's potential stars.

The acclaim did little to offset Anne's growing feelings of loneliness. To make matters worse, her marriage plans with John Ericson had fizzled. In Chicago with *Stalag 17,* John met a young singer named Milly Coury. After completing the road tour, he tested for M-G-M, got the job, and took the advance to buy an airplane ticket to Chicago. He and Milly were later married and moved to Hollywood where they became known as one of the industry's model young couples.

Tiring at last of the town's tedium, Anne hurled herself headlong into the Hollywood social scene. She partied, held forth for gossip columnists, and attended premières in sequins and furs. Also, she made movies.

George Jessel was producing a film about the celebrated impressario Sol Hurok. It was to be a tribute, more pastiche than biography, but a prestige picture just the same with guest appearances by such noted classical performing artists as Isaac Stern, Roberta Peters, Tamara Toumanova, and Ezio Pinza. Jessel signed David Wayne to play Hurok and Anne to play his wife, Emma. Anne's was a curious bit of casting. While the screenplay by Harry Kurnitz and George Oppenheimer adopted a long view beginning with Hurok's Russian youth, the principal action took place many years later which meant a mature Emma would be depicted. Anne would be playing a character at times twice and as much as three times her actual age. But Jessel wanted Anne for the part, confident that he was not merely casting a young actress but "discovering" a new star. As it turned

out, mostly he was discovering how not to go about making a
motion picture biography.

It was entitled *Tonight We Sing*, completed on June 12,
released the following February, and soon mercifully forgotten.
Despite able direction by Mitchell Leisen and ennobling classical cameos, the picture succumbed to all the built-in traps of
movie biography plus several more of its own invention. Added
to the predictable foreshortened perspective and chronological
compression, there was an active mythologizing going on with
the character of Hurok which at best was a kind of innocent classical name-dropping and at worst a quasi-historical pageantry.
The result was an episodic and breathless plot sprinkled with
music and dance, in a tone more befitting a Broadway musical
than the classical repertoire at hand. It was not entirely clear
where the blame belonged, but Hurok himself had served as
technical advisor on the production.

Anne went down with the film, although her Emma possessed
a simplicity and grace more befitting a mature character actress
than a virtual ingenue. At the very least, Anne succeeded in
impressing those around her, particularly Isaac Stern, who, while
the first to admit uneasiness about his own acting was quick to
admire her apparent facility, her "quickness in getting inside an
idea and demonstrating it cleanly before the camera." He was
also eager to point out that in contrast to much of the other
bravura acting that worked against any semblance of realism,
Anne "managed to convey with some accuracy the feeling of
the period and the person she was portraying." Whether she was
making progress in motion pictures or in spite of them was not at
all clear.

Her next picture, *Treasure of the Golden Condor*, required
even less acting. Completed before but released after *Tonight
We Sing*, it was a Technicolor swashbuckler (in movie parlance a
"costumer") starring Cornel Wilde and a great deal of location
footage in Guatemala. Anne was billed fifth and cast in an ingenue part as "Marie." The movie was harmless enough, just
more Hollywood candy-colored derring-do. What it did not do
was provide her with any remotely actable material. Anne, of
course, had done bit work on television, but there at least the

stress was more on line reading than wardrobe. Anne was getting a small sample of what it was like to be a Hollywood clothes
horse.

There was a prolonged lull between jobs broken finally by an
assignment that hardly seemed worth the wait, a little baseball
fable written by Jack Sher called *The Kid from Left Field*. It
told of a nine-year-old boy and his rise from knotholer to batboy
to manager of a major-league baseball team. Of course, success
had its pitfalls—envy, truant officers, and finally the common
cold. But it all served to reveal the fact that the boy had been
acting as mouthpiece for his father, now a vendor but once a
player who had fallen from baseball grace. It wasn't much, but
it provided Anne with a contemporary role and more screen time
than she had enjoyed in any of her first three pictures. As the
story's love interest opposite Lloyd Bridges, she was surprisingly
sexy and adult and yet warm and sincere in scenes with the kid
of the title. Still, this was clearly a budget film—black and white,
inexpensively cast and mounted—and it did not wear its penury
particularly well. The picture, completed in March of '53 and
released the following summer, did nothing to add to Anne's
stature as an actress.

So far Fox had offered Anne little more than a choice of
evils. But if she was dissatisfied with large roles in small pictures,
she was soon to have a crack at a small role in an old-fashioned
Hollywood extravaganza. In 1953 Fox had resoundingly resurrected the epiphanic spear-and-toga genre with *The Robe*. Hoping to exploit its own vogue, Fox quickly followed with another
gladiatorial spectacular starring Victor Mature and entitled *Demetrius and the Gladiators*. The sequel, like the original, spared
nothing by way of ornamentation from the Technicolor and Cinemascope to the hordes of extras. It traced the progress of one
indomitable Christian (Mature) from peasant to slave to gladiator to demi-tyrant to gladiator again and finally to born-again
freed man. Running him through the paces was essentially an ex-
cuse to work in everything from sweaty eviscerating gladiators to
women in various states of diaphanous undress. There was even,
at odd moments, room for acting.

Anne did not appear until the story was nearly one quarter

told, and then only as a novice courtesan at her first bacchanalia. (Demetrius all but asks, "What's a nice girl like you doing at an orgy like this?") She bore up well under the circumstances, and despite being rouged and pawed projected a certain kitteny innocence that suited the role. Less anticipated was the sense that with her high cheekbones and short curly black hair, she seemed to mirror Mature's vaguely androgynous quality. But there was little time to notice since Demetrius spent most of his time skewering adversaries in the arena. For her part, Anne was permitted one chilling dramatic moment, but then all but vanished until the movie's sanctified conclusion.

Demetrius and the Gladiators was completed in early summer of 1953. Anne was increasingly aware that her work at Fox had shown little progress and that she lacked the autonomy to do anything about it. Between divestiture and the rising popularity of television, the studio system was in decline, and studios were less consumed with talent than with slick and novel technology. Hollywood was obsessed with doing what television could not, and while television had access to estimable acting reserves, it could not as yet rival Technicolor nor the gargantuan panoramas of the movies' latest toy, Cinemascope.

Twenty or even ten years earlier, Anne might have been carefully and steadily groomed for stardom. But the studio lacked patience and seemed to have taken a dim view of her star potential. Anne was left to languish and, seeing no reason to extend her indenture with Fox, prepared to go freelance.

With her career seemingly on a frustrating treadmill, Anne did what she could to inject some excitement into her life. But she tired of dating and found herself wanting instead to establish a security in her personal life that was entirely missing in her professional life. She was, in other words, looking to get married. A girl friend of Anne's had left town on vacation, leaving behind a boy friend, Martin May. Martin was slightly older, a law student at USC. He started spending time with Anne in order, she thought, to cry on her shoulder about his absent girl friend. His motives turned out to be anything but lugubrious. On July 1, 1953, Anne and Martin eloped.

7

On June 6, 1952, the *Nieuw Amsterdam* steamed slowly out of New York Harbor. At the deck railing, waving amid the streamers and confetti, stood Lucille Kallen, Estelle Jacoby (Max Liebman's secretary), Peter Goode (Sid Caesar's valet), and Mel Brooks. The festivities subsided and as the Statue of Liberty slowly receded on the horizon Lucille turned to say something to Mel and noticed that the color had drained from his face. Mel excused himself and went below to his cabin. Lucille was puzzled. The water was calm, the sun bright, and the voyage too young for *mal de mer*. Then it occurred to her: the recognition and renown both of them had earned in association with "Your Show of Shows," the acceptance which had so long eluded Mel, was confined to American television, and American television, along with its practitioners, was literally unknown in Europe. The shock of impending anonymity was evidently more than Mel had anticipated.

The passage was uneventful, blue skies and clear sailing, still Mel was subdued. He not only missed meals, the social cynosure of any ocean voyage, but also the leisurely conversation surrounding meals, a ready-made audience if ever there was one. Peter, Estelle, Lucille all agreed they had never seen Mel this way. Were there any cause for concern, it vanished the moment the boat docked in Europe. Mel's mood changed abruptly, and he was his old joking self again, though uncharacteristically relaxed. Even so, a relaxed Mel Brooks was no study in stasis. While Lucille, Estelle, and Peter divided their time among beaches, landmarks, and bistros, Mel shot off on private sorties. For instance, when in Paris, he learned that John Huston was in town on location for United Artists shooting *Moulin Rouge*, which starred Jose Ferrer as Toulouse-Lautrec. Mel made regular visits to the set, returning to his room at the shank of the night, leaving strict instructions for his roommate Peter to avoid unnecessary noise. Each morning Peter would tiptoe over to Lucille and Estelle's room just to spare Mel the buzz of his electric shaver.

Mel's style of vacationing might have been eccentric but it was not purely egocentric. Before departing from the States, he and Lucille had exchanged itineraries with Imogene Coca, who was scheduled to sail to England later that summer. Mel and Lucille flew in from France to greet Coca, who had no sooner disembarked than Mel rushed up to her clutching a bouquet of flowers and kindly cautioning: "Now, Coca, they don't know you here like they do back home." Mel having himself suffered the pangs of anonymity wanted to spare her any unnecessary grief. The truth of the matter was that Coca, the wiser by years in the business, had no illusions about the limited frontiers of her current television fame. Besides, she was unassuming by nature and could do quite nicely without the notoriety. Still, she was touched by the gesture of friendship and flattered that Mel would want to try to protect her.

The innocents abroad returned rested and restored. It was the first time the others had seen Mel in anything resembling repose —and very nearly the last.

Television refers to it as "hiatus," a pseudoscientific expression for the simple practice of a summer break in production. For borderline shows, hiatus is the time to sweat out option renewal. For failed shows, it is a time to seek new projects. By 1952, "Your Show of Shows" was an unqualified hit, a minor institution, and hiatus was a time to recover from the season just past while gearing up for that just ahead. But show people are often like thoroughbreds, and too much rest is a fearful thing.

By fall, the "Show of Shows" regulars were back to work revitalized and in superb voice. The show had long since moved into a spacious suite of offices on West Fifty-sixth Street in the City Center. It was a model complex of rehearsal and writing space for which Max's large, unadorned rectangular office—with its floor-to-ceiling bookcases, desk "el," furniture in waiting-room vinyl, and Steinway grand piano—served as nucleus. Max's office was in many ways a clearinghouse for the show's creative accounts. Mostly it was a workshop, and looked it. There were half-eaten sandwiches, mustard-smeared pages, containers with last week's cole slaw, and a haze of cigar smoke that suggested Pittsburgh in July.

At the City Center, Lucille and Big Mel occupied a small cubicle, where they would retreat for domestic sketches and songwriting, venturing into the neighboring maelstrom of Max's office only at their own peril. Little Mel went anywhere he pleased, everywhere, including the boss's desk, where he would often plop down, prop up his feet, and chomp on one of Max's cigars. The first time Max witnessed the charade, he was unsurprised but also unsettled at the image, as if seized by a split-second prescience. It was an odd sensation since had anyone asked Max the likelihood of his staff dynamo's becoming a major force in show business he'd have placed the odds between slim and none.

As the show took root, personalities became more pronounced and styles more entrenched. Lucille was organized and orderly. She gave nothing away by way of raw creativity or ready imagination, but she was the one who arrived at work on time, she was the one who shuddered at the unkempt office, she was the one who was stationed at the typewriter for rewrites and revisions when nobody else thought or deigned to. She was the one who winced when the unpunctuality and sport of others resulted in late hours.

Little Mel was the staff enfant terrible, volatile, supercharged, vociferous. His humor was very often as unusable as it was spectacular. His delivery was floodlike and flashy, sometimes

blurring the line between saying things funny and saying funny
things.

Big Mel was the dean of the writing staff and his writing was
an extension of his intelligence but not the extent of it. Lucille
was quick to point out that intellectually, he was "head and
shoulders" above the rest (Big Mel was a big reader, especially
fond of nineteenth-century Russian novels). Where Little Mel's
delivery was fluent, Big Mel's was flat and colorless, virtually
requiring, as Lucille liked to tease, "seven UN interpreters."
There was much of the big and little brother about the two
Mels, complete with counsel, competition, and occasional tension.

Carl Reiner, who replaced Tom Avera (and who, although he
had been hired and billed solely as a performer, figured in the
writing more with each season and, with his own raunchy off-
the-wall sense of humor) found a ready friend, playmate, and
kindred spirit in Little Mel.

Coca was shy and retiring, Sid shy and imperious with a full
guttural and gestural vocabulary which he used to express approval or disapproval. Max, aside from his specific responsibilities as producer, was the staff's paterfamilias and, by needs,
its amateur Freud. None of them, not even Max, had known
fame on such a national basis, and the interplay of mood and ego
seemed to increase exponentially with success.

Max exercised his seniority in an effort to keep the program
on an even keel. But with the fueled egotism and niggling insecurity of sudden, unprecedented success, it was an often thankless task. There were tempers, fits, and tantrums, squabbles and
feuds, fatigue and frustration. And always the spiraling production schedule that swept grievances under the rug in favor of the
pressing business ever at hand. The key to Max's method was a
compassionate professionalism. Quirks and idiosyncrasies were
tolerated and in many ways encouraged (a tame mind might
spawn tame material), extroversion was given room to flex and
introversion shelter from the storm. But nothing was permitted
to impair the quality of the show, that was where Max drew the
line, and the others were in complete accord.

Where Max felt perhaps less comfortable was in vaguely pa-
ternal capacities. At face value, Sid was an insulated potentate,

Little Mel a puckish free agent. But both had lost their fathers at an early age, and both fathers had been named "Max." Moreover, Sid's father, like Max Liebman, had been Austrian by birth. And while nobody on hand would have described Max's relationship with Sid and Mel as particularly fatherly (Max and Sid were mutually respecting peers, more older brother-younger brother; Max and Mel were carefully regarding sparring partners, more schoolmaster-class clown), an observer might have noticed the tiniest particle of transference. For one, Max was more worldly, more cultivated than either Sid or Mel. Max traveled abroad each summer and regularly returned with the canvases of struggling young artists that he displayed in the office corridors. Similarly, Max's passion for the classical performing arts (his wife, Sonia Glazer, had been an operatic soprano) was imparted to those around him. Outside of professional topics, neither Sid nor Mel was inclined to ask Max for personal advice (Mel even less so than Sid), but there were enough intimate moments to lend some credence to a relationship that was something more than sheerly businesslike. As Mel would much later confide, he still needed "to learn how to be a father instead of a son."

The stability and prosperity which "Your Show of Shows" brought those associated with it was a godsend for Mel Brooks. He was able to slacken the singlemindedness and exhibitionism that had typed his behavior as an outsider, and let down his guard enough to grow as a writer. At Mel Tolkin's suggestion, he began reading the Russian novelists and soon became a devotee of Dostoyevsky, Tolstoy, and Gogol. That, in turn, helped him see television within a broader perspective, not as the be-all and end-all of his creative energy, but as an ideal in-service training ("Your Show of Shows" was unmatched in this regard) a potential springboard into other areas of writing. Mel had no reason to complain. Working for the top show in television was a good sight better than hustling cotton velvet in the garment center.

Inevitably, his interests turned to the legitimate theatre. Of all the "Show of Shows" principals, Mel was the only one without a major Broadway credit. True, not all of their experiences had been pleasant ones (Kallen and Tolkin became eligible for Max's "One Week Club" with their short-lived 1950 musical *Tickets Please*) but that did nothing to still Mel's fascination.

The opportunity came in 1952. Leonard Sillman, whose "New Faces" revues had effectively introduced new talent since the maiden show in 1934 (which featured among others Imogene Coca) was at it again, and Mel was engaged to collaborate with his friend Ronny Graham on the show's sketches. Mel went at it hammer and tongs and, with some additional dialogue by Peter DeVries, words and music by Graham, June Carroll, Arthur Siegel, Sheldon Harnick, and Michael Brown, staging by John Murray Anderson, choreography by Richard Barstow, sketch direction by John Beal, and a powerful young cast which included Eartha Kitt, Paul Lynde, Carol Lawrence, Ronny Graham, Robert Clary, and Alice Ghostley, *New Faces of 1952* opened in May to unanimous critical approval. The *Times*'s Brooks Atkinson called it an "excellent light revue," John Chapman of the *Daily News* thought it "young and peppy and handsome and funny." Walter Kerr, at the *Herald Tribune* termed it "high-spirited." Eartha Kitt was most often singled out for praise, and that surprised no one. Her spellbinding feline beauty, her cool command of lyric, and her unique vocal timbre halfway between a purr and a hiss defied neglect. Paul Lynde also won a fair portion of notice with the rudiments of the head-bobbing, hand-wringing, campy comedy that was to become his trademark. Clary and Ghostley were deservedly complimented, as was Ronny Graham.

The writing, in particular the comedy, was roundly applauded as high-toned in step with the chichi vogue that was sweeping New York's nightclubs at the time. There was some concern that the revue's urbane style might discourage summer attendance, which relied heavily on out-of-towners understandably less attuned to city chic. Despite these and other apprehensions, *New Faces* drew well, ran for 365 performances, and was even sold as a film to Twentieth Century–Fox.

Mel shared in the good fortune and was credited with having written the production's comic showstopper, a longish sketch satirizing Arthur Miller's *Death of a Salesman* (which had taken Broadway by storm three years before under the direction of

Elia Kazan with the heavy overtones of the Method). The sketch is vintage Mel Brooks (some say the best of his early career) using the form of parody with the grammar of farce to assault the selected subject matter. At center is a simple switch. The Willy Loman character, a dour and distraught Paul Lynde, is an over-the-hill second-story man who now can't even lift a wallet anymore without getting the shakes. His hopes for a son who will follow in his lightfingered ways are shattered when that son, Stanley, brings home a school report card with straight "A's" and talks about taking up the violin (an oblique reference to Clifford Odets' *Golden Boy*, itself mainstream Group Theatre). The mother (Alice Ghostley) holds out a last, faint hope for her son: "Steal something, anything. I know you can. I know, deep down inside, down where it really counts, you're rotten." But Stanley insists on pursuing the righteous path, exits, and Lynde slumps to the floor, clutching his heart.

The sketch was heavy-handed, as much of its own accord as in imitation of the visceral, thumping Method. And yet it made its parodic point without relying completely on the subject matter for comic invention, which is where the elements of farce enter in. Mel's instinct for comic disproportion, the Brooks Method, was tightening into a style that combined separate comic forms without diminishing the whole. It was by no stretch revolutionary (the Marx Brothers had for years mingled alien forms to excellent advantage) but it was a signpost for Mel's progress as a writer, an indication that he could contain his straying wit while paying at least lip service to formalism.

Mel's Broadway success did not alter his status on "Your Show of Shows." The refinement and prestige of legitimate theatre notwithstanding, he was still considered the show's resident Katzenjammer Kid (his patron saint, the Ritz Brothers). That spoke no ill of his income. Mel's earnings jumped with the show's popularity, and, far from the former fifty-dollar handouts, he was now making over a thousand dollars a week (a fact that did not escape the ever-skeptical Kitty who periodically asked, "Have they found out yet?"). Ironically, of all the accoutrements of success—the notoriety, the prestige, the creative license, the intellectual growth—prosperity proved the most difficult for him to handle.

Rather than instill in him, as it might in others, feelings of gratitude or greed or magnanimity or even modesty, in Mel it instilled nausea. When he was an outsider pocketing Sid's tips, the
least usable scrap of material more than justified the outlay. As
Mel's wages improved arithmetically his comic drive increased
geometrically. Instead of accepting the money as recognition of
his contribution, he seemed to take it as a challenge to top himself. As Mel saw it, there were only three ways for him to write—
funny, funnier, and funniest. His compulsion was inherently
self-defeating since for fifty dollars or five thousand dollars nobody topped Mel Brooks, not even Mel Brooks.

The signs of psychological strain, which many thought went
hand in glove with the Brooks style—phobic, hypochondriac, and
lunatic—finally stepped over into the seriously psychosomatic.
Mel, already prey to insomnia and dizzy spells, took to vomiting
between parked cars. Mel Tolkin came to the rescue, first by extolling the virtues of psychoanalysis (both he and Sid were on
the couch), then by recommending his analyst. With the help of
Dr. Clement Staff, Mel began slowly to learn the virtues of
Freud and a more normal metabolism all of a piece.

"Your Show of Shows" improved with age. The writing never
seemed to wilt nor the cast to wither. Max Liebman University
was turning out weekly diplomas with vitality and verve, and
gave no sign of faltering. Each year brought the show new
awards and citations from sources as different as: *Variety, Look*
magazine, the *Radio Daily* Poll of TV Editors, the Academy of
Television Arts and Sciences, the *Radio Daily* Poll of Radio Critics, the *Saturday Review of Literature* Poll, the *TV Guide* Gold
Medal Award, the Sylvania Awards, the *Motion Picture Daily*
Poll; the list goes on. But the accolades were secondary to the
satisfaction of knowing that the staff had grown into a highly
productive, dynamic, professional albeit often frazzled, creative
working unit. While, for the viewing public, the show had
passed from novelty to popularity to near institution, it had
from within evolved from staff to ensemble to virtual family.

Work was no substitute for an actual family, but Mel was soon
contemplating steps in that direction. A few years before, Mel
had met two women who were friends and, at the time, dancing

GARD
n Street
Culture
t Weav-

MARILYN JACKERSON
237 Rodney Stre
Biology Club; Personality Clu
Honor Roll; Class Presiden
Typing Certificates; Class Se
retary.
Jay—To make some man happ

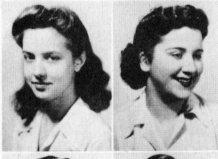

ng Street
Certifi-
b.

ALICE R. JONAS
409 Grand Stree
G. O. Treasurer (4); Preside
Official Class (2); Secretary
Mrs. Epstein, Mrs. Arnold; Hone
Roll; Vice-Pres., Senior Grade.
Ally—Treasurer to Morgentha
(What the G. O. has done fo
me.)

Avenue

MELVIN KAMINSKY
III Lee Avenu
Class Day Committee; Senic
Council; Dean's Assistant; Fen
ing Team.
Kaminsky—To be President o
the U. S.

Avenue
etary to
nor; Sci-
ciety.

ANNETTE KATZ
190 Wilson Stree
Senior Arista; 90% Averag
(5); Honor Roll (every term)
President of Annex Dramati
Society.
Puppit—To be affiliated with th
Broadway theater world.

ki Street
P Son-

CHARLOTTE KATZ
344 South Fourth Stree
Honor Roll (4); Typing Certifi
cate; Hebrew Culture Club; Vic

Class of '44, Eastern District High School.

(COURTESY OF DONALD M. KIRSCHENBAUM)

Anne's screen debut opposite Richard Widmark in *Don't Bother to Knock*, 1952. (FROM THE PENGUIN COLLECTION)

Anne, a Twentieth Century-Fox starlet, 1952. (WIDE WORLD PHOTOS)

Part of the "Your Show of Shows" brain trust. Left to right: Sid Caesar, Mel Tolkin, Lucille Kallen, and Mel. (COURTESY MAX LIEBMAN)

The "Graduation Picture" of "Your Show of Shows." Mel is second from left in second row from the front; others include Lucille Kallen, Carl Reiner, Imogene Coca, and Sid Caesar. (COURTESY MAX LIEBMAN)

A publicity shot for *The Kid from Left Field*, 1953.

(FROM THE PENGUIN COLLECTION)

Anne as Annie Sullivan with Patty Duke during a performance of *The Miracle Worker*, 1959. (WIDE WORLD PHOTOS)

Anne with producer Fred Coe (seated center) and director Arthur Penn (seated right) during a set break for the filming of *The Miracle Worker*, 1959. (WIDE WORLD PHOTOS)

On the set of *The Pumpkin Eater*, 1963, during a union work stoppage at Shepperton Studios, a poker game with, left to right: Anne's stand-in, Anne, Peter Finch, and Janine Gray. (WIDE WORLD PHOTOS)

1963. During a curtain call of *Mother Courage* at the Martin Beck
Theatre, Joan Crawford presents Anne's Oscar for *The Miracle Worker*.

(WIDE WORLD PHOTOS)

Anne as Gittel Mosca onstage with Henry Fonda during a performance of *Two for the Seesaw*, 1958. (FROM THE PENGUIN COLLECTION)

on Broadway in *Gentlemen Prefer Blondes*. Their names were Mary Katherine and Florence, and Mel and "M.K." (as she was called) soon began dating. They enjoyed each other's company and Mel later proved himself a loyal friend when he helped arrange an audition for M.K. for the Broadway revue *Curtain Going Up*, to which Mel had contributed a piece entitled "Fathers and Sons." M.K. got the part, and she and Mel remained friends although they soon stopped dating. In midsummer of 1952, M.K. prepared for a trip to Italy, and just before she departed, Mel started to date her good friend, Florence (Baum). Like M.K., Florence was a talented dancer, a lovely, leggy brunette, intelligent with an irresistible smile and a warm, engaging manner. By the time M.K. returned from her travels, Florence and Mel had married.

Mel was not the only member of the writing staff to settle down. Lucille had also married, which created no particular problems. What did was her pregnancy some time later. Since the show's inception, the staff had essentially increased only twice—once to absorb Mel, a second time to sign a superb young writer, Tony Webster. Since the addition of Webster, however, the staff had pretty much stood pat. Now, with Lucille's coming leave of absence, Max was forced to admit that the remaining staff was already too overburdened to even consider picking up the slack, just as he realized the fact that even the most skilled writer would enter this case-hardened exclusive club at his own risk (although any writer would have given his eyeteeth for a chance to try). Finally, with Lucille listing heavily toward the maternity ward, Max reasoned that two recruits might stand a better chance of survival than one, and hired a team of sketch writers who had established fine comic credentials, brothers Danny and Neil (Doc) Simon. They signed an interim agreement to cover Lucille's absence (six weeks) leaving Max an option for renewal at the end of that period.

In due course, Lucille was back in the thick of things and Max decided against renewing the Simons' option, confiding that they: "Just didn't throw off enough sparks," although that said more of the ironclad staff-family than of the Simons.

As much as anything, momentum kept the writing staff going. As Mel Tolkin would later admit, "We were too young to know it's impossible." The demands were made more stringent by the show's credo (always fiercely original) and by Sid's personal code (he wanted to do nothing that Bob Hope could do as easily). That left the comedy on its satirical tightrope with no safety net of tried-and-true one-liners. "Your Show of Shows" was voracious and required a steady infusion of fresh subject matter. But while the show's focus made useless any encyclopedic command of jokes and gags, it did draw on life situations, and when the staff went dry, it had only to prowl jointly or separately into everyday life. A walk down the block might suggest a crowd sketch, a stroll past a church a wedding monologue, a restaurant episode an eating scene. The show demanded imagination and perceptivity, and the trained eye of a keen-witted social critic.

Within the show's weekly context, "classic" really had no meaning. Some sketches were better than others, some unusually good, some unusually bad. There were pieces that examined new facets of Sid and Coca, of Carl and Howie, just as there were those that charted new terrain for the writers. The finest sketches were instructive, sublimely satisfying, and, in cases of crisis or critical acclaim, repeated. But for the most part television was like flash paper, brilliant and brief, with only the crude, pre-video kinescopes as visual record. It was an unjust fate since, given a more lasting medium, the show's satirical edge would have held up beautifully.

Some of the sketches had fun with familiar settings (the "cliché" sketches), as with a high school graduation ceremony:

COCA: There's my daughter . . . fourth from the right.
CAESAR: Oh, I see her. The redhead with the plunging neckline and the high heels.
COCA: It's a stage she's going through. In a couple of weeks, she'll be back to her natural brown hair. Where's your son?
CAESAR: He's the one standing right next to your daughter with his mouth open.

Other sketches took aim at the banal, such as dog stories:

CAESAR: I like a playful dog. I once had a Great Dane. They're so playful and affectionate, you know. Whenever he'd see me, he'd jump up and knock me down, tear my clothes, and drag me all over the living room floor . . . I was afraid to go home.

COCA: Dogs are really faithful. We had a neighbor of ours who treated his dog miserably . . . never fed him on time. Well, one day he just up and left. That dog didn't leave that front porch. He was faithful. Well, about two years later, the master returned. The dog just stood there, watching his master come down the path and onto the porch.

CAESAR: And then what happened?

COCA: Ripped him to pieces.

The sketches were by no means all discontinuous. The show inaugurated its own pint-sized situation comedy with Sid and Coca as Charlie and Doris Hickenlooper. The Hickenloopers were pure fifties middle class, Doris obsessed with upward mobility, Charlie content with social inertia. Doris ordinarily prevailed, as when she dragged Charlie to an East Indian restaurant with the sort of waiter (Carl Reiner) who is too fulsomely exotic to be authentic:

CAESAR: What have you got to eat?

REINER: Klochomoloppi. We also have lich lock, slop lom, shtocklock, rishkosh, and flocklish.

CAESAR: Yuch!

REINER: We have "yuch," too. Boiled or braised?

The Hickenloopers were master squabblers. Doris was the articulate one, verbose, verbally intimidating. Charlie had the barely contained temper of a brawler, a man of few but well-chosen words:

COCA: You know what the trouble is with you? You have no spirit of adventure! Don't you ever try something new, strange, unusual, a little off the beaten path, something

a little weird, something you thought you'd never have
anything to do with?

CAESAR: (a mean, measuring glance) Once.

Charlie was not always so laconic. Given a chance, he could
weave his own elaborate logic, especially when rebutting Doris'
frequent attacks on their marriage:

COCA: You never treated me like this before we were married.
CAESAR: That's the biggest lie of all. What a lie! I always treated
           you rotten—that's the one thing about our marriage. It's
           honest and aboveboard. You knew what you were get-
           ting into. I'm a rat!

The Hickenloopers showed off the writing staff's double-edged
facility for convention. These domestic sketches worked many of
the same plot combinations as conventional television sitcoms,
but arrived at radically different results using a mild camp,
which effectively exercised a relatively banal form but carica-
tured it as well. The Hickenloopers would follow the mindless
mores of situation comedy, but only up to a point. Then they
would break free of the frivolous situational syntax and work
their real satire. The writers had it both ways, earnest and arch,
using the form and mocking it.

To the extent that terminology mattered, the domestic
sketches were broad, but pointedly satirical. The staff's treatment
of movies, on the other hand, was in fact more specialized, virtually surgical in its comic dissection, which is to say, that more literate side of satire, parody. This, arguably, was the show's comic
vertex, where distinct and separate outlooks converged in unison
and precision. The movie pieces highlighted the cast's versatility
and the staff's virtuosity. And inspiration was only a movie house
away. Hollywood's more commercial fare was an endless source
of comic fodder, obvious, stylized, and practically inviting mockery. But bad movies were easy targets, which cheered the staff
only to a point and then sent them after bigger game. So-called
classic movies offered up any number of generic conventions and
clichés, tenuities and pieties, all ripe for demolition. But even
that could lose its challenge and so the staff carefully laid for

that most sacred cow of the fifties cineastes, the foreign film. The writers would frequent the tonier art houses or reconnoiter four blocks down the street from the City Center for the afternoon screenings of more esoteric films at the Museum of Modern Art. The foreign films completed their satirical panoply and the results were devastating and marvelous.

First on the chopping block was the Hollywood musical. No other popular art form is more nearly its own caricature which, in a sense, almost preempts parody and certainly requires a sharper critical eye. The staff nonetheless proved itself a deadshot in this area and found an inviting target in the *42nd Street* sort of backstage melodrama. Coca might play "Mary Stumbler:"

COCA: Oh, Buzzy! I don't think I can do it! I'm scared! I can't sing for Mr. Crane, for the lead in the show! I can't do it! I'm just a little chorus girl! My voice will crack! I'll forget the lyrics! I can't sing for Mr. Crane! (to the accompanist, with sudden, steely aplomb) Key of C, please, and not too fast.

Or keeping step with Hollywood twists on Hollywood musicals, Sid might play the washed up leading man, Rod Rodney, suffering the meteoric rise of his young wife Mary Sweet whom he discovered and coaxed to stardom, in a deflating treatment of the old warhorse *A Star Is Born,* "Star Struck":

COCA: (beamish and selfless, accepting an Oscar) I must be dreaming. I don't believe it's true. Ever since I came to Hollywood, it's been like a dream. I hope I never wake up because it's a wonderful dream. But I don't really deserve this award. It should go to the man who made all this possible . . . Thomas Edison!

CAESAR: (staggering in, boisterous and bombed à la Frederick March and James Mason) One day they give you statues, the next day they throw mud in your face! The public! The great public! You forget pretty fast, don't you? Remember me? I was America's sweetheart. Me! Ron . . . Phoney! (A sweeping hand gesture delivers a chop to Mary's jaw)

COCA: (reeling slightly, coughing up some dental work) It's all right, darling, they were only caps.

The musical spoofs were not only hilarious, they were downright threatening. "Your Show of Shows" was already starting to overshadow current stage musicals and revues while at the same time playing a major role in the TV conspiracy that was shaking the movies' hold on the public. Filmmakers visiting from the West Coast would drop by rehearsals at the International Theatre and gripe to the writers that the satires were mocking the musicals as fast as they could turn them out. These men could at least take some comfort in the fact that the musicals were merely one target among many.

The gangster picture, still enjoying its latest cycle, was apportioned its quota of parody. Sid might twit the standard convict epiphany:

CAESAR: While I was in solitary, I spent a lotta time thinkin'. I did a lot of thinkin'. I got a lot of thought . . . I thought about the walls . . . the bars . . . the guards with the guns. You know what I figured out?
REINER: What?
CAESAR: We're in prison.

The tough, wisecracking newspaper romance was no more immune than the musicals or mobsters:

CAESAR: (bursting with a news tip) There's gonna be some action at the club Hi Ho tonight. Somebody's gonna get bumped off!
COCA: You've got printer's ink in your veins.
CAESAR: So that's what makes me nauseous all the time. (She seductively removes her horn-rimmed glasses) Sally! I've never seen you without your glasses. (Appraisingly) Put them back on!

Westerns, especially the early and mid-fifties variety of message Westerns, formed an irresistible foil for the staff's urbane sensibilities. In a parody of *High Noon* entitled "Dark Noon," Caesar plays the determined sheriff (singleminded, phlegmatic,

and monotone à la Gary Cooper) and Coca, his wholesome, un-
comprehending wife. The hour approaches in which the re-
venge-minded outlaw has vowed to return:

COCA: I don't understand it! How can you stay here and wait
          for a man to come and kill you?
CAESAR: Cause I'm stupid, Mary Ellen.

Later, the sheriff's dutiful sidekick (Howie Morris having at
Walter Brennan) tries to rally town support as the hour of reck-
oning nears:

MORRIS: Before he became the sheriff, this town was a wild,
          lawless town, full of drinking, gambling, and shoot-
          ing. Since he's been the sheriff, it's different! He
          closed down the saloon, he cut out the gambling,
          he stopped the drinking!
TOWNSMEN: Kill the sheriff!

Not long after the *High Noon* send-up, Sid and Mel Tolkin
caught a screening of Alan Ladd's highly touted Western, *Shane*.
That became the kernel of still another parody which eventually
found its way to the air as "Strange." The opening seems every
bit as portentous as the movie's. Sid (in the title role) arrives,
parched and tired at the Higgins' farm, where the owner (Howie
Morris) and his obnoxiously venerating son (Coca camping
Brandon de Wilde) look on as the stranger guzzles water by the
bucketful.

MORRIS: You seem mighty thirsty, stranger. Have a long, dry
          ride?
CAESAR: No, had a herring for breakfast!
MORRIS: What's your name?
CAESAR: Folks call me . . . Strange.
MORRIS: Strange? What's your first name?
CAESAR: Very. But you can call me Strange.
COCA: Gee, that's a nice gun, Strange. That's a nice holster,
          Strange. Nice gun belt, Strange. I like you, Strange. You
          got nice boots, Strange. You're nice, Strange.
CAESAR: Get away, kid, or I'll blast you.

Strange's feelings for the kid change little, even after he is confronted by the town bully, Carl Reiner (the swarthy, menacing image of Jack Palance).

REINER: You know what you are? A lemon-and-lime lollipop-lickin' sodbuster!

CAESAR: Did you call me a lemon-and-lime lollipop-lickin' sodbuster?

REINER: And not only that, you're a lily-livered lemon-and-lime lollipop-lickin' sodbuster.

CAESAR: Did you call me a lily-livered lemon-and-lime lollipop-lickin' sodbuster?

REINER: You're a low-down, lip-eared, lily-livered lemon-and-lime lollipop-lickin' sodbuster.

CAESAR: Are you calling me a lily lowie lolly limey lemon eared . . . are you calling me a coward?

REINER: Yeah. (heaves the obligatory whiskey in Sid's face)

CAESAR: Barton, don't push me too hard.

Sid backs down, and the kid is shattered.

COCA: Ahh, you're a coward.

CAESAR: (tossing his own whiskey in the kid's face) Nobody says that to me.

With the boy's help, Strange guns down Barton and his gang and then takes to the road *sans* explanation, as the admiring boy calls after:

COCA: Come back, Strange, come back.

CAESAR: Shut up, you rotten kid.

Spy movies took their lumps:

CAESAR: Here are the diamonds. You vill take them vis you onto the train to Istanbul. Ven you arrive at Istanbul, you vill valk through the station and out onto the main street. Three blocks avay, a man vill run out from behind a building and scream at you, "giff me the diamondss!"

MORRIS: Vat do I do then?

CAESAR: You don't give them to him. Now . . . you vill valk another two blocks and then a very beautiful blonde vill come up to you and she vill say softly to you, "giff me the diamondss."

MORRIS: I don't give her the diamonds?

CAESAR: Yes, you vill give them to her! That girl vill be me!

MORRIS: Oh, I see. You'll be in disguise.

CAESAR: No! I'm in disguise now!

But no parodist, however entertaining, is truly worth his salt if he only goes after safe subjects. Westerns, musicals, melodramas, and the like, were all deserving but relatively risk-free. That is not to say that their treatment was in any way comically guaranteed (few things are in comedy). Less likely, perhaps, were the rash of foreign films then in vogue among "serious" filmgoers. Where domestic movies were regarded with a wary eye and viewed as merely diverting, lowbrow, vacuous, commercially tainted, unimaginative, or purely frivolous, imports were ascribed every manner of meaning. The themes were taken more literally, as dense and complex if sophisticated, as naturalistic and pure if simple. As it happened, the foreign parodies were among the funniest and best received. They included: "Das Hertzig Glockenspiel or: My Beer Is Your Beer," "Ich Die Halls of Ivy," "Ess Is Nicht Quiet Auf Der Vesten Front," "Der Prince Und Der Poppa," "The Sewers of Paris," "Le Grand Amour," "I Love You Strongly," "Hate," "Au Revoir, Ma Cherie," "Ubetchu," "Il Sono Mariago, or: Say You'll Be Mine," "Presto," "Bambino," and "The Grand Disillusion."

While, for the writers, the foreign films were at least as inviting as the domestic, there were complications. The viewing audience could be counted on to have seen most popular American movies, or if not the specific movie, something akin to it. Foreign films, on the other hand, were less widely known. The commonplace and corn and mediocrity of many American movies prefigured indigenous parodies, but the foreign parodies had first to establish their text.

They worked splendidly. Viewers who had never even heard of Vittorio DeSica's 1949 classic *The Bicycle Thief*, let alone seen it, loved "La Bicycletta." A great deal of the success here depended on the casts' redoubtable dialect double-talk. Carl had demonstrated his knack for this specialty, Howie owned a like facility (particularly with the Germanic), and Coca, with her wonderfully elastic facial expressions, made up in visage what she might have lacked in language. And, of course, there was Sid, the master, who raised foreign double-talk to a high comic art. Nobody quite knew how he did it, not even Sid. But the gift was there, fluent and fast, crammed with phonetically credible nonsense patois, seasoned with just enough foreign-phrase dropping to suggest authenticity.

Beyond both the domestic and foreign movie parodies was a full complement of silent-movie take-offs which showed off Sid and Coca's command of pantomime. In all, the number of movie parodies exceeded one hundred.

No other single enterprise—stage, screen, or television—could have provided Mel Brooks with the same diversity, scope, and license as did "Your Show of Shows." The show was culturally eclectic, the creative outlets many and varied, and creativity given primacy. If Mel was not much of a formalist he was phenomenally original, and some of the show's best comic moments were his. But, for all the show's range and flexibility, there was one outlet it did not afford him—performance. Granted, Mel's style of writing was strictly kinetic. He enacted his material as he thought of it, what professionals refer to as a "talking writer" in contrast to a "writing writer." His office bravado was very much like the hard-won approval of his old street-corner comic machismo, but nothing like the larger audience acceptance he had enjoyed as a stand-up in the mountains. In truth, Mel was envious of Sid and Carl and Howie.

Only once was Mel allowed to perform on air, and then only disembodiedly. The staff had written a parody of the recent Joan Crawford suspense movie *Sudden Fear*. The opening sequence showed the Crawford character stroking a pet cat when the phone rings. She puts down the cat, answers the call which turns out to be a death threat, hangs up the phone, steps back onto the cat, which then screeches ominously. The sketch was written and everything set except for the cat sound. Max sent someone to rummage through sound effects, but nothing would quite do. Max summoned Mel. There was very little in the Brooks repertoire that anybody connected to the show was unaware of, up to and including his caterwauling, perfected over many years in the closes and alleyways of Brooklyn. Mel served up a bloodcurdling sample for Max and then received his instructions: "Mel, you're going to stand backstage. You'll be at a microphone, and when the stage manager cues you, make the sound."

Mel screeched flawlessly through early rehearsals, right up to the dress rehearsal. Max was situated in his customary control-room seat, the sketch began, the phone rang, the receiver slammed down, the character stepped back, the stage manager gave his cue—nothing! Mel blew it. The sketch continued—dress rehearsal stopped for nothing. Afterwards, Mel apologized and promised to deliver next time. In the break between dress and air time, Mel was frantic, pacing backstage as if he were about to go on as Hamlet. Showtime arrived, then the sketch, then the cue —as terrifying a cat screech as ever graced television. Unseen and fleeting, it was, nonetheless, Mel's network debut.

Undaunted, Mel found other outlets for his passion to perform. While there were relatively few cast parties, there were occasional gatherings usually at the invitation of Coca and her husband, Bob Burton. Mel seized these affairs to entertain the entertainers and improvised routines with Mel Tolkin and especially Carl. Carl played off Mel much as he did Sid, pressing, poking, probing for response. Mel, who lacked Sid's flair for aggressive visual comedy, revived his own trusty aggressive verbal comedy and struck a rapport with Carl which, while it might in some respects have resembled Sid's style, was distinctly its own. Carl and Mel loved the cat-and-mouse game of straight man and comic, and in time evolved a handful of standard routines to back those that were continually invented and improvised. And if they seldom failed to stir a laugh at parties, they were reliably their own best audience.

The show proper meanwhile continued its established metronomic pace. There was no sloughing or repetition, but toward the close of the 1953 season there were the barest signs of the show's yellowing at the edges. Ratings had slipped only slightly, and yet some sensed the slightest trace of weariness. Rumors circulated to the effect that there was enmity at the show's top rung and that things might not last a new season. Rumors abated when the show returned the following September with a somewhat redesigned format. As the season progressed, there was renewed speculation over the show's fate and, judging by what many perceived as a telltale listlessness, it was not to be passed off lightly.

In February 1954 the news finally broke. NBC was ready to revamp its Saturday night schedule and it would begin by redistributing the wealth of talent that had come to be concentrated in "Your Show of Shows." It was prototypal spinoff thinking, a way of shaking loose the creative spores of a successful program. The network had already negotiated a contract with Sid, giving him artistic control over his own show. NBC had also talked with Max who, rather than simply continue as he had, was once again eager to experiment and was given carte blanche to invent a new species of one-shot programs which Pat Weaver immodestly termed "spectaculars." Coca had also been approached by the network but hesitated to make any commitments, preferring instead to first play out this last season.

"Your Show of Shows" had its swan song on June 5. The show encored several of its most prized pieces and finished with a tearful last curtain call and touching valedictories. It was a moving conclusion to a monumental undertaking which, including the "Admiral Broadway Revue," had endured for four years and 160 shows.

For Mel Brooks, the show had at times been life itself, education, maturation, self-awareness, creative succor. While he had fared well at various extramural ventures, Mel had come to identify with the show and, in large part, with Sid. It was not entirely clear where Mel would go from here, but one thing was above doubt—"Your Show of Shows" had left him with credentials that were now like hard currency. Virtually any of those connected with the show could pick and choose his next job.

Mel had begun as little more than a comic foundling and emerged as a creator in charge of his own fate. If the show had been Mel's matriculation as a writer, this was to be his graduation.

8

The divorce became final on February 13, 1957. It had been more a symptom than a source of problems.

After a succession of appearances in undistinguished films, Hollywood's high gloss had begun to look nickel-plated. The studio, which Anne had once looked to for protection and direction, seemed impersonal and feckless. She was typecast and miscast, her talent repeatedly misspent. Her growing disenchantment with work had prompted her to look elsewhere for attention but Hollywood's fast set, with its cruelties and caprices, only undermined what scant self-confidence she had acquired. Anne was primed for marriage, so ready, in fact, that she later confessed, she might even have married George Jessel had he proposed. Martin May was no Jessel. He was tall, good-looking, blond, the scion of a landed, oil-rich Texas family. When he and Anne eloped, he was just completing law school at USC, and, to all appearances, could provide the sort of dependability and shelter Anne so desperately wanted.

The marriage had gotten off to a shaky start. May wanted to break the news personally to his mother, and while he awaited the right moment he wanted the marriage kept secret and insisted he and Anne maintain separate apartments. Anne reluctantly complied, and for six months they continued the pretense. However, even after they adopted a more open and normal conjugal arrangement, Anne's reservations persisted. For one thing, May was in the habit of keeping a loaded gun under his pillow, and Anne, whose New York was in its way at least as wild and woolly as her husband's Texas, was dumbfounded. For another, May was having no luck at passing the admittedly difficult California bar exam and that did nothing to instill confidence in him. For still another, his total estrangement from the acting profession left little common ground for the newlyweds.

But more important, and certainly most divisive, was the utter disparity of their backgrounds and temperaments. May's moneyed WASP, western, hinterlands upbringing hadn't the least congruence with Anne's poor, Italian-Catholic, eastern urban youth. They were virtual opposites and each difference seemed to magnify the next. Anne's own professional concerns and preoccupations were only one more wedge in a marriage that few friends gave much chance of survival.

If married life offered little refuge, work offered even less. Anne had yet to find a comfortable acting niche nor had she any palpable acting persona that could precede her into a picture. That meant no particular publicity strategy, no concerted build-up, no tailor-made vehicles, in short, nothing approaching stardom or even demi-celebrity. The best she could hope for was to learn through trial and error the curious art of movie acting.

Unfortunately, there was nothing akin to artistry in Anne's first filmwork of 1954. Shot practically overnight early in the year, *Gorilla at Large* might well have been the antithesis of what Anne had hoped to find in Hollywood. Both the budget and the screenplay were impoverished. The story revolves around a series of murders at an amusement park. What at first appears to be the work of some diabolical gorilla turns out to be a killer in simian clothing.

Anne is billed second (a big fish in a little potboiler) and is cast as a sideshow aerialist whose act has her dangling dramatically over the cage of an actual ape. It is a fatuous role, calculated to deposit Anne's figure into a succession of skimpy outfits, not least of which is that familiar staple of bygone beauty con-

tests, the Catalina swimsuit. As Laverne Mills, Anne is trapped in
a thankless role, the sort that later led her to wisecrack: "I
wanted to develop my acting, not my body."

Anne's next film was more seemly, a Civil War period piece,
The Raid. Though it too was without benefit of budget, it had an
able director in Hugo Fregonese and a fine cinematographer in
Lucien Ballard. Anne played a war widow, again a character
nearly twice her age, and supplied a credible womanly com-
posure that went beyond the calico and hoopskirt confines of the
role. While the film failed to stir any critical fires, it was a good
indication of what Anne could do with even a modest role in a
minor production.

Anne's marriage was approaching its first anniversary. Martin
had begun to speculate in local real estate with developments in
the San Fernando Valley. Anne was pulling five hundred dollars
a week at Fox, and, even if her career wasn't getting anywhere
at least it wasn't giving any ground. The Bancroft-Mays were
making do. Their impulsive elopement might have been stock
Hollywoodiana, but a world away in the Bronx, Millie Italiano
was having none of it. Anne was lectured on the virtues of a
proper church wedding and in time came around to her mother's
way of thinking. Anne and Martin packed up the family car and
headed east. Roughly midway, they detoured north and stopped
in Chicago so that Martin might begin to bone up on the Illinois
bar exam, which he planned to take later that month.

While in Chicago, Anne received a call from a producer at
Warner Brothers, Edward Small, who just two years before had
produced a minor film noir classic, *Kansas City Confidential*.
Small had just paid $10,000 for the rights to a book by Jack Lait
and Lee Mortimer which formed the nucleus of yet another *Confidential*, this one set in New York among warring mafiosi. Small
wanted Anne for the movie, but first Warner wanted her to hop
the next flight to Los Angeles in order to test for the part. Anne
refused. She had no intention of leaving Martin to drive on
alone, let alone disrupt Millie's wedding plans. Besides, as she
told Small: "There's plenty of film on me around Hollywood."
Nothing more was said. Anne and Martin continued on to New
York. The two of them had a brief vacation, Millie had her

church nuptials, and, upon returning to the West Coast, Anne had her next part in *New York Confidential*.

The production had much to offer. With Broderick Crawford and Richard Conte, it was Anne's strongest cast yet. Then too, her role was quite substantial and figured in several meaty scenes. And finally, the picture was scheduled for location shooting in New York, which gave her still-faltering marriage breathing room.

New York Confidential is mainstream film noir. It opens with a shadow-bathed New York City skyline, a driving, jazzy score, and it quickly dispatches a passel of hoods before the credits are even cold. Broderick Crawford fairly ripples with menace as the graying mobster chieftain Charlie Lupo. Richard Conte plays his young henchman, Nick Magellan. Anne is Katherine Lupo, a hot-blooded college graduate who is upset by the fact that her father's goons keep shaking down her blueblood boy friends. She bursts into Daddy's office wearing a daring spaghetti-strapped gown, trailing a fur, and pausing only long enough to slug down a glass of his private stock before tearing into him. Anne matches Crawford decibel for decibel, but his Lupo has problems enough what with rival gangs and police investigations. At length, Katherine vows to go out in search of fun, by which she does not mean a beer, a burger, and a double-header at Yankee Stadium. She succeeds only in killing herself in a car wreck, as Charlie's empire comes down around him.

It was a fine movie of its sort, and Anne gave as good as she got. Her Katherine was petulant, potent, sensual, with just a touch of the fifties femme fatale. Unfortunately, as a gangster picture the action consisted mostly of gunplay, backroom summits, and back-street machismo, none of which invited feminine intrusion. Paradoxically, Anne had mastered an essentially misogynistic genre.

Anne traveled to Mexico City in early February 1954 for location shooting on *A Life in the Balance,* a Fox thriller from Georges Simenon's novella, *A Matter of Life and Death*. The film starred Ricardo Montalban and was directed by Harry Horner, whose last project had been an adaptation, *New Faces of 1954*. The story concerns Montalban's attempts to clear him-

self of a grisly murder committed by a knife-wielding psycho-
path, Lee Marvin, and concludes with a taut chase on the campus
of the University of Mexico. Anne was mostly along for the ride.

Meanwhile, United Artists had seen *New York Confidential*
and hired her for more of the same with *The Naked Street*. It
was a convoluted tale of gangster brothers-in-law, with Anne as
Roselle Regalzyk, the naughty but nice little sister of mobster
Phil "Regal" (Anthony Quinn). The unwed Roselle has managed
to get herself pregnant by Nick Branda (Farley Granger), another crook who is soon on his way to the electric chair. Phil no
sooner has Nick sprung so that he can marry Roselle, than Roselle miscarries, making the shotgun wedding unnecessary. In
lightning succession, Nick muscles in on Phil, Phil kills Nick, the
police kill Phil, and Roselle runs off with a dashing investigative
reporter (Peter Graves). *The Naked Street* was completed in
February 1955, released the following November, and all but
forgotten by December.

If Anne's career was quickly going nowhere, her marriage was
just as quickly deteriorating. The church wedding had done
nothing to stabilize the relationship, nor had a series of trial separations. There were repeated squabbles, feuds, and standoffs.
Anne would respond by either retreating into herself (she was
capable of prolonged stony silences) or by camouflaging herself
with the company of friends. May, already alienated from Anne
professionally, was further shut out by the increasing number of
actors and actresses which crowded their home life.

With her film career spinning its wheels, Anne began to dab-
ble once more in television, which had been slowly working its
way West. Strictly speaking, the "B" movie, which had come
into prominence with the Depression and post-Depression dou-
ble-bill, had died in the early fifties with the double blow of
divestiture and television. In practice, however, much of the
talent and energy that had once gone into making "B"'s was now
diverted to television. Studios started their own television production outfits, and shared in the very medium which at times
seemed to threaten their downfall. For an actress like Anne, this
expanded the job market, although a good deal of the television

work was not so much an escape from the perils of filmmaking as an extension of them.

By early 1955, Anne had appeared in ten motion pictures and had nothing to show for it. There was no discernible picture-to-picture progress. There was no apparent logic or design to the roles she was offered. There were, save one and a fraction of another, no "A" projects to her credit. And, although she had freed herself of contract work, there was no sign that the supposed freedom of freelancing had in any real way enhanced her autonomy. She seemed hopelessly mired in low-budget exercises. Anne could take some comfort in the knowledge that she was consistently better than the movies in which she appeared, but there was little artistic consolation in not so much acting in movies as surviving them with dignity. If she had inadvertently fallen into a no-win rut, it stood to reason that she had little to lose by way of experimentation. With that thought Italiano went Western.

The Last Frontier (from a novel by Richard Roberts) started shooting in early spring and was completed the first week in May. The story is a kind of lopsided Hollywood revisionism which sides with neither the Indians nor the cavalry, but with some vaguely Cooperian natural man. Anne (blond for the occasion) plays the wife of a crotchety cavalry colonel (Robert Preston), but becomes enamored of a much-abused trapper (Victor Mature). By movie's end, the colonel is conveniently disposed of by Indians, leaving his widow and the trapper free to commune with nature.

Despite the skilled direction of Anthony Mann, *The Last Frontier* received only middling critical response. However, Westerns were making money for the studios, and since Anne was in the business of making movies, she was soon again making Westerns. In late summer 1955 she signed with M-G-M to play an Indian maiden in a picture called *The Last Hunt*, and reported to Rapid City, South Dakota, for the initial location footage. An early scene had Anne on horseback riding tandem with Stewart Granger. The cameras were rolling, the two riding, when suddenly the horse skittered, throwing Anne jarringly to the ground. She was rushed to a doctor, and what was at first thought to be a fractured vertebra turned out to be a severely pinched nerve. The injury would mend but would require three months of bed rest. M-G-M paid Anne in full and replaced her on the picture with Debra Paget. The Bronx equestrian was left to endure a tedious recovery which she spent not with her husband in California, but with her family back East.

The mishap might have been chastening for Anne, but was not. She returned to Hollywood and immediately signed with Universal for another Western, this one with the working title *Apache Agent*. However, if her injury had not moderated her penchant for horse opera, her recovery did seem to ease other matters into perspective. The picture was scheduled for location shooting in Tucson. Three days before Anne was due to depart, she publicly announced her separation from Martin May.

Apache Agent was taken from a reputedly true story in which a Bible-toting Indian agent attempted to create a miniature Utopian society among a tribe of Apaches. Anne played an Indian squaw, her hair straight and close-cropped, her print outfit snug and flattering, her dark eyes liquid and soulful despite an exaggerated Coppertone complexion. That was the best of it. The worst of it was the story itself, naïve, paternalistic, implicitly racist. It was given no life whatever by Audie Murphy, whose portrayal of the agent was sanctimonious, simplistic, and phrased in bland preachments. Anne on the other hand, spoke in traditional Hollywood-Indian staccato with little packets of dialogue that read like Western Union telegrams. The script's more fluent moments were no less ridiculous, as when the agent asked: "Why do you Apaches use the word 'maybe' so much?" to which the squaw replied: "Because we are never sure of anything." The film was retitled *Walk the Proud Land*.

It was a year to forget. Anne returned from Arizona and moved in with her agent, Richard Powers, and his wife. Anne and Martin had had separations before—over two dozen by some counts—but this one had the look of permanence. There was no immediate move for divorce, none for reconciliation. Anne went back to work, back to Columbia, and back to cheesecake. She played Marie Gardner, a model who aids an artist wrongly suspected of murder, in a melodrama by a Fox publicist recently

turned screenwriter, Stirling Silliphant. *Nightfall* was directed
by Jacques Tourneur (responsible for such "B" classics as *The
Cat People* and *I Walked with a Zombie*) and starred Aldo Ray
as the artist looking to exonerate himself.

It was a serviceable plot—certainly a Hitchcock staple for many
years—and Silliphant worked it for some nifty dialogue. But
unlike Hitchcock (who made no secret of the fact that plot was
merely a loose framework for directorial pyrotechnics) Tourneur
played it more or less straight, and the movie, though only
eighty minutes long, sagged under its own weight.

With her private life a shambles and her professional life little
better, Anne was thoroughly demoralized. In the past when
things were bleak, she would seek escape, a new apartment, a
new relationship, a marriage. All had failed dismally. Anne knew
she needed help and needed it soon, when she remembered a
friend whom she considered to be an "intellectual" and whom
she knew to be in psychoanalysis. She phoned him and asked the
name of his analyst. In the summer of 1956 Anne began psychoanalysis, and within one week of beginning, she and Martin were
legally separated.

Anne's filmwork soon slipped to its low point with her performance for United Artists in *The Girl in Black Stockings*. It
was another dollar-book murder mystery, directed by Howard
W. Koch (a fine former screenwriter—*Sergeant York, Casa-
blanca*—whose directorial work was markedly less accomplished
—*Untamed Youth, Andy Hardy Comes Home*) and featuring Lex
Barker, Mamie Van Doren, Ron Randell, and Marie Windsor.
Following location work in Utah, the movie wrapped on August
8, and went mercifully unreleased until nearly fourteen months
later, when it surfaced only briefly.

Anne was still stuck in unrewarding movies but she was taking
positive steps to extricate herself from her marriage. On October
23, she and Martin signed a property settlement, and on December 13, Martin's lawyer, Bentley M. Harris, filed papers for divorce with the California Superior Court. Anne attempted to
have the marriage annulled (on the tenuous grounds that the
union was childless) but learned after the first of the year that

the request had been denied. On February 13, 1957, Martin was awarded a divorce on the grounds of extreme cruelty. It was, under the circumstances, a rather polite conclusion to a wretched marriage. The divorce received relatively little publicity in the local scandal sheets, and even less in the legitimate press. Martin's testimony had been to the point, but still gentlemanly and guarded. He stated that Anne's professional need to travel had been a serious difficulty, explaining: "When she was here, she worked from 4 A.M. to 6 P.M. She came home and couldn't talk. . . . We couldn't get along or have any understanding or any real marriage at all," adding: "There was a lack of companionship, with millions of people tracking into the house." Later, and with more perspective and understanding than might by rights have been expected, he offered a fitting epitaph for the marriage: "She tried to combine two loves—one a marriage and the other a career. The career turned out to be the greater of the two."

For Anne, there seemed to be no malice, no recrimination, and no self-recrimination. Much as divorce violated the letter and spirit of her upbringing, it was strictly unremarkable in Hollywood. It did however signify an important reordering of priorities. She had indulged herself in what she would later term a "late adolescence," substituting one shelter for another, using relationships as a hedge against self-awareness. She was ready now to confront life, to assert her identity, to reconsider the direction her career had taken. Anne was soon announcing to friends and reporters alike: "I'm interested in only four men: my father, my agent, my press agent, and my analyst." That said it, clearly and bluntly. When, in the aftermath of it all, she was asked by columnist Sidney Fields to explain the collapse of her marriage, she replied: "Call it different temperaments. He's blond and I'm brunette—in temperament, too. He's from Texas and I'm from the Bronx. Texans will never understand Latins, and vice-versa." Anne accepted part of the blame and that was a departure from her old habit of holding her men friends responsible for failure. Confession was good for the soul. Anne had learned to take responsibility for her life, and that was soon reflected in her work.

She began by diverting attention from movies, which at the budget level had provided nothing but frustration and obscurity. She turned again to television, but this time with an eye to serious drama. On January 17, 1957, Anne appeared on the prestigious "Playhouse 90" in a ninety-minute production called *So Soon to Die* (written by Marc Brandel from a magazine story by Jeremy York). Anne played Isobel Waring, a young heiress due to inherit a fortune the day she turns twenty-five. There is another party with a secondary claim to the estate who hires an out-of-work London actor, Lionel Amblin, to murder Waring before the decisive birthday. The would-be assassin becomes enamored of the young woman and, far from killing her, ends up marrying her.

The show, while a production of Screen Gems which was a television subsidiary of Columbia Pictures, had a strong theatrical bent. The director, John Brahm, although then in transition from a string of ordinary budget movies to television, was the son of a renowned theatre family and had established himself as a highly respected director in the early thirties at the Burgtheater in Vienna, and the Deutsches Kunstlertheater and Lessing Theater in Berlin. Similarly, Anne's leading man, Richard Basehart, had distinguished himself onstage as well as in film.

Every bit as interesting as the show itself were Anne's personal reflections at the time. Television, like film, heralded its productions with press releases. Ordinarily, these were half-truths couched in the breathless prose of press agentry. This time, however, the obligatory interview caught Anne in an introspective mood. She began with an observation about the temperament that seemed to accompany acting: "I don't mean you have to be crazy to be an actor, but I do say that you have to be slightly neurotic in order to act." She went on to explain: "We're exhibitionists, with moods, probably because of some basic insecurity. But you must be a person of moods in order to understand and express emotion." She even took that a step further and said that an actor without anxiety "would just be another normal, average person, and who ever heard of a good actor who was normal or average?" She had a point, and seemed to be implying that what was behaviorally toxic was creatively tonic, posing what for her was the logical correlate: "Every acting hopeful should first ask herself: Am I neurotic enough? . . . or talented enough?" Anne seemed eager to certify the former. Brahm and Basehart confirmed the latter, each was immensely impressed with Anne's work.

As Anne's ties to the film community slackened, her interest in television intensified. She would, however, make one last film, a Western for Fox which starred Scott Brady and was called *The Restless Breed*. The picture was completed in June, and following an abortive release was not again heard of until a reissue some time later.

With that, Anne's Hollywood term came frustratingly full circle. She was not only back at Fox, but there for a motion picture that was having difficulty finding national distribution. If Anne had failed in movies it was not for want of trying. She had been a tireless worker, always doing her homework in preparing a role and indulging no peevishness in performing it. She had been, perhaps, too co-operative: "I learned my lines. Then they said move here and move there, and I did. And they said bark, and I barked, or, you know, whatever they'd tell me, I'd do." When her career had been in need of refurbishing, she had freelanced and roamed generically. But she was repeatedly sentenced to pinch-penny productions and stymied by scripts that habitually demoted actresses to auxiliary and ornamental roles.

In just over five years, Anne had appeared in fifteen films, had worked at one time or another for most of the major studios, had not given a single slipshod performance, and had nothing at all to show for her conscientiousness. Television work had provided some relief, though it was really little more than a studio backwater. Her marriage had been ruinous, and might have been worse in its aftershock were it not for her decision to enter analysis.

For it all, there was still one faint hope of redemption. The previous December, Richard Basehart had been approached by a gifted producer, Fred Coe (the driving force behind television's "Philco Playhouse") to come to Broadway to star in an unusual two-character play by William Gibson. Basehart read and liked the play, and though he personally vacillated, he twice recommended for the female lead a young actress with whom he had

just worked on "Playhouse 90," Anne Bancroft. Primarily as a
courtesy to Basehart, whom he was eager to please, Coe agreed
to meet Anne during her brief visit East in late February for her
sister's wedding. Anne's chances had been enhanced when, unknown to Coe or Gibson, Basehart showed her his copy of the
play allowing her to marshal her Bronx-Italian background behind the character's, which was Bronx and Jewish. The meeting
went splendidly, as did a second meeting with Gibson. Her charade was quickly apparent to both men who merely took it as evidence of her acting ability. The production only awaited Basehart's acceptance of the offer and the endorsement of Anne by
the play's director, Arthur Penn.

Anne met Penn upon returning West and he made the approval of her unanimous, underscoring the point by signing her
for an April 7 "Playhouse 90" production which he was to direct.
Only Basehart's commitment remained. Anne seemed at last on
the verge of emancipation from her Hollywood drudgery. Then,
in mid-March, word arrived that Basehart had refused the play,
which instantly upset the intended strategy—a talented "name"
actor co-starring with a talented "no-name" actress. Anne's
prospects slipped precipitously. Without Basehart, she was
merely one of many actresses in the running for the part. Casting
for the male lead continued to hang fire with consecutive re-
fusals by Paul Newman, Van Heflin, Jack Lemmon, Barry Nelson, Eli Wallach, Jack Palance, and Robert Preston. The playwright all but despaired of ever finding a leading man or of
seeing his play staged.

Whether on the strength of this near-miss with the legitimate
theatre, or a hard look at the bankruptcy of her Hollywood experience, Anne suddenly found herself radically rethinking the direction her acting career had taken. Late one night, she was sitting alone in her apartment, facing the fact that she had been
fooling herself to think her filmwork was going anywhere. It had
all been like some maddening palindrome that read the same
way forward or backward. Anne had finally run out of money,
out of self-deceit, out of patience. She walked into the bedroom
and packed her things, then went to the phone, called Millie,
and said: "I'm coming home."

9

NBC was hedging its bets. At the first sign of creative entropy the network dismantled "Your Show of Shows" and divided the spoils. As Pat Weaver put it, NBC was taking ". . . the opportunity to strengthen its own programming schedule with three hits and thus expand the talent of its stars," not to mention expanded advertising revenue. Max Liebman was soon mapping out his first spectacular. Sid Caesar was well into the planning stages of his own weekly variety show, due for September 1954 as "Caesar's Hour."

Imogene Coca proved more elusive. She was deluged with movie scripts and television deals, but found none to her liking. Her devotion to "Your Show of Shows" had been total, and when the show dissolved she was without any convenient contingency plan. By her own admission, Coca was not especially "career wise." She was slow to exploit her current fame, reluctant to accept the first fairish property handed her. And so while Max and Sid busily set about their own next steps at NBC, Coca sidestepped television and entered a Dallas production of *Wonderful Town*.

The "Show of Shows" writing staff likewise splintered off at odd angles. Mel Tolkin threw in with Sid as head writer on

"Caesar's Hour." Lucille Kallen took time out to become reacquainted with her family while staying abreast of Coca's plans. Mel Brooks, leery of prolonged identification with either star, declined an offer from Sid and went temporarily independent. There had been some rumors of Mel getting his own television show to write, but nothing materialized. Meanwhile, his growing infatuation with literature coupled with his fractional theatrical success encouraged him to look beyond television.

His thoughts again turned to theatre. "Your Show of Shows" had transposed any number of stage values to its production methods. Furthermore Mel had dreams of making a substantial and personal creative statement and there was the chance that theatre would take him seriously where television would not. Mel's incalculable work experience and professional exposure plus the financial cushion television provided, seemed to give him a leg up on other aspiring playwrights.

There was only one problem. Mel had learned to write in a crowd. His writing, like his primordial corner shtick, was by nature interpersonal and competitive. He worked best as a comic provocateur, a verbal gymnast with spotters. He would take the ordinary or commonplace and shake it off its axis, leaving it to spin and flutter for comic effect. His comedy began where others left off, and while the results were wildly inconsistent (though less so as his writing matured), his occasional sharpshooting was dazzling. And while a writer of the absurd is not necessarily a refined satirist or farceur, Mel, in the company of more structure-minded colleagues, was able to harness his excesses within their form. In the creative communal atmosphere of the show, Mel had been less the jester than the comic terrorist and whatever the expense in waste and frayed nerves, the benefit had been mutual.

When Mel went independent his technique was suddenly deprived of context. What was formerly stylistically reactive now lacked the all-important countervailing force. Alone, there were no rules to violate, no deadlines to footrace. There was no discipline other than that he himself enforced, and for Mel—much of whose comedy had been studiously undisciplined—the solitude was stifling. This was neither the time nor juncture for him to attempt a solo project. He missed the companionship and rivalry, the "noise and cigar smoke." He shelved his playwrighting ambitions and reconsidered television. If he was anticipating anything akin to the old "Show of Shows" alchemy, he was sadly mistaken.

Coca, still contentedly ensconced in Texas, was weathering the exhortations of her manager who naturally enough wanted her to return to television while "Your Show of Shows" was still fresh in the ever-dwindling public memory. The manager at length won out, but Coca remained at a safe remove until the details could be resolved. Entirely on the strength of Coca's name and without so much as a working draft or agenda let alone a format, NBC volunteered a weekly thirty-minute spot for whatever it was Coca was to do. Just what that would be stayed a mystery, even as hiring began. Marc Daniels was designated producer-director and Lucille Kallen head writer, with Max Wilk and Ernie Kinoy as staff writers.

Where "Your Show of Shows" had been fashioned after a carefully considered, time-tested model with Max Liebman as its rock-ribbed guardian, the Coca show was uncertain and ill-defined from its inception. It began halfheartedly, even haphazardly, and as the première date rapidly closed, the writing staff collected itself and started to wrestle with the question of form.

There was neither the time nor resources to sustain a revue and that narrowed the options automatically. One formula that had survived half-hour programming was the celebrity situation comedy, which began with a star or personality and engineered a kind of deductive comic logic. It was just a matter of knowing the celebrity's strengths and playing to them. With production hurtling toward an autumn air date, the decision was made to sample Coca in a situation comedy. The only problem was which Coca to use, because as Max Wilk noted at the time: "She can be anything."

In roughly three weeks' time a first script was pieced together which cast her as a celebrity who has consented to an Edward R. Murrowesque televised home interview. With the twists and turns of story that are situation-comedy staples, she confuses the dates and realizes the mistake while out pleasure driving. Her car then breaks down and she is stuck at a garage as the show, "Face to Face" (i.e., "Person to Person") begins, leaving all to stall, with Coca arriving a split-second before sign-off. It was a clever premise and was strongly cast with Ruth Donnelly and Billy DeWolfe as an unconscionably fussy Ed Murrow. The show aired at 9 P.M. on October 2.

It was an unmitigated disaster. Coca bore up admirably, but she was sorely out of her element. At the heart of the failure was a gaping misconception which rested largely with Coca's personal manager. What had figured principally in the success of other situation comedies was the outsized personality of the star. The broader and simpler the persona, the better the show's chances, since the comedy was little more than antic logic that inevitably reverted to type. Coca, of course, had never succumbed to type. She was, first and foremost, a comic actress who expertly submerged herself in character. She could credibly play a clown, a ballerina, a nagging housewife, or a dowager, and in her agility she was all of them and more. But in reality she was none of them. The situation comedy form, which had for others made a virtue of limitations, had for Coca made a vice of versatility.

Two days after the première Coca sent out distress signals for more substantial material, which quickly translated to more writers. The William Morris Agency, which had hastily packaged the show in the first place, brought in Hal Goodman and Larry Klein, who did what they could but ended up by throwing their hands in the air and saying "Gevalt!" The second week's show consisted of a pair of scenes which fared not appreciably better than the previous single story.

The norm for any writing in live television at that time was essentially variations on a theme of panic. But the atmosphere at the show's offices in the Mutual of New York building (then the home of the William Morris Agency) was impenetrably gloomy. Lucille would retreat to a nearby couch, clutch at her stomach, and ask as of some errant divinity: "What is the concept for the show?"

No answers were forthcoming, so the producer did the next best thing, and hired another writer, who arrived briefcase in hand with musty material that brought the show to its third week in as much disrepair as either of the first two. Again the call went out for writers, but this time William Morris turned to someone they thought sure to shake things up—Mel Brooks.

"Shake things up" was a colossal understatement. Mel's entrance was described by one staff writer as "convulsive." He quickly took the existing chaos and turned it into anarchy. Mel was funny—there was no disputing that as he went through his legendary improvisational gyrations in search of inspiration, and got only as near to a typewriter as it took to be overheard by the person at the keys. In many ways the other writers were in awe of his comic fearlessness. But the fact remained, what was before a rudderless show was now rudderless on seas made rougher by Mel's presence. That, despite the fact that he was not always present, but often off at the studio gamboling about the aisles and stage, making impracticable suggestions and, as one writer put it, ". . . substituting energy and noise for any ideas."

The show refused to focus, and as the season wore on, the gray areas that had gone unresolved in preproduction merged in a kind of shroud. The show was clearly doomed, and the comedic mastery that had been so beautifully understated when Coca worked with Sid (a weightlessness that counteracted his comic gravity) became somehow formless in the absence of a strong partner. The entire project was confirming Coca's worst fears regarding an overhasty return to television.

At the creative level, everything was in turmoil. Mel's comic dogmatism (a foreseeable by-product of his over-all comic *modus operandi*), which had been held in check on "Your Show of Shows" alternately by Max, Sid, or Mel Tolkin, now intensified and ran roughshod over the staff. Lucille, who had her hands full just staving off total creative collapse, found herself in a power struggle with Mel. The other staff writers, uninitiated in the ways of Brooks, were by turns alienated and demoralized. The tension, never especially subtle, finally jutted through the fragile peace during one sketch conference. Mel pitched a joke which was funny, but which not uncharacteristically had nothing to do with the task at hand. Lucille, in a modest exercise of her authority as head writer, said: "That's very funny, Mel, but we can't use it." Mel was incensed and he turned on her, all the humor flushed from his voice: "Don't you tell me what's funny, you just type." Lucille quietly stood, left the room, and approached the producer: "We've been having a lot of trouble with Mel, and I think it's come down to a point where it's either him or the rest of us." After some diplomatic give and take, they agreed instead to split the difference—Mel would stay, but there would be no more writing by committee. The staff was separated and sequestered, submitting work in writing only, and that was the final nail in the coffin. The show did not last the season.

It's possible to underestimate Lucille's strenuous efforts which bravely forestalled the inevitable. It is also possible to overestimate the role that Mel played in the show's demise. Coca, although skeptical at the administrative level, had complete faith in Lucille and Mel. The three of them had maintained a certain closeness and a high professional regard for each other. Granted, the bond between Lucille and Coca had been stronger to begin with, since Lucille's writing sensibilities had long been in harmony with Coca's acting strengths. Together they had suffered the backroom bravado of "Your Show of Shows" and it was more or less assumed that they would eventually come to collaborate in its wake.

Mel's inclusion on the other hand, however attributable to timing and availability, was a curiosity if not an outright incongruity. While with "Your Show of Shows," Mel was largely identified with Sid. His specialty, a kind of visual absurdity with verbal captions, was somewhat alien to Coca's style, which worked best either with nuance or with material that was broad but not extravagantly stylized. But whatever their creative differences, Mel and Coca were good friends. They enjoyed one another's company immensely, and, above all, they had fun together.

Mel betrayed a side to Coca that few other colleagues ever witnessed, a calmness and a confidential tone that stopped just short of actual confidentiality. Coca sensed in Mel a vulnerability which she saw as the logical counterpart and possibly even the taproot of his staunch extroversion. Mel saw in Coca none of the pragmatic assertiveness he considered imperative for survival in a hard-nosed profession: "Coca, you're so talented, you're so avant-garde—you're never going to get anyplace." She simply took this as an expression of friendship and said what she could to allay his fears. The basic contrast in their personalities was obvious to Coca, as was the fact that Mel and Sid were far better suited to each other. She had been glad to have Mel writing for her, but mystified that he had not instantly gone to work for Sid.

The network reasoned that the show had failed Coca, not the reverse, and it prepared another vehicle for her, while dismissing the present production and writing staff. Once again, Mel was out of work. For Mel, the debacle was, if nothing else, educational. Twice now he had miscalculated, first prematurely opting for autonomy, then writing for Coca despite incompatible styles. Mel was getting ahead of himself, taking off on tangents that hadn't allowed him to do what he had done best—write for Sid Caesar.

Mel was only twenty-nine years old, too successful and certainly too original to fear becoming merely a house writer, an anonymous hack. He was young, and much as he might argue the fact, still learning his craft. In the past, working with Sid had hardly been an inhibiting experience. They were like-minded in their respect for character comedy (spun integrally from a given character or source) and their disdain for joke comedy (the workaday chintz of the field). Furthermore, one did not solely write for Caesar but for a cast of Caesars. For his new show, Sid had spared no expense in hiring some of the best writers in the business. To be identified with "Caesar's Hour" was to be identified as a comic Brahmin. If Mel wanted to assert his creative independence, it could be better done with Sid than without him.

On September 9, 1955, a year and a day after it first aired, "Caesar's Hour" began its second full season on NBC. There were numerous changes made over the summer hiatus, but one of the most notable ones went unnoticed by all but insiders and aficionados—the addition of Mel Brooks to the writing staff. It was a welcome homecoming. Mel was reunited with Sid, Carl Reiner, Howie Morris, and Mel Tolkin, and the rest of the company was the best of company. The show, which was initially written by Aaron Rubin, Phil Sharp, Charles Andrews, Shelly Keller, and Mel Tolkin, had a rolling admission that at one time or another would include: Danny and Doc Simon, Mike Stewart, Larry Gelbart, and Joe Stein. It was more than an impressive roster, it was Caesar's praetorian guard.

Barely three years before, the Simons had tried and failed to infiltrate "Your Show of Shows." The show's strict equilibrium had proved their undoing. Max Liebman's genius for organization had provided the show with a low center of gravity that was as sturdy as it was impervious to outsiders. Balance prevailed. For each extrovert, a gentle soul; for each fastidious manner an effusive mania; for each temper an elastic ego; all unified behind Max as guiding spirit and resident peacemaker.

"Caesar's Hour" turned Max's blueprint on its head. It was built from the top down, starting with Sid and his host of characters, categories, and idiosyncrasies, and ending with the cast and staff. It fell to the writers to extract the essential Caesar, to challenge and stretch his imagination, to serve the show, which was synonymously Caesar. Personnel aside, "Caesar's Hour" was not "Your Show of Shows," and Mel's late arrival posed few problems. For one, he already had the master's ear, and was willing to turn backflips to hang onto it. For another, the show's philosophy and working style fit Mel like a second layer of skin.

The Liebman formula had held that comedy exclusive of music and dance was comedy unedited and diminished. Max believed firmly in parceling comedy over a larger production and he was the first to point out that the conviction was hardly original with him but was the backbone of vaudeville, Ziegfeld, the Broadway musical, and for that matter, the Marx Brothers. Max's adherence to this general tenet was reflected in his staff's working style, which, like the show itself, was co-operative and complementary but often compartmentalized. That is not to say that the writers were individually chained to typewriters—the approach was collaborative, at times almost communal—merely that the "pitch session" as such was never the dominant mode.

Sid, who believed that "Your Show of Shows" had often made comedy a second-class citizen and been given short shrift opposite overstuffed production numbers, was eager to exercise crea-

tive license with "Caesar's Hour." Paying little more than lip
service to production numbers, the show was designed as a vehicle for comedy, though comedy in the full Caesar sense—satirical, physical, antic, absurd, pantomimic. And he was helped
in no small way by Carl, Howie, and Nanette Fabray, who had
earned a spot on the cast roster.

With "Caesar's Hour," comedy was sovereign, and that in turn
governed the working style of the writers. It was the apotheosis
of the pitch session, boisterous, contentious, and often cutthroat.
Each bit had its unique genealogy; the seed might be an anec-
dote, an incident, a newspaper item, an argument, another bit, or
it might arrive fully formed as if by magic or immaculate conception. The gestation of a sketch was even more variable and
complex. But in either case, the proof of the plotting was in the
laugh. Something that read funny but didn't play was excised. It
was a lunatic sort of dialectical materialism, comedy evolving by
collision to a higher material form. It was not always a pretty
process. Nanette once compared the writing conferences to "sitting in the black hole of Calcutta."

The pitch sessions were intended as a kind of spontaneous
combustion, primed for the least spark. It was the perfect setting
for Mel's pyrotechnics. His vocal and bluff humor had been marginally muted with "Your Show of Shows," irrelevant when writing alone, and very nearly muzzled when writing for Coca.
"Caesar's Hour" found him in full flower and in full voice. It
recalled his youth, where humor was power, and power coaxed
the humor to still giddier heights. Inevitably, the pitch gestalt
served some writers better than others. Doc Simon, the younger
Simon, was more subdued (a writing writer) and his comparatively impassive nature cost him the full recognition he would
later receive working alone. Similarly, during a later incarnation
of the show, another Caesar veteran, Milt Kamen, interrupted a
writing session to introduce a young find whom he described as
"the young Larry Gelbart," causing Gelbart to look up from his
discussion with Sid and exclaim: "The young Larry Gelbart is
here." The newcomer, a short, wiry redhead whom Sid hired,
also was more cerebral than vocal, and it was not until some
time later that Woody Allen would come fully into his own.

"Caesar's Hour" was a writer's haven because it preserved the primacy of comedy. There was apparently no network politics to play, since Sid's assumedly ironclad contract with NBC, signed in 1954, guaranteed him ten years at something over $100,000 per year. If Sullivan was winning audiences with trained seals or jugglers, that was of no concern to Sid. If Lucille Ball was attracting a vast following with her brand of screwy situation comedy, that was her affair. Sid generated his own comic ethos and stuck by it doggedly. This commitment to comedy, upheld by the network's commitment to Sid, gave the show its own aura of security approaching sanctuary, a miniature *Zeitgeist* which enveloped the players, particularly the writers. If writing for Sid was in many ways its own reward, it was not the only reward. Sid was fiercely loyal to his troupe, and that was generously reflected in dollars and cents. By the time Mel had established himself on "Caesar's Hour," he was making something in the neighborhood of $5,000 weekly, but even that was a fraction of the astronomical production tab which leveled off at about $110,000 and was second only to "The Perry Como Show."

Although the budget seemed liberal, it was at least partially justifiable on the grounds of perfectionism. Everyone associated with the show worked to Sid's standards and specifications. Sid was every bit the workhorse and precisionist he had been with "Your Show of Shows," and perhaps more so now that his name graced the title.

Naturally, some of the comedy material was reminiscent of the old show, but mostly as a continuum of the Caesar persona. Mel continued to work dialectical wonders with the German professor. Likewise, the show extended the tradition of the movie parodies, including the silent melodramas, a gem entitled "Cyranose," and a hilarious take-off on *On the Waterfront* ("On the Docks"). There were pantomimes (one of his most memorable as a concert pianist), portraits (Sid as bop saxophonist "Progress Hornsby" speaking the barely intelligible jive in which Larry Gelbart specialized), and musical spoofs (Sid, Howie, and Carl and "The Three Haircuts" rocking with "Going Crazy" and "You Are So Rare to Me").

There were also domestic sketches with Sid and Nanette as

"The Commuters." Aside from the more overt differences between "Your Show of Shows" and the present venture, the domestic sketches were a handy index to the change that had taken place. Here, the absence of Max, Lucille, and Coca was perhaps most noticeable. Many of the "Commuters" sketches seemed to lack Max's sense of structural tightness and economy, leading the *Times*'s television critic, Jack Gould, to refer to a particular episode as "an unrelieved bore." Also missing was the special touch of satirical incisiveness Lucille had brought to "The Hickenloopers." And, finally, without detracting from Nanette Fabray, a gifted comedienne in her own right, the domestic sketches lacked Coca's rubbery but surefooted lunacy. But comparisons were useless. "Caesar's Hour" was on and successful and "Your Show of Shows" was, by the incessant television clock, a matter of antiquity.

Astride the prosperity of the show, Mel was not only a man of means, he was now a family man. Florence had given up dancing for motherhood and within three years had given birth to two children, a daughter, Stefanie, and a son, Nicky, named for Mel's literary hero, Nikolai Gogol. And though the television season bred the now-familiar signs of overwork and strain, most summers found retreat in the convenient seaside tranquillity of Fire Island where the Brookses were blessed with an ever-widening circle of friends that included childhood friends, fellow professionals, and artists from other fields.

Mel's work for Sid, and the fealty that exacted, seemed to excite rather than sublimate other writing urges. For a writer working television and living in New York, Broadway was eminently seductive. On balance, television paid more for less work, and although it too was a high-risk medium, it was tame next to theatre, which was always a crapshoot. But unlike television, the rewards of theatre were not to be so simply gauged. There was the prestige, the notoriety (in theatre the writer's name adorns the playbill and occasionally the marquee, whereas in television, the credits are merely a cue for viewers to retreat to the kitchen or bathroom) and the satisfaction of reaching a strictly live audience, eight shows a week, four weeks a month, for the extent of the run. For someone who has succeeded repeatedly with a mass audience, the lure of a concerted "small" success can be irresistible. Mel was again thinking Broadway.

Back in the summer of 1953, lyricist Joe Darion and composer George Kleinsinger (who had collaborated on a successful stage show for the Bil Baird puppets) hit upon the idea of anthologizing and scoring the popular Don Marquis stories *archy and mehitabel*. The idea was eventually to take form as an LP for Columbia Records, but the existing material was only enough to fill one side of a record. More material was written, and the final recording featured vocals by Eddie Bracken and Carol Channing, with narration by David Wayne. In part as promotion timed with the album's release, the piece was presented in concert at Town Hall in a single performance by The Little Orchestra Society. A theatrical producer, Peter Lawrence, saw the show, and suggested afterward that it be turned into a full musical comedy for Broadway.

The property, then "Back Alley Opera," passed from Albert Selden and Morton Gottlieb to Lawrence. Darion and Kleinsinger added still more material, and Darion wrote a libretto. The show was capitalized at $220,000, and Eddie Bracken and Eartha Kitt were soon announced for the leads (they were to be understudied by Tom Poston and Chita Rivera). Orson Welles, who was given credit for discovering Kitt, was mentioned briefly as a possible director, but that job was eventually handed to Norman Lloyd. The talented young John Morris was signed for additional musical routines. The show was to begin rehearsals in late February 1957 pending the completion of filmwork abroad by Kitt. Meanwhile, Mel had been hired to assist Darion in the libretto chores, which included trying to shake the wrinkles out of a troublesome second act. The show was scheduled to open on April 15 as *Shinbone Alley*, without an out-of-town tryout.

Mel's moonlighting, far from sedating his "Caesar's Hour" activity, seemed to embolden it. He continued his practice of comic oneupsmanship while also developing a certain reputation as a comedy writer's comedy writer. Mel's imagination not only embraced the disproportionate and extreme, but his free-style behavior fell into a similar pattern as if to turn rhetorical fancy into adjectival reality. If it was fanaticism, it was not joyless. Mel's clowning was not reserved for the script, but it coiled like a viper and lay for anything that moved. Oddly, his most reliable target was the boss, Sid. In the throes of a characterization, a sketch, or a monologue, Sid Caesar was possessed of an astonishing fluency. But Sid as Sid could be ponderous and almost willfully inarticulate, except for his lexicon of monosyllables and shrugs which served as a communicative shorthand. By contrast, Mel was quicksilver and nearly always "on," and he would often haze Sid, teasing and taunting about everything from his shoes to his jewelry. And yet aside from one brief scuffle, there were never any physical altercations, a blessing for Mel who stood a full head shorter and who was not nearly so fleet of foot as in the Brooklyn days. Sid mostly took the razzing in stride, aware that its author was actually in his service, as one time when Sid took Mel by the head and announced: "This is mine!" just as Mel fished out Sid's wallet and, waving it for effect, said: "This is mine."

The rivalry that drove the writers within the show merged at the staff level as a friendly rivalry versus other comedy shows. There was an element of pride as well as an appetite for public recognition, and both seemed due their day in the sun when "Caesar's Hour" approached the 1957 Emmy Awards with nominations in every major category including writing. The ceremony took place on March 17, and from the start the show walked away with the lion's share of the honors. Sid won handily for the best continuing performance by a comedian, Nanette in the equivalent category as comedienne (a minor coup since she had parted with the show over pay disputes and had been replaced the previous September by Janet Blair). Carl Reiner was named best supporting actor, and Pat Carroll (a later addition) best supporting actress. The show proper won as the best series of one hour or more, but when it came time for the Emmy for best comedy writing, Nat Hiken, Billy Friedberg, Leonard Stern, Tony Webster, Arnold Rosen, and Coleman Jacoby of the "Phil Silvers Show" edged Caesar's boys (at that time Mel Tolkin, Larry Gelbart, Neil Simon, Shelly Keller, Mike Stewart, Gary Belkin, and Mel Brooks). While the others took the loss with whatever good grace they could muster, Mel climbed the table at which they were seated and in full view of the assembled and the cameras declaimed: "Coleman Jacoby and Arnie Rosen won an Emmy and Mel Brooks didn't. Nietzsche was right! *There is no God! There is no God!*"

Mel's demonstration notwithstanding, it was a minor setback. "Caesar's Hour" had shone and the show seemed unshakable. In May, the bubble burst. Sid announced that he and NBC were parting ways, and as the details came to light, it was apparent that the decision was really the culmination of a series of events. The show had developed a slow leak.

At issue was what had come to be known in the industry as the "bread and butter" school of thought. Network executives, armed with ratings, evaluated shows not on quality but on viewership which translated directly into advertising revenue. A good show with a high tab and slipping ratings was bad business. As television ad prices began to soar, competition for a larger share of the viewing audience stiffened, with the result that the public and not the creators dictated taste. Networks, increasingly pragmatic, expedient, and venal, were pandering to some mythical-statistical lowest common denominator in search of the broadest possible audience base. The predictable trend was toward innocuous hosts (a kind of video eyewash) as well as panel shows, quiz shows, and the ever-popular television pulp Western. For a series with any sophistication and élan to survive, it first had to warrant its continued existence via ratings. When NBC scrutinized "Caesar's Hour" it saw only two things: it was overpriced and underwatched.

This sort of corporate reductionism was anathema to Sid. He had not been wanton or wasteful in his management of the show. He had set what was, to his thinking, the highest standard of professionalism, suffered no shoddiness or laxity in its pursuit, and wished only to reward the ensemble that assisted him in his comedic vision. When the network's misgivings came to a head, Sid was adamant, protective of his staff and audience, determined that the show not suffer cutbacks of any sort. As early as April 18th he told *Newsweek:* "It's no secret that my Saturday night show is out. If NBC comes up with a good idea, that's fine.

The NBC executives offered no panaceas, but they did mount a very compelling argument. The entire matter was, they contended, really out of their hands. The rating slump was an uncontestable fact, and sponsors were no longer willing to foot the staggering bills. In order for the show to continue uneconomized, NBC would have to subsidize its costs which, added to lost ad revenue, would run into the millions. NBC was not suggesting that the show be eliminated, only that its air time be reduced by half.

In truth, the argument was academic and the changes a *fait accompli*, since thirty of Sid's weekly sixty minutes had already been auctioned off to a show starring Gisele MacKenzie. Sid knew, as Coca had painfully learned, that a half hour was too paltry a forum for an expansive style of comedy. He was not a monologist who could arbitrarily halve his joke list. He was a character comedian and satirical actor who required some breathing room for the detail work upon which his humor rested: "There are only twenty-four minutes in a half-hour show and I have nothing to say in twenty-four minutes."

That alternative flatly refused, NBC recommended fewer shows of longer length, in other words four or five yearly specials. Here Sid simply pointed out his contractual arrangement that guaranteed him twenty hour-long shows through 1957 and 1958. With that, negotiations broke off for good. In all fairness, there was merit to both sides. Sid had delivered himself wholly to NBC and was justified in wanting the network to live up to its obligations. As for presentational matters, Sid knew precisely what Sid did best.

What Sid did not know was the malady that the young medium itself had only recently and pointedly become aware of—overexposure. Saturation was an inescapable problem of which attrition had become an ineluctable symptom. Unlike radio stars, who accumulated popularity slowly but held onto it stubbornly in a medium that left much to the imagination, television stars found mercurial success closely followed by sudden often inexplicable backsliding in a medium that left nothing to the imagination. Sid's nearly continuous run of close to nine years was in itself a phenomenal defiance of the odds. In that time, scores of others had passed abruptly into and out of public favor. Even though Sid's material had remained extraordinarily fresh, his image was beginning to stale before the public's rapidly shrinking attention span. In that sense, NBC was acting in behalf of its ten-year pact with Sid, hoping to ration him over a number of years rather than spend his popularity in a single binge. And, if the network could be permitted a note of altruism, it could be said to be acting in Sid's best interest in this regard. There was, of course, an enormous mitigating factor in their reasoning—the emergence of ABC as a serious competitor in the market place. This third network, although still ramshackle in many respects, was taking a sizable bite out of the audience block formerly shared by the two majors, causing them to foreclose on certain shows they might otherwise carry at a loss.

An overriding irony was the role the writing assumed in the show's fate. The bulk of television programming still originated in New York, but demographics showed that audiences were increasingly distributed over a wide national base of middle- and lower-income families. New York was no less the country's cultural center, but ratings-minded network executives were worried about a comedic outlook that might be accused of New York provincialism. If the staff occasionally dipped into comic esoterica (no great crime to begin with), it never adopted anything like a public-be-damned attitude. At worst, Sid and his writers were guilty of refusing to condescend to their audience. Taste was becoming an unpardonable sin.

The upshot of it all was that Sid asked to be let out of his contract, and NBC, breathing a sigh of relief, released him with its blessings. The final show was set for May 25, and in anticipation of this farewell, Sid took a moment on air to invite fans to write in requesting favorite pieces they wanted to see reprised. The response was awesome, which did nothing to reverse the decision to discontinue the show, but did seem to vindicate Sid's contention that he was reaching a large and loyal audience.

The show aired and the series ended, despite requests from fans and critics that Sid reconsider. The parting was described as amicable, and NBC President Robert W. Sarnoff added his official *bon voyage:* "We regret his decision, but we wish him the best of good fortune in whatever ventures he undertakes in the future." As others picked over the ashes, there was revealed one crowning irony. The crippling decline of "Caesar's Hour" in the ratings was attributable in large part to the competition ABC had offered in the same Saturday night time slot—"The Lawrence Welk Show."

Mel might have seemed luckier than the others. At least he could look to Broadway to break the momentary fall from television grace. But *Shinbone Alley* was having its own problems. One week before the opening, the director, Norman Lloyd, left over differences with the producer and writers. Added to that was the unsolved eleven-scene second act. The show had opened to what were at best tepid reviews. There was agreement among critics who saw the musical as a show of parts, some of which excelled, but all of which never really integrated into a complete entertainment. Walter Kerr, writing for the *Herald Tribune*, was especially critical of the libretto, observing that: "Joe Darion and Mel Brooks are working the obvious mathematics of man-into-insects," offering as example Eddie Bracken's labored line: "I could lick you with five hands tied behind my back." Tom Donnelly, with the *World-Telegram and The Sun*, complained of the absence of "a coherent narrative," concurring with John McClain of the *Journal-American* who cited "Long lapses when the story falters." Thomas R. Dash, with *Women's Wear Daily*, made the point less bluntly, referring to several "languid patches," and the *Times*'s Brooks Atkinson noted the problematical second act, while Richard Watts, Jr., of the *Post* took the play to task for an "ineffectual" and "chaotic" framework that was all the more culpable for wasting what good material and performances there were. Writing for the *Mirror*, Robert Coleman cast the lone dissenting vote, complimenting the authors for their "amazing job in adapting the esoteric essays of Don Marquis," and insisting that the show had scored a blow for entertainment that was, of a piece, "Intelligent, sophisticated, and sexy."

As had happened with *New Faces*, most of the favorable remarks gathered about the performance of Eartha Kitt. But that did not outweigh the libretto's shortcomings, its failure to distill a story from material that was originally serial and episodic. *Shinbone Alley* was no hit, but there was some consolation in the fact that it was a near miss. It closed after forty-nine performances.

Television gave and television took away. Sometimes it did both at once. In late September, ABC announced the planned reunion of Sid and Coca in a regularly scheduled program. Beneath the glow of anticipation was the glaring reality that while the network was giving them the chance to rediscover their lost audience, it seemed too to take away the time necessary to their art. The show would run Sunday evenings, but for only thirty minutes, or rather the twenty-four minutes that had so stuck in Sid's craw during the late negotiations at NBC. Still at this point, a half hour was better than none, and the optimists among them viewed this as a beachhead from which to re-establish the two stars whom television had treated so coldly in recent months.

Sid and Coca redux. In many ways it was to be old home week. The obvious omissions were Max (still up to his ears in spectaculars over at NBC) and Lucille (still smarting from the first Coca debacle and enjoying her self-imposed exile from television). The two Mels, little and big, were on hand, as were Mike Stewart and Doc and Danny Simon. As for producer, Hal Janis (a veteran of both "Your Show of Shows" and "Caesar's Hour") left security at NBC to join the show. The cosmetics firm Helena Rubinstein agreed to sponsor the show through late spring (with a budget less lush than Sid had grown accustomed to) with an option to renew through a '58–'59 season. ABC, of course, wanted the show to succeed, but it had no intention of padding its chances. The designated time slot pitted the show against two perennial favorites, "The G.E. Theatre" and "The Dinah Shore Show."

"Sid Caesar Invites You" premièred at 9 P.M. Sunday, January 26, 1958, amid fears that time might have eroded the Caesar-Coca magic. The show, intermingling the classic with the new, went smoothly and briskly, with the steady-going Carl Reiner supplying polish and comic punch, and help from newcomer Paul Reed. The show flew by without a hitch, and everybody sat back and awaited signs of fate, not from the critics (whose reactions were of passing interest but otherwise superfluous) but for the Trendex rating, that oracular bit of science which estimated audience size. Later that week, word arrived—G.E. had reached some 21.6 million viewers, Dinah Shore another 14.5. Sid and Coca topped the list with 25.8. ABC was ready to admit, albeit gingerly, that it had a winner.

Then the ratings started to fall off, first gradually, then sharply. The initial strong showing was attributed to curiosity, not so much a fluke as a curio—old fans tuning in to see if Sid and Coca were fully returned to form. Comedically, the pair had given up nothing, but the half-hour allowance was insurmountable. Aside from the old saw, that character comedy demands time, there was the corollary that bit comedy demands diversion, preferably music and dance. Thirty minutes allowed neither, and Sid and Coca, their comedy reduced to crystalline form, did not hold the viewer's attention. Through no fault of theirs or the staff's, the show seemed stark and even arid. It was as if someone had extracted their teamwork from "Your Show of Shows," crammed it into an abridged anthology, and in the process robbed it of life. In April, Helena Rubinstein announced that it was withdrawing its sponsorship and that if the show's option was to be picked up, it would have to be by some other concern. No sponsor filled the void, and "Sid Caesar Invites You" aired its final installment on May 25.

Before anyone could file a proper post mortem for the show, Sid announced that he had been in touch with representatives of BBC, and that a deal had been made to transport the show to London for a thirteen-week trial summer run. This would mark the first time a show consisting exclusively of American talent, would appear on British Public Television, and Sid, embittered by recent network mishandling, was fully prepared to let America's loss become Britain's gain. The show made its transatlantic transplant, debuted, and promptly found more of the same. The BBC, in competition with private networks, was no less ratings-conscious than its American counterparts, and when the audience response proved less than was hoped for, the show was canceled despite favorable reviews.

The company disbanded, and Sid re-entered negotiations with NBC. This time, he agreed to a series of specials, which was nothing less than the network had held out for a year and a half prior.

The first signs of television's effect on Sid were already apparent to Mel. Earlier he had taken Sid aside and said: "Enough, let's do movies." Sid refused. He had risen by television and if need be would fall by it. Artistically, Sid was still Sid, but that now seemed too intense for the cool medium, and the constant shuffling between networks could only portend television's eventual orphaning of him. And for Sid, who was chiefly a product of television, with no abiding interest in stage and no particular affinity for film, it was an uneasy prospect.

The lot of the television writer was a world apart. Where the star was virtually foredoomed by exposure (hypothermia in the cool medium) the writer was safe in his relative invisibility. The public's appetite for a given star was easily sated and networks were loathe to argue the point. On the other hand, networks saw writers as an elastic commodity that might serve one star as well as another. It was an often exasperating conformity and conservatism but it did work to the advantage of the television writer who, if he remained flexible, pliable, and portable, stood an excellent chance of longevity. In short, whatever became of Sid, Mel had good reason to believe that television would be willing to employ him so long as he was willing to work for it.

A continued income was very much to the point for Mel. In the first place, he and Florence now had another child, another son, Eddie, and the family obligations were that much more. In the second place, family life was soon to take on further complications. The marriage, impulsive at the start and in many ways the whimsy of two young and largely inexperienced people, had fallen on bad times. There was later some unpleasantness about infidelity, but the real problem seemed to be that both Florence and Mel had simply gotten in over their heads at too tender an age; 1958 had, in its vicissitudes, been a year to forget. The following year, Florence and Mel were separated.

10

Homecoming. For Anne it was not so much an arrival in New York as a departure from Hollywood. It was retreat but not escape. To have remained in Hollywood would have been escape. Coming home meant admitting the disillusionment of the last five years, addressing the personal setbacks, reassessing herself as an actress. Coming home also jolted into perspective the double life Anne had slipped into, the flip Hollywood life style that had been hers by some accultural osmosis, in sharp contrast to the concrete values that had been hers by upbringing.

Anne's misguided career was strictly secondary to her botched personal life. She may have taken divorce philosophically, but never lightly. According to the Hollywood example, marriage was little more than an impermanent arrangement, a convenience. But according to the Catholic Church and the Italiano example, marriage was permanent and sacred, the cornerstone of the family which in turn was the capstone of life. Anne returned to New York with a gnawing sense of shame and pain, not so much that she might have disappointed her parents as that she had violated her own values.

Hollywood had been demoralizing; New York would have to be cleansing. Although the prospects for work were drastically curtailed by the move, Anne was far more concerned with ridding herself of the bad work habits she had picked up in movies. She had come to Hollywood with no clear technical understanding of how best to prepare or perform a role and she left town not appreciably better equipped. Movies, especially "B" movies, were all surface and simulation, and most directors preferred to reshoot or simply shoot around acting deficiencies rather than attempt to correct them. Anne's approach had been painstaking and diligent, but left entirely to her own devices she could do little more than memorize her lines and hope for some slim identification with the character she was playing.

There had been one time, during the shooting of *New York Confidential*, when Anne was to play an agitated scene that was to prefigure her character's suicide. She had been working at a literal-instinctual-empirical level, and consequently had no idea how to handle the scene. The director offered no counsel and merely resorted to take after take (thirty-three in all) hoping to capture by accident what by rights should have been generated dramatically. The incident was indicative of Anne's movie experience. Most of what she learned in Hollywood would have to be unlearned.

One of Anne's first decisions upon returning to New York was to enroll at Herbert Berghof's HB Studio. Berghof, who had studied with Alexander Moissi, Max Reinhardt, and Lee Strasberg, and, with Strasberg, had been a charter member of the Actors Studio, had opened his own studio in 1945 which he operated with the help of his wife, the fine actress and teacher, Uta Hagen. Aside from the studio's excellent reputation, there might have been another attraction for Anne. Berghof had worked extensively in theatre, but not exclusively there. He had appeared on television, in radio (he was once a guest on "The Goldbergs"), and, in 1952, had appeared in four movies for Twentieth Century–Fox. In Berghof, Anne might expect an instructor who was both remedial and sympatico.

Studying acting did not by any means preclude continued professional acting, and Anne kept in touch with producer Fred Coe while the fate of William Gibson's play continued to fluctuate. The play, *Two for the Seesaw*, was something of a tragicomedy involving a man and a woman, alone and lonely in New York City. Jerry Ryan, a dour and defeatist Midwesterner meets Gittel Mosca, a buoyant and neurotic Bronx-born dancer manquée, who, like Ryan, has elements of doubt and self-destruction, but unlike him, tries to put a comic mask on her problems instead of a scowl.

In early February, Anne had successfully interviewed for the role with producer Fred Coe. Prior to the visit, she had read that theatrical producers sometimes lacked imagination and that it was a good idea to "be the part from the minute you walked in." Bolstered by an advanced reading of the script on loan from her friend Richard Basehart, Anne transformed her least inflection and gesture. When admitted to the waiting room of Coe's office, she carefully posed herself carelessly, one shoe off, absently scratching her foot. Coe invited her in, and she stood shoe in hand, and before he could say another word, she blurted out in exquisite Bronx inflection: "Do you have a john?" He answered: "Yeah," and she elaborated: "Oh, I have to go so bad." She went to the bathroom, counted off what seemed a reasonable length of time, and rejoined him tossing off a casual "Thanks." Anne stayed with the characterization, and when she finally left, Coe phoned his playwright, who was on the Coast with a teleplay, and proclaimed her "the best Gittel yet," asking Gibson to meet her during his stopover in New York enroute to his home in Stockbridge. The endorsement was more meaningful than it might at first have seemed. It was not uncommon for an actor to reward a paramour with a reading. While Coe knew little of Anne and nothing of her relation to Basehart, he was half prepared to greet an actress whose primary attributes were not acting. As it happened, he was entirely unprepared for the winning impression.

Anne was asked back for a second meeting at Coe's office the next day, February 8. Gibson was seated there, calmly, expecting little, when Anne appeared still sporting her Bronx dialect (which, incidentally, took some doing after five years of Hollywood diction) and popped a prepared question-statement that startled Gibson for its fidelity to Gittel: "How was the Coast, lousy, huh?" Gibson did a mental double-take, Coe sent for an

actor-reader, and Anne launched into a stunning reading of Gittel. She departed, with Gibson convinced not that she was the
part, but, better, that she could play the part to perfection. With
the endorsement of playwright and producer, Anne was asked to
see the play's director, Arthur Penn, upon her return to Los Angeles. Penn's response was brief and explicit: "Gittel on the
hoof."

That was in February. By March, Richard Basehart had
begged off the project and the fate of Anne, a Broadway un-
bankable, was again in jeopardy. In the ensuing weeks, Coe,
Gibson, and Penn went fishing for a "name" leading man, but no
one rose to the bait. The three of them were veritable Broadway
neophytes, and the thought of depending primarily on a likewise
uninitiated actress, despite the fact she seemed born to the part,
was unthinkable. The question of a leading man was foremost in
its irresolution and Anne was left to languish.

The suspense lingered through spring and into early summer.
By mid-June, Anne was just one more unemployed New York actress, with nothing in particular to look forward to. Then she received a call from Gibson asking her to meet him the next day at
an address in the East Seventies. The apartment belonged to
Henry Fonda, who had been sent a copy of the play by Coe,
with whom he worked in television. Fonda liked *Two for the
Seesaw*, with certain serious reservations, and agreed reluctantly
to a quick reading of the first act before repairing to Europe and
a summer-long vacation on the southern coast of France. Anne's
grasp of the part had improved with time and Fonda marveled
as Gittel came "blazingly alive." He asked her to put off a shop-
ping date with Millie and to stay and join him in a reading of
the second and third acts. Afterward, Anne left, but Gibson
stayed behind to discuss what had become painfully obvious in
the course of the reading—that the part of Jerry was underwrit-
ten and overshadowed by Gittel. Fonda remained noncommittal, aside from his enthusiasm for Anne, and Gibson volunteered to improve the man's part, to which Fonda replied:
"Fine, any way you make this guy come as alive as Gittel is, I
think you've got a marvelous play."

Gibson devoted the next two months to revisions and by late

summer sent a copy of the first two acts to Fonda who was still in Europe. Fonda was no more pleased with Jerry and continued to withhold decision when he received a lengthy cable from Coe saying in essence that the moment of truth had arrived, that a commitment was necessary in order to book a theatre for the coming season. Fonda thought to himself: "Anybody who can write a part like Gittel has got to be able to write a part for Jerry." After two weeks he cabled back: "Start it rolling, I am yours."

Anne was notified of the good news, and, while the others plowed into the myriad details of production, she was left to fill time until the start of rehearsals in early November. Part of that time she spent researching the character of Gittel. There were a number of external facets and foibles she already felt a natural empathy for, especially a history of unsuccessful relationships with men. But, past one or two kindred areas, Anne was not Gittel, and her Hollywood sojourn had done much to erase many of the Bronx sensibilities and idiosyncrasies essential to the role. Anne looked elsewhere for a model and settled immediately on her older sister, Joanne. Anne saw in Joanne the sort of emotional polarity Gibson attributed to Gittel, an exterior that was witty and earthy contrasting a sensitive and guileless interior. Anne made a point of spending extra time with Joanne as an objective method of studying and getting acquainted with Gittel.

Of course, there were aspects of the character which neither Anne nor her sister encompassed, a passion for modern dance, for instance, and that led the research to other climes. Gittel was a frustrated dancer, but an enthusiast nonetheless who liked to advertise her expertise by sprinkling her conversation with offhand references. Gittel was especially fond of the work of José Limón, whose name she dropped with a chummy and phony familiarity—"José." Anne, who in her research was careful to leave no stone unturned, promptly joined the classes supervised by Limón's company. For three weeks she attended regularly, fixing an eye on the less gifted dancers who frequent such classes and who might in ways lend insights into Gittel.

Anne also carried her research into the streets of Greenwich Village where she observed the sort of bohemianism of which

Gittel's manner was an individual but imperfect copy. In time, Anne came to impersonate Gittel as she went about the daily mundane activities of her own life. In that sense, she not so much pretended to be the character, as met the character halfway. Anne Bancroft began to occupy that common ground between Anne Italiano and the fictional Gittel Mosca.

Permitted a luxury of time, Anne was cataloguing observations and experiences which she might later consult in service to the role. It was very much in keeping with the training she was receiving at HB Studio, which, like that at the Actors Studio, was of a Stanislavskian bent. Uta Hagen stressed techniques such as "identification," "substitution," and "transference" to help bring observed and even imagined sensations and events into line with character. There was particular emphasis on role-specific homework, which Anne went about as she did most everything, with discipline, vitality, and thoroughness.

Not all of Anne's time was spent in preparation for the play. A few months before, while Gibson and Coe were still rummaging for the male lead, it seemed that the play might stall indefinitely, and with it Anne's hopes for a quick reclamation of her career. It was during this maddening lull that Anne started seeing a man named Mario Ferrari-Ferreira, a distant relative of the famous Ferrari automobile-manufacturing family. The two had scarcely announced their engagement when Anne received word that Fonda was in and the play was on. Her first reaction was to tell Coe to count her out, and that she intended instead to get married. She soon reconsidered. There was, she decided, no reason to assume that a marriage and career need be mutually exclusive: "I can do it and be married." She got back in touch with Coe and reported she would not be withdrawing from the production. As it turned out, Mario would have to be away anyway just about the time the show was scheduled to go into rehearsal and out-of-town tryouts. At long last, it looked as if things were starting to fall into place for Anne.

Meanwhile, behind the scenes, Gibson continued his rewrites, enlarging and improving the role of Jerry Ryan, as company manager Joey Harris set about turning the playwright's fiction into a financial reality. The production was capitalized at $80,000 and the promise of an innovative play with the solid insurance of Henry Fonda in one of two leads made fund raising a delight. In less than two weeks, the project was underwritten to the last nickel, with Fonda himself accounting for a full quarter of the show's backing. That, in addition to a weekly pay check of $2,500 against an eventual 15 per cent of the gross helped further sharpen the actor's interest in the play's success.

Anne's contract terms were far less lucrative. Where Fonda could ask out of the play after six months, Anne was bound to it for as long as two years, but on the short end, could be dismissed before the play ever reached town. Her weekly take was set at $550, allowing for regular increments of $100. Anne, despite her uncanny affinity for the role, was to be paid commensurate with her shaky credentials. The same investors who besieged Joey Harris with the mere mention of Henry Fonda, displayed a distinct indifference toward Anne. In fact, one producer who earlier had been approached by Gibson's agent claimed to have seen Anne work before on the Coast, with the ungenerous appraisal that she was "lousy, stank, like a dead thing." The comment went no further than Gibson and his agent, but it was clear that Anne's success would be measured not by what she brought to the play but by what she got out of it. In any case, Anne's relative anonymity had been no deterrent to the siege of eager subscribers, many of whom had to be turned away with an apology and a shrug. In all, there were thirty-nine angels with none but the highest hopes for a substantial return on their investment.

The first rehearsal began on the morning of November 4, in a room on Fifty-seventh Street. Two things struck the playwright as he entered the room: a certain air of detachment about Fonda, and an easy joviality about Anne which did not hide the fact that since last seen, she had put on close to thirty pounds (most of which she would shed by opening night). With the producer, playwright, and director on hand, and all positioned around a table littered with coffee cups and note pads, Anne and Fonda shared a first read-through. Everyone broke for lunch then returned for a second reading, and aside from some paperwork which Anne had to fuss with for an Equity functionary, the balance of the afternoon was spent with Penn and his cast discussing interpretations. Everyone knocked off around six, and reassembled the next morning for a scene by scene read-through/seminar which became the routine for the next few days. Things went reasonably smoothly except for several persistent problems in the male role and a timed reading that ran roughly twenty minutes longer than expected.

As the first week of rehearsals neared an end, a subtle friction began to reveal itself. Penn worked deliberately and patiently with Anne in probing the play's more submerged meanings, in effect, reading between the lines. The approach was consistent with their theatre training, in many respects psychological, and it seemed to bring about the desired result. Fonda, meantime, was an old-school actor, who, at fifty-two, was twice Anne's age and whose technique was a world apart from hers and Penn's. His approach was more literal, he essentially read the lines and not between them. Fonda required far less time to review a given segment, and was left to sit by with waning tolerance as the others went about their analysis. Gibson, who had adopted something of an observer's posture, quickly noticed the disparity and later mentioned it to Penn, who in turn divided his time more evenly between his two actors. That helped considerably, but it did not hide the fact that in a cast of two, there was a serious divergence of acting method; one, traditional and more objective, or "representational" (Gibson's background as well); the other modern and more subjective, or "presentational." It was to remain a point of difference, but not an insurmountable one. Anyway, it was soon overshadowed by the unsolved difficulties with the male role.

After eight straight days of readings, the company took a day's rest then reconvened for the first onstage rehearsal. It was a compact, musty space atop the New Amsterdam Theatre at 214 West Forty-second Street, once the private domain of Florenz Ziegfeld and his exclusive "Danse de Follies." All hands were there, including the stand-bys, Kevin McCarthy and Gaby Rodgers, and the stage manager, Pete Van Zandt. As Penn set about blocking the play by placing Anne and Fonda onstage and working from their natural movements, the disposition of the early rehearsals took a sudden and not altogether unexpected reversal. Fonda, until now impassive and remote, took to stage majestically. Anne, a marvel at the table-side readings, was suddenly awkward and unsure and all but overwhelmed.

By the end of the day the first two scenes had been blocked fairly effectively and without incident. Fonda's stature was, to Anne, "breathtaking." Even Penn, who till then had found little to smile about, commented to Gibson, "He stalks that stage like a stallion." Of Anne, in contrast, Penn told himself: "She can hardly find the stage." And to the voice in his head were added the voices of a number of the show's lawyers and agents who told him: "She's no good, dump her." But Penn was confident that with time he could tone down Anne's broad overprojection and smooth the rough edges of her gawkiness.

There was every reason for his conviction. Anne had been totally receptive to his instruction, and had been so selflessly accepting of his criticism that she began to shy away from his compliments. She was finally finding all the directorial sensitivity and seriousness she had wanted but missed in filmwork. Her inquisitiveness and conscientiousness which in movies had been more of an impediment than an asset, was now respected. She could search out meanings, explore nuances, and fully grow into a role rather than give some programmed imitation before cameras. Onstage, Anne was dismal at first, but fast improving. With work, and nurturance, she would adjust to the theatre setting. One thing was certain, she would not fail for want of enthusiasm.

As the first day of blocking drew to a close, the theatre emptied of most hands. Gibson sat alone in the audience section; Coe, Penn, and the publicity agent stood off to the side; but Anne lingered onstage and on a girlish impulse said: "It's just like it is in the movies!" to which Penn responded, not without irony: "How else do you think we learn how to do it?"

Penn's commitment to Anne had its practical side. She required attention but offered no resistance or temperament. In fact, since much of Gittel's dialogue took place over the telephone, Penn would often call her at home and the two of them would improvise. By contrast, he had his hands full with the brewing tensions between playwright and leading man. There had been from the first a gap between the character as conceived by the writer and the character as perceived by the actor. Rehearsals, instead of bridging the gap, only widened it. Finally, Fonda stopped cold one day and said of Jerry Ryan: "Too many complexes, I can't follow this guy!" Anne retreated to a nearby cot, Penn engaged Fonda in an impromptu tête-à-tête, and Gibson did his best to get some drift of what was being said. Tête-à-têtes became the director's most valuable tool. Penn, in sneakers and chinos, would shuttle from Anne to Fonda, in effect doing the work of two distinctly different directors: "Out of one side of my mouth I'd be talking to Anne about a semi-Freudian adjustment, and out of the other side, like George Abbott."

The second day saw two more scenes blocked and more difficulties reared with Jerry Ryan. After rehearsal, Penn and Gibson worked into early morning deciding what to do with the character, whether to leave him as was and risk alienating Fonda to say nothing of the audience, or to rework the part and risk undercutting the author's conception. The result of the meeting—three lines were changed. During the next few days of rehearsal, with the character still unrealized, animosity welled up and soon no one was pleased with Jerry Ryan.

Halfway through the third week of rehearsal, the third act was blocked. That left a week and a half of rehearsals which were to culminate in a dry run before an invited audience. While the others worried whether tempers would be on the mend by then, Anne, who till then had been flexible but astonishingly unshakable, began to wonder how she would fare before a live house.

The test date arrived, Penn briefly introduced the cast, staff, and play, and the show got under way. There was no trace of nervousness or reason for despair in Anne's performance, which went quite well despite one or two muffed or misplaced lines. Fonda did not drop a beat or a word but his disenchantment seemed to show through, as the play finished to polite applause from an audience which had seemingly conspiratorily refused even a ripple of laughter at what had been intended in large part as a comedy. There was a backstage meeting yielding a half-dozen line changes which were inserted the next day and readied for the second dry run before a Saturday night audience. The response was tremendously improved over the previous night, complete with laughter and a curtain call. All egos appeared soothed. A brief rehearsal was scheduled for Sunday, and Monday the show packed off to Washington, D.C., for an out-of-town opening that Thursday, December 5.

There were three persistent problems, all of them of the playwright's own making. The first was structural. The play was meant to swing over a wide field of emotion, from a facile and vernacular comedy to a deadly earnest series of emotional and physical crises. It was textually ambitious and required constant structural refitting to establish dramatic equilibrium. But that was what road tryouts were for. The other two problems were really just twin faces of one. Fonda was no fonder of Jerry Ryan, and he was understandably reluctant to offer himself up in some act of blind faith since his own theatrical experience surpassed that of the other principals combined. Experience is not automatic or quantitative, but the simple fact was that Fonda was the ranking veteran in a difficult two-actor play about which he had serious reservations. Were it a musical, he might hope for upbeat camouflage; were it a cast play, insulation and distraction. But as a full 50 per cent of the cast, onstage nearly 100 per cent of the time, Fonda knew instinctively that the least doubt or conceptual flaw would show through, and his instinct for self-preservation led him onstage to retreat from the role, to underplay. Offstage, he was not violent but admittedly "loud" in his protestations.

Fonda's undisguised dissent was inadvertently compounded by Anne's enthusiasm. Gittel was a plum role—offbeat, charismatic, sympathetic—which Anne could not only play but practically inhabit. The more lifeless Fonda's performance, the more lively Anne's. The growing imbalance was starting to push Gittel beyond dramatic truth to a level larger than life, which violated the play's concentrated semblance of realism. That meant, in short, that Jerry had to be toned up and Gittel toned down. But that, thought the producer and director prayerfully, was what road tryouts were for.

On arrival in Washington, the more pressing problem proved to be the set, which for reasons technical, financial, and union had not been introduced in rehearsal in New York. Since the action of the play required two separate apartments that could be called into use in quick alternation or simultaneously, set design presented a challenge that George Jenkins had solved imaginatively, though not uncomplicatedly. The set had arrived in town Sunday, and despite continuous work by stage managers and hands, was still mostly in disarray by Tuesday. That evening after dinner, the company met at the Shubert Theatre for a first technical run with cast onstage reading. Pausing for the least and most details, the rehearsal crawled through fits and starts when, past midnight, with the end of act two barely in sight, things ground to a halt. The slackening morale was done no favor with word of a sluggish box office.

Rehearsal resumed its snail's pace the following afternoon, again slogging through midnight with tempers at times nearing the breaking point. Thursday, there was finally a stumble-free dress rehearsal which wound up only a few hours before that evening's opening curtain. Everyone adjourned for dinner. Fonda was in a funk. Anne was in a buzz of anticipation, heightened by the arrival en masse of her family from their present home in Yonkers.

The curtain was twenty minutes late. The audience was patient, and, as the first act unfolded, attentive and appreciative. Fonda's performance was, to the insiders, noticeably subdued, but Anne's work more than compensated. Penn, Coe, and Gibson had, for the time, abandoned efforts of muting Gittel for fear of a general soporific effect.

Audience response was heartening and sustained through several bows. Afterward, backstage, Anne was besieged by what seemed to be half the Italian population of Yonkers, while Fonda sat in his dressing room trying to put the best face on what was for him a bad situation. The company branched off for separate post-performance outposts, and finally to bed awaiting the first salvo of reviews. Gibson retired with the nagging fear that his leading man had been miscast.

The notices allayed some doubts while confirming others. Most objections centered on the play itself, although criticism was in each case wisely qualified by the individual Washington critics whose lot it was to see works in progress. If the diagnosis was in some cases pointed, the prognosis was uniformly cheering. Reaction to the performances was somewhat mixed, but nothing like the lopsidedness many had dreaded. Jay Carmody, of the *Evening Star*, found the play in many ways self-important largely as a result of the central theme of alienation—in its several comic and tragic variations—which he termed "overpowering." He seemed to squirm with the characters' problems, which indicated that the playwright had not only achieved audience identification, but perhaps had overachieved it.

Tom Donnelly, with the Washington *Daily News*, focused more on the play's playful side. As a result, he was somewhat put off by what started as an adult and humorous romp but, with the second act, became "increasingly solemn." He objected to the manner of shared introspection which for him turned into an unnatural and unremitting inspection. Pressed by repeated dramatic turns of plot, he saw the story as edging perilously close to soap opera in many instances. Still, he heartily applauded the performers, describing Fonda "as always a most ingratiating performer . . . he succeeds in putting a pleasant gloss on Jerry," while noting that Anne "sometimes overplays Gittel in the preliminaries" but quickly added that "she soon settles down to giving a performance that is altogether delightful."

The Washington *Post*'s Richard L. Coe better understood the delicate balance of the "amusing and touching" qualities and predicted both would sharpen with performance. He also recognized the underlying division of labor: "Miss Bancroft has the more ingratiating assignment . . . Fonda's role is infinitely more difficult and he plays it with a fine actor's intelligence of its pitfalls." Along the lines of Jerry's intricacy and ambivalence he added: "Fonda must capture us on two levels. . . . However, he plays the fellow with ingenious skill, shifts of command, and nice mixtures of dry humor and appeal."

The notices were intriguing, frustrating, and instructive, but they weren't gospel. The consensus at the production level was

that Anne was an extraordinary talent in a superb role, and
Fonda, a proven excellent actor saddled with a thankless role.

The play settled in for the balance of its seventeen-day Washington engagement while Gibson set about rewriting Jerry and
tightening the second act. Anne, still in the first flush of her
creditable stage debut, could not ignore the implications this had
for her personal life. She had begun by believing in her dual
commitment to a career onstage and an eventual marriage to
Mario, and had kept up a faithful correspondence. But as Anne's
involvement in the play grew, her letters to Mario grew fewer
until, by the time she was in out-of-town tryouts, she had
stopped writing entirely. The break was neither calculated nor
callous, nor, for that matter, purely the result of a harried production schedule.

Anne had first come to the play on the ebb of what had been a
devastating and vulnerable period in her life. In returning to New
York she was forced to admit the folly of her immediate past,
and there was no guarantee that the about-face would have any
but catastrophic effects on her career. Her reading of Gittel had
no sooner been unanimously ratified by all, than she was left
hanging with the ensuing delays and complications. Meanwhile
she'd become involved with a man whom she had every intention of marrying. But then the show coalesced, and the career
hopes that had only begun to surface in her work at HB Studio,
suddenly were real and within reach.

Anne was not setting aside her engagement because of some
raw ambition. Rather, for the first time, she was involved in a
project where her colleagues not only viewed and valued themselves as dedicated artists working in a commercial medium but
accepted Anne on the same terms. For once, she was not just a
face or a shape who could recite her lines intelligibly and not
upset the scenery, but an actress, in need of more schooling and
experience, but an actress just the same. She felt respected,
trusted, and appreciated as an artist and as a person, which in
turn allowed her to accept criticism openly and to grow. Self-
doubt had in the past caused her to seek shelter in marriage. As
the self-doubt receded, so did the urge for escape in marriage. It
was not as if she were now using her work as a surrogate mar-

riage. Instead she was coming to see that she had been using marriage as a substitute for absent artistic-emotional compensations. Anne had not outgrown her need for relationships, merely the need for protective, encircling relationships.

Anne's decision to break the engagement had one other principal mitigating component. Her sudden departure from Hollywood had been both a rejection of a freewheeling life style, and a reaffirmation of the values with which she was raised. The fact that she had not obtained religious annulment of her marriage to May meant the Church did not recognize the legal fact that she was now unmarried. To wed again would require a rejection of the Church, and that was more than she was willing to face at the moment. Her involvement in the play was now total, as was the self-esteem that involvement gave her. Her personal growth had at last caught up with her professional growth, and the long-awaited sense of wholeness and well-being was not something she cared to surrender.

The show completed its Washington run on a firmer footing than it had begun. But there was more work to be done. Not all the kinks had been removed from the second act and Fonda's faith in Jerry Ryan had improved hardly at all. While the sets were dismantled, the rest of the company moved on to Philadelphia in preparation for the opening there, Christmas Day. Gibson answered the unceasing call for rewrites, and the discord over Jerry became such an open topic that even Anne volunteered advice. She had phoned Gibson one night and appeared in his hotel room the following morning with ideas on how to best fortify the role. Instead of making a verbal or written presentation, she acted the part as she saw it. Gibson presided over the command performance with an admiration that nearly outweighed the absurdity of seeing a comely actress impersonate the manly grouch, Jerry. It was an oddly interesting rendition, actually, but the playwright was already nearly buried in second opinions and politely declined Anne's.

In Philadelphia the play's stubborn blemishes seemed to magnify with New York on the horizon, and the growing edginess worsened as a full afternoon's rehearsal was lost when Anne was all but incapacitated by severe menstrual cramps. Gibson was afforded little peace of mind when some simple arithmetic revealed the cyclic fact that the Broadway opening was precisely twenty-eight days away. As if the production needed any more upset, the uneasy truce with Fonda drew unwanted attention in a column by the New York *Journal-American*'s Dorothy Kilgallen, who surmised that the ongoing rewrites were solely for the purpose of beefing up Henry Fonda's role because Anne Bancroft's performance drew so much attention from the critics.

The character disparity had been addressed from nearly every possible angle and always it pared down to a simple truth—Gibson was unable to do for Jerry what he had done for Gittel, that is, create a fully realized character. It wasn't so much that Jerry was unsympathetic but that he was unsympathetic and two-dimensional. As the sage Fred Coe saw the problem: "put Hamlet and a clown on the same stage" and an audience will gravitate toward the clown.

If there was one unbudging inequity it was that the actor on whose fame and clout the production counted was left to play an unsavory and almost second-class character. It was the source of all the behind-the-scenes wrangling. Fonda's dilemma was that he had inherited what all conceded was a largely unappealing part in what he above all conceded was a most appealing play. The question was how to prevent Jerry from being swallowed whole by Gittel without ruining the play, and the answer was there was no answer. Fonda was understandably anxious to see that his role had no obstacles other than what were absolutely necessary. He felt that he was "up against a wall, fighting for survival," and with the play in preview in Philadelphia, suggested that a handful of seasoned directors be invited to view the play and render opinions. The subject came to the attention of Coe, who, with Solomonic sagacity, quickly vetoed the whole idea.

Anne, for her part, was riding the wave of critical approval, and with the unburdening that brought, had successfully scaled down the overplaying that had re-emerged in Washington. Of all those involved in the production, she alone seemed to be having some fun. Offstage, she palled around with the show's production secretary, Jessica Levy, while her stage work mellowed and matured to the point where no one, including Anne, questioned whether she would ultimately shrink under the New York critics' gaze.

For a Broadway-bound play, Philadelphia is no theatrical whistle-stop. It is a major city with a well-grounded critical establishment and, given its nearness to New York, is easily accessible for snooping, scouting, and general reconnaissance. Ideally, a play is meant to come of age in Philadelphia, to assume the identity it will carry to, through, and, with luck, beyond Broadway. The scrabbled pieces of *Seesaw* seemed at last to fall into place. Fonda had come around to a reading of the part that enlarged upon Gibson's original conception. That, in turn, further galvanized Anne's performance, which could now be more reactive and reserved. Above all, there was agreement that, in theatre argot, "Hank was taking the stage."

Peace of mind was not to be so readily won. In the days just prior to the opening, Anne had been experiencing difficulties with her throat. What started as a tickle soon turned into an irritation, and that edged to the brink of laryngitis. In the final preparatory reading at the Forrest Theatre on the afternoon of Christmas Day, Anne spoke in little more than a whisper, hoping to save what voice was left for the evening performance. By curtain time, Anne was feeling not at all well, but she went on gamely and audibly though sapped of the verve that had been hers from the very beginning. Fonda helped carry the show with a performance which, if not his best, was certainly among his better. Penn, Coe, and Gibson sat by with all the anxiety and mental pacing that attends any theatrical siring. It was soon apparent that most of the structural gremlins had been exorcised. The audience was generous and approving, the show proceeded apace, and the performance (nothwithstanding Anne's infirmity) was blessed with several bows.

There was a post-production gathering at a nearby restaurant which broke up before the first word of criticism had been printed. By morning, the production was the better by three mostly favorable notices. Jerry Gaghan's review for the Philadelphia *Daily News* was highly complimentary of Fonda, whom he thought compensated for various structural flaws and whose "intelligent grasp of a role makes credible the self-tormented attorney from Omaha." He was less than enchanted with Anne: "In contrast to Fonda's repressed style, she mugs unashamedly and ranks as one of the year's busiest performers."

The Philadelphia *Inquirer*'s Henry Murdock had a distinctly different impression of Anne's work: "Miss Bancroft, heading for Broadway for the first time, lights up the stage with her funny, explosive, warm-hearted gamin heroine." He was careful to point out the skill with which Fonda performed and was downright eager to note that the veteran had not been upstaged by the newcomer: "No one can take such liberties with that lean and sometimes saturnine master of underplaying." But the most encouragement came not in the approval of the play's separate parts but in the testimony to its ensemble work: "One gets the impression that Gibson wrote a two-character play not just as a display of virtuosity but because, given his plot, and given a pair of players of such force and resource as Henry Fonda and Anne Bancroft, two characters were all that were needed."

Max de Schauensee provided the icing in his *Evening Bulletin* piece. He commended the writing, directing, and set design, applauded the "remarkable fine performances," and furnished the most intelligent grasp yet of what Anne had accomplished with the often coarse Gittel: "It is a triumph on Miss Bancroft's part that she is able to enlist the gradual warmth and even nobility. Nothing that Miss Bancroft has shown in her numerous movie roles gave any indication of the talent she displays here." What a difference a play makes.

Then came the casualties. Gibson took to bed with bronchitis. Anne took to hobbling about on a knee strained through scripted onstage contortions (which if nothing else, helped take her mind off her throat which had continued to trouble her and had required outpatient medical attention). And Fonda was unconsolable in his belief that Jerry was still dimensionless and that the playwright seemed powerless to do a thing about it.

But the real nemesis was rewrites. Penn and Coe continued to requisition them, Gibson supplied them only grudgingly, Anne and Fonda did what they could to unscramble and insert them. In some cases, the changes were helpful as with Anne in the af-

termath of her recent critical mugging for "mugging." In
Fonda's case, however, the changes had quite another import. As
both backer and actor, his interest in the play was acute and
uncontestable. By the same token, he was doubly determined
to see the production done properly, and the unabated stream of
changes struck him as an imposition and an impropriety, and beyond that, as a sign of unprofessional conduct. His long stage
background dictated a simple practical axiom—beginning with
Thursday of the last week in Philadelphia, the director should if
at all possible "freeze" the performance. The idea being that in
all fairness to the actors, ongoing line changes should not be
added to their list of worries with Broadway lurking just ahead.
There was also the implication that what could not be fixed in
two months of rehearsals and tryouts wasn't likely to magically
mend in the intervening hours before the opening.

Anxieties came to a head during an afternoon rehearsal when
tempers finally erupted and Anne, though a bystander, was overcome with a sudden fit of nausea. The outburst not only failed to
clear the air, but darkened the pall that was settling over the
production. The final Philadelphia performance was on Saturday, January 11. It proceeded uneventfully and by midnight, the
crew was again dismantling the sets. The next stop was Tuesday,
the Booth Theatre, and the first Broadway preview.

Anne took up temporary quarters at the Hotel Manhattan at
Forty-fourth Street and Eighth Avenue, a convenient block away
from the Booth. There was little recuperative time, and most of
what little there was was devoted to rehearsal and the chronic
line changes which, by now, were the production's equivalent of
a nervous tic or stammer. The first preview was Tuesday night
and the select audience was clearly charmed by what it saw. The
response was bracing for Anne, less so for Fonda, who bolted out
of the theatre within minutes of the final curtain. In rehearsal
the following day, there were more polemics over readings, more
line changes, and more frazzled nerves. The Thursday night preview was at least as reassuring as Tuesday's. Afterward Fonda
made another hasty exit, while Gibson treated Anne to an ice
cream soda before joining his producer and director at a bar and

learning that they wanted yet more rewrites (something to do
with transitional dialogue in the next-to-last scene). The material
ultimately proved unnecessary, but Penn and Coe's fastidi-
ousness seemed pardonable in light of the recent knowledge that
the production tallied some $14,000 in cost overruns. That meant
that in the event of a flop Coe would have to suffer the added
mortification of approaching his angels for a surcharge.

Friday, January 17. Anne, who had been suffering insomnia of
late, napped during the day. She awoke, spooned down a bowl
of pea soup (as daring a meal as a recent gastritis would allow),
and then made her way to the theatre. Gibson paid her a brief
visit in her dressing room, and she told him that she was experiencing no jangled nerves per se, only a keen desire to have
opening night quickly behind her.

Out front, the first-nighters were taking on the usual expectant
glow. A corps of critics dotted the orchestra seats, and at eight
o'clock sharp, the house lights dimmed, the audience hushed, the
theatre darkened, the curtain went up.

Jerry Ryan and Gittel Mosca meet in passing at a party. He
phones her the next day under the pretext of buying her refrig-
erator and ends by asking her to dinner. They return to her flat
for a nightcap of warm milk, bottled beer, and conversation. She
is a frustrated modern dancer with a pert openness, an unlaun-
dered vocabulary, and a duodenal ulcer. She earns a nominal living sewing costumes for other dancers. She is single, but the
worse for several misfired affairs. He is an attorney on the run
from a successful Nebraska practice, a recently sundered marriage, and a wealthy, meddling father-in-law.

There is an attraction in their oppositeness which soon becomes less opposite when Gittel's ulcer starts to bleed, and, after
an emergency hospital visit, she returns to convalesce in Jerry's
room. It is a sunny reversal. Gittel, the bubbly, self-destructive
giver, is forced into passivity. Jerry, the sullen, self-hating taker,
must try his hand at care and compassion. They grow in one
another's company but realize their relationship is ultimately
doomed. At close, Jerry departs for a fresh start in Nebraska
while Gittel prepares to sort out her messy personal life.

The Booth thundered with applause. The audience was on its feet and clapping through repeated curtain calls. Backstage was pandemonium. At the eye of the congratulatory storm stood Anne tearfully calling for her mother and father, whom she soon found and embraced. The rest of the company circulated with less a sense of joy than of relief. In time, the crowd dispersed, and Anne was joined by her close friend Mrs. Ruby Rick, who had flown in from the West Coast for the occasion. Together they made their way over to the apartment of Fred Coe's agent for the opening night party *cum* vigil, where there were already whispers of good reviews. The place thronged with theatre people and well-wishers, but Fonda was nowhere to be seen. He had sought refuge in his own apartment.

The *Times*'s Brooks Atkinson and the *Herald Tribune*'s Walter Kerr were the first to file, and the text of their reviews was called in to the party before the city editions had even hit the news-stands. Atkinson thought the play was superbly written, directed, designed, and acted. If his review fell short of a rave, it had little to say that was not positive. Kerr, on the other hand, had some reservations about the play's professed theme, but he was other-wise complimentary, and could not say enough about Anne's performance, adding the unrestrained announcement: "We have been handed, gratis, a brand new, first-rate performer." On the strength of those two reviews, the show was virtually insured a large measure of success, and for once, the fog of the recent or-deal began to lift.

Anne left the gathering around four-thirty, newspapers in hand. She and her friend went back to the hotel room where they paged through the reviews, placed the papers and elation aside, and started a conversation that was notedly non-theatrical. They talked, at times philosophically, about life and other things. At eight-thirty, they went to sleep.

Anne woke up that afternoon, riffled through the remaining re-views, and learned that she was the "find" of the season. Some of the praise came at the expense of the play, or at least much of what was said in favor of the vehicle paled beside the panegyric allotted the star. The critical infatuation was astonishingly unani-mous. Richard Watts of the *Post*: "Anne Bancroft gives so brilliant a performance . . . that Mr. Fonda is pushed to keep from seeming almost her straight man." Robert Coleman of the *Mirror:* "She completely captivated the first-nighters at the Booth, who were happy to sit in at the birth of a new star." John Chapman of the *News:* "Her timing of movement and speech are flawless, and her warmth and personality is more than considerable." John McClain of the *Journal-American:* "Anne Bancroft makes her Broadway bow and threatens at times to take the entire theatre under her arm and go home."

That day, Broadway's darling had more mundane matters on her mind. She eagerly checked out of the Hotel Manhattan and into an apartment in the East Fifties which she sublet from another actress. That left her just enough time to get back to the theatre for the evening's performance. The mood there was anything but that befitting a runaway hit. Fonda was little consoled by the reviews, despite the ample praise of his performance. What's more, he had had it with Gibson and his habit of peppy backstage visits, and had left the unequivocal request: "I don't want that son-of-a-bitch in my dressing room."

Penn and Coe were again talking assorted minor changes, and Anne suffered the sudden downdraft of interview requests. The final, fitting irony came three days after opening when Fonda succumbed to the flu and was lost for a week. *Seesaw* had never been anything than just that.

Anne's personal reaction to sudden acclaim was decidedly mixed. The fame that had seemed so desirable yet elusive while in Hollywood was now hers in full. But it was not quite the glittery prize she had once expected it would be. The show's disagreeable history dulled much of the luster, as did the sobriety of Anne's rededication to acting. Anne explained her sentiments to the *Times*'s Gilbert Millstein:

> If I had any idea that what happened to me was going to happen, I might never have done it. How can I say it? What has happened is I'm very tired. That's what has happened as far as I'm concerned. I'm too tired to work up any kind of emotion. The only time I can work up any kind of emotion is at 8:40 every night and then, you know, it works itself up.

Opening night, it was just like any other show. I was at a point where I was ready to say I am what I am because of what I am and if you like me I'm grateful, and if you don't, what am I going to do about it? I swear to God, no reaction. I swear.

Anne had discovered the truth behind the old adage—fame is just a paint job.

11

Mel took a fourth-floor walk-up on Perry Street in the West Village and watched his world come down around him. Complacency was a vice he had never known. Throughout the glory days of "Your Show of Shows" and then "Caesar's Hour," Mel had never allowed himself to simply slip into the safe workaday routine of a staff writer. But if he always seemed to have some surplus energy for other projects, replenishment was only ever as far away as Sid's current hit. Through nearly ten television seasons, Sid seemed invincible. And though common sense said otherwise, it sometimes seemed as if he could go on forever.

Forever came in 1959. Following the abortive "Sid Caesar Invites You" and the short-lived BBC resurrection, Sid and his entourage were left without a regular series for the first time in almost a decade. However, within weeks of the ABC washout, NBC was back and bidding, and soon Sid was signed for the series of specials that had seemed so repugnant just months earlier. But something was lost in transition from series to special—the constancy of a regular staff and ensemble which in its brilliant resilience had been a kind of creative trampoline on which Sid could turn his comic somersaults.

For Mel it was all like being suddenly pushed from the nest and told to fly. From the start, he had taken care to avoid being overidentified with the powerful Caesar persona. Still, his creative spacewalks all seemed to have had some invisible umbilical tie to Sid. And if Mel was at times to think of television writing as beneath him, his vanity was grounded in the assumption that television would always be there when he needed it. But his tenure with Sid had made him something of a comic specialist. He was overqualified for some shows, unqualified for others, with none but qualified success in other areas.

Professional directionlessness was compounded by Mel's disjointed family life. He had left nearly everything of value to Florence and the children, beyond which he was obligated to considerable alimony and child support. Despite years of healthy pay checks, Mel had saved no money. Virtually overnight he went from parvenu to pauper, and was left to unriddle his fate in a cold-water flat decorated in orange crates.

Added to these all too real worries was a rising irrational fear of death. Passing acquaintances knew Mel as a comic social lion, a reveler, a tummler. He was not just the life of the party, he was a portable one-man party. It was a delirious, aggressive optimism, the sort of outlook that had prompted him since his youth to tell friends, "I always expected to be the King of France." Nonetheless, Mel's social ebullience was attached to a tortured fatalism that was manifested as a near obsession with mortality (a kind of psychological Möbius strip). Mel was about to turn thirty-three. Max Kaminsky had died at thirty-four. Though Mel enjoyed generally vigorous health, there was a latent fear that he too might die at an early age (a false sense of insecurity). The accumulated anxiety was relieved in part by a passion for medical literature that nearly exceeded his passion for general literature. But the intellectual could only go so far toward easing what was essentially emotional and irrational. What must have seemed the symbolic death of joblessness could only have fed Mel's *Angst*. Friends would later recall that he was frenetic and at times grossly inconsiderate; in short, not terrific company.

Fortunately, the tether to Sid was not entirely severed. Mel worked on some, though not all, of the NBC specials, and after-

ward, when Sid switched to CBS for another package of hour-
long specials, Mel went along for the ride (a later Caesar special
would win Mel an Emmy). The first program was sponsored by
U.S. Steel and entitled "Holiday on Wheels." It aired in October
1959 with Leo Morgan (late of "Caesar's Hour") producing, and
Mel Tolkin sharing writing duties with Mel and Sidney Zelinka.
The show met with enthusiastic response and was followed by
two others before the year was out. Still, the specials merely
echoed the best of the past. They lacked the spark, the spontaneity, and they lacked Carl Reiner.

Carl, like Mel, had enjoyed the security of the weekly shows,
but was less unstrung by their passing. In the course of his long
association with Sid, Carl had grown from an accomplished
straight man to a formidable comic actor and creator. On "Your
Show of Shows" and again on "Caesar's Hour," the performers
were not segregated from the writers but were encouraged to
make creative contributions. Carl never received writing credit
per se, but he was at the very least a "talking writer" who could
hold his own in a crowd. After parting with Sid, Carl vacationed
at his summer place on Fire Island where it occurred to him late
one night that he was a "writing writer" as well. One short story
later he was ready for bigger game, and the result was a successful semi-autobiographical novel, *Enter Laughing*. But writing
more supplemented than supplanted his other work. He made
assorted guest appearances and signed to host a celebrity quiz
show, "Keep Talking," which was designed to fill the void left by
the scandal-ridden "$64,000 Question."

Carl was experiencing certain frustrations, however. He had
spent the better part of the summer of '58 on Fire Island, sifting
through scripts which had been submitted to him as possible television series. It was an anemic lot, and by late July he was close
to despairing of ever finding a worthy comedy vehicle when his
wife, Estelle, suggested he simply create his own. Inspiration followed quickly as Carl adopted the general rule of thumb for any
beginning writer and drew on what he knew firsthand. The
premise he devised described a television writer whose time was
divided between his zany colleagues at work and his wife and
young son in suburban New Rochelle. Carl completed a script

which then found its way to Peter Lawford, who agreed to produce the pilot. Morty Gunty and Sylvia Miles were cast as the two assistant writers, Barbara Britton as the wife, and Gary Morgan as the son. Carl played the writer in what was to be known as "Head of the Family." The pilot turned out well and seemed certain to be picked up, even though there were no immediate takers for the series. Carl, optimistic and motivated, prepared another dozen scripts so that as soon as a host network was found, the show might move directly into production. By the following June, there were still no takers, and in the face of a growing television vogue of detective shows and Westerns, prospects for "Head of the Family" faded and flickered.

Carl and Mel, once television's prodigies, were finding the medium increasingly inhospitable. If there was little to laugh about in their careers of late, they still amused themselves and friends with the impromptu routines which had their genesis at Coca's parties during the "Show of Shows" days. It was essentially a man-on-the-street setup with a distinct flavor of "Nonentities in the News." Carl posed as interviewer, skeptical and probing, Mel played any number of characters, many of a markedly Jewish bent. When Carl wasn't available, Mel would often perform with Mel Tolkin, who enjoyed the routines but was partial to more intimate audiences. On at least one occasion the two Mels worked before a large and illustrious gathering. In October 1959, Random House was hosting a party at Mamma Leone's restaurant to celebrate the publication of Moss Hart's autobiography, *Act One*. The guest of honor was to be entertained by a stellar lineup of show people, and the somewhat less-than-stellar Mel and Carl. However, Carl was detained on the West Coast and Mel Tolkin substituted, betraying little stage fright and considerable prowess as a straight man. Big and Little Mel worked fifteen minutes and brought down the house.

Still Carl and Mel performed together most, best, and most often, and virtually anyone who knew them knew their routines. Years before, in 1953, one particular routine had taken form which was to loom large in Mel's future. Carl had purchased a little novelty item, a portable tape recorder which at the time was anything but commonplace. One night during a party at the

Reiner's Westchester home, Carl brought out the gadget, threw
the switch, poked the microphone at Mel, and said something on
the order of: "Sir, I understand you were living at the time of
Christ." Mel raced off on that theme, Carl chased him into other
mock-historical realms, and the bit became the crown jewel of
their repertoire. The character in time was known as "the 2000
Year Old Man," a quaint, curmudgeonly, "spectacularly Jewish"
bimillenarian through whose eyes Carl and Mel replayed recorded history. The premise was as fertile as it was funny, and
over the years, and especially with the encouragement of playwright Joe Fields, the Old Man helped win Carl and Mel their
own elite cult of fans.

Mel was still doing no better by free-lance writing. It was a
bumpy ride that was taking him nowhere. Mel's past work
within the Caesar sphere had been a larger part of his life than
even he had realized at the time. It had been almost organic and
the disruption, traumatic. For months after the last regular show,
Mel continued to rise early in the morning as if girding himself
for the morning pitch session, rewrite, or rehearsal. He was still
governed by some inner clock which woke him but left him
nothing to do except "bang my head against the bathroom wall,"
which was a habit without a future—his Perry Street atelier had
plaster walls.

New York was one clue to Mel's predicament. Television production had been gravitating to the West Coast, and that way
went style (the Dodgers being a case in point). The sophisticated, theatrical comedic influence of New York was lost in
transit only to be replaced by slick, insipid situation comedies
with laughter that was canned and writing that ought to have
been. The new breed of contrived comedy did everything for the
viewing public, including instructing it where to laugh. Au-
tomated comedy wanted no part of any imagination that might
engage the mind, such as satire, parody, pantomime, and old-
fashioned full-blooded farce, all of which required something
more than mere conditioned response, all of which comprised
Mel's working vocabulary. The question that increasingly confronted New Yorkers who made their living in television was

whether to move to Los Angeles and go on making a living, or
stay in town and starve.

Some ventured West while guardedly leaving behind bread
crumbs (families, houses, friends) so that if need be they might
find their way back out of the woods. In July 1959, Carl took the
giant step, moving to California, and signing on with "The
Dinah Shore Show" in the dual capacity of writer and actor. In
1960, Mel decided to test the western waters. It was not his first
experience with Hollywood. A few years earlier, Mel had landed
some work with Columbia but came quickly back to New York
and the television lap of luxury. This second foray would be better planned. Time and again, Mel had run a mental inventory on
which working comedians might embrace his special brand of
humor. The name of Jerry Lewis kept coming to mind, and if the
Lewis style was nothing like Caesar's, it was certainly like nobody else's and that filled at least one of Mel's prerequisites.
Then too, Lewis was not a stand-up comic but a purveyor of
characterizations, human, subhuman, and unhuman, and that
seemed amenable to Mel's free-floating writing.

Mel signed on for a Jerry Lewis spectacular, and that led to
work on a feature film, *Ladies' Man,* which Lewis produced,
directed, starred in, and helped write. Mel's association with the
project began during the summer of 1960, and ended suddenly
and unceremoniously thirteen weeks later. Whatever the vague
similarities between the Caesar and Lewis comic style, the work
styles were worlds apart. Mel's cocksuredness and total lack of
inhibition, so catalytic with Sid, was disastrous with Lewis, who
eventually had the script rewritten. The stint was profitable if
not otherwise fruitful, and Mel departed some $46,000 to the
good. But the figure was misleading, since Mel had little other
outside income, and his arrangement with Florence accounted
for $1,000 per month. By October, he was short of work, short on
his alimony payments, and perilously short of alternatives.

With Carl coasting and Mel more or less "between jobs," the
appeal by friends that they go public with their two-act looked
less whimsical by several shades. They had already ventured beyond the padded politeness of party claques and stood the act
up in front of paying customers at Danny's Hide-a-way in New

York. They were an unqualified hit, but that still left room for doubt about the prospects of a record album. To begin with, they did not work from a script, and aside from bare categorical preparation and sheer familiarity with character, the routines were improvisational. They also knew that the inspired dynamics of a live, extemporaneous performance could be lost in translation to record. And finally the character of the 2000 Year Old Man was unmistakably rooted in the Brooklyn-Jewish-immigrant experience—Mel's accent was impeccable "American-Jewish"—and while many of the features and foibles were universal, there might have been a concern that the material would be considered provincial or esoteric and ignored.

The routine remained little more than a lark until 1960, when Mel dropped in on Carl, who was then on the Coast, and Joe Fields collected a party of notables before whom they were to perform. Afterward, they were approached by George Burns who teased, "Listen, you better put that on a record, because if you don't, I'll steal it." Steve Allen, who was also present, was in a position to make good Burns's suggestion, and put Carl and Mel in touch with a small label, World Pacific Records. Carl by then, was working steady and had no need to branch out into recorded comedy. Mel, on the other hand, was in bad shape financially, with no better offers and nothing to lose. After several days' delay, Carl and Mel reported to World Pacific and before a hastily assembled audience dredged up old material and improvised new for over two hours.

The performance tapes were edited down to roughly forty minutes, or two sides of an LP. The album featured the Old Man primarily, but not exclusively. The audience was small but vocal, the audio cuts nearly seamless, and the comedians well miked. As for the quality of the material, it begins in grand style. Carl discloses in a confidential reportorial voice that we are about to meet a man claiming to be two thousand years old. Carl asks him to confirm the claim and Mel prefaces his reply with a prolonged, labored, wheezing sigh, that could just as easily be a bimillenarian or a sixty-year-old yard goods salesman after a day's work and four flights of stairs. And that's the precise orientation, the perfect exhalation that anticipates the entire routine before Mel has ut-

tered a word of dialogue. By the time he speaks and corrects Carl
—he is not quite two thousand years old but will be on October 16
—the audience is already in his pocket. Carl continues with all due
gravity, Mel energizes his voice somewhat, and they're off, ranging through the customary interview framework, veering off at
odd angles, digressing, editorializing, but never losing hold of
form. The topics roll by: the discovery of ladies by someone
named Bernie; "rock talk" as the first primitive language ("Hey,
don't throw that rock at me."); the key to a long life being the
avoidance of fried food, also never running for a bus; ancient
history; middle history; famous historical acquaintances; contemporary pontification. Whenever the interview hints of becoming a checklist of historical gags, Carl adroitly steers it to more
personal territory: the Old Man's first job, his personal life (hun-
dreds of wives, and 42,000 children, not one of whom writes or
visits), and his choice for mankind's single best accomplishment—
Saran Wrap. There is an undercurrent of familiarity with character which acts as an infrastructure for the piece. Also, there is
the unmistakable air of spontaneity, of ad libs and asides, uncharted topical areas, and the sense that the comics are time and
again startled at their results, choking back their own laughter,
straining not to break character.

It is a brisk 12½ minutes that plays like an ingenious jazz
improvisation on a standard melody. Granted, the setup is superb, but its execution could easily wander into predictable
areas, or snag in decrepit gags. Carl guards the tempo, and the
moment he senses a given theme is nearing depletion, he moves
on. Sometimes he intentionally interrupts, teasing with just the
tip of ideas. Other times he lingers for a thorough treatment,
squeezing variations and inversions that might have otherwise
escaped notice. He is by turns doubtful and gullible, accepting
one claim at face value while discarding the next. His timing is
magnificent, his tone unshakable.

Mel is protean, running off on various riffs, returning suddenly
to form, weaving in and out of Carl's tempo in remarkable fits
and starts. His dialect is exact, allowing for small lapses, and his
beautifully muddled syntax is the synthesis of every Jewish immigrant who ever remodeled English. His language, down to the

last inflection and short-circuited phrase, is like perfect pitch. It tells the audience that the Old Man is not so much literally two thousand years old but a comic synecdoche for all old men who seem to carry with them the weight and wisdom of antiquity. Mel's reading of the character is surprisingly lyrical, with certain leisurely lines that work like grace notes. There is also an authentic ellipsis of various prepositions and predicates that creates a staccato effect which pushes and punctuates the material. By end, the old man is like some golden-ager at a testimonial dinner, dispensing appreciation and advice and enjoying the simple sanctity of survival. The routine ends on a distinct up note, and like the best comedy, leaves the listener wanting more.

"The 2000 Year Old Man" segment was a tour de force, and as the record's opening band, it overshadowed much of the rest. The second cut has Carl interviewing a wildly popular young singer. Mel, as "Fabiola," gets off a number of good lines in the brief two-minute piece, but the characterization is a bit fuzzy and the voice lacks the sureness of the Old Man's. What seems at first to be some dissolute rock star, starts to stray into the bohemian-beatnik-bopster area. Still, the bit has at least a degree of cohesion which is wholly missing from the side's final interview, "The Astronaut." It is four minutes of groping which is the virtual opposite of the synchronization on the title sketch. The straight lines and setups are there but the responses lack punch and punctuality. The digressions which worked so beautifully with the Old Man here turn into blind alleys. The problem is that Mel never really finds a handle on the character and starts to strain for humor, and finally mild shock effect, as in his repeated reference to the side-effects of training in the centrifuge: "You puke your guts out."

Side two begins more promisingly. Carl describes the setting, a coffeehouse, and proceeds to interview a quartet of offbeat characters. The last and best is a rather hip folk singer whose command of his string bass is severely limited, and whose knack for improvisational lyric is no better. Mel is nicely on target with a strumming, monotone accompaniment and an interchangeable nonsense verse. As satire, it is soft and makes no special comment on the sort of musical minstrels who habituated coffee-houses in the sixties. But the tone is suitably low-key, indifferent, and hip, and Mel diligently follows each of Carl's leads, all of which bear comic fruit. At just under three minutes, the interview is a model of economy, with no unnecessary detours. The next routine lacks focus. Mel is a Peruvian coffee-plantation owner, native by claim but clearly Nazi by accent and demeanor. It is a serviceable, if not especially original premise, but the humor takes only the more familiar turns. It gives Mel a chance to exercise his German—which drifts to the German-Jewish—but beyond that there is little else to recommend it. For the record's final four minutes, Mel portrays a psychiatrist (the character introduced at Mamma Leone's) who, if not nominally the Old Man, is a very close relative. Carl inquires as to techniques and specific cases, Mel responds with a kind of Old World moralism that is utterly divorced from anything resembling the accepted analytic mode. Faced once with a patient who was emotionally involved with his dog, the psychiatrist cured him by saying, "Hey, you can't do that. Vatta you, crazy?" It is another variation on the Gospel according to the Old Man, and the results are just as satisfying. The bit is trim and tight, and it provides the album with a certain character symmetry as well as a bright finale.

The album was cut and released by World Pacific in January 1961, and the immediate reaction of insiders was mixed. Those who had been lucky enough to know the material firsthand through parties missed much of the former raunchiness and freewheeling zaniness. Actually, a good deal of spicy humor had found its way onto the tape only to be weeded out in the editing phase. By sixties standards the "laundered" final version was still anything but pristine.

Another complaint that was raised concerned what many considered to be the derivative style of Mel's comedy. Naturally, any routine which used an interview format, Carl Reiner, and eccentric character-dialect humor, was bound to beg comparison with Sid Caesar. Many were calling Mel's Old Man a second-rate imitation of Sid's German Professor. But any close look showed that despite a certain congruence, the two characters were discrete in concept, style, and execution.

Once listeners brushed aside the niggling comparisons and petty snipes, what remained was a highly professional and original comic creation. Carl and Mel worked wonderfully together, and when they were on target they were brilliant. Even when they were off the mark, their rapport was such that they could extract a few good laughs, then close. Their sense of self-editing was superior.

The record quickly found a substantial cult following, which was as much as might have been hoped for at the outset. None of those involved in the project was prepared for what followed. The album received considerable radio airplay, especially on William B. Williams' popular late-night program on WNEW in New York. The cult quickly took on new converts until it was no longer a cult but a goodly following. Since the album had been released with relatively little fanfare, the popularity had come chiefly by word of mouth.

Record sales soared and soon outstripped the label's production capacity. By the first of the year Alan W. Livingston of Capitol Records stepped in with a bid to purchase the rights from World Pacific. The transaction was completed, and later footnoted with a press release remarking that it was "the first time Capitol has acquired material previously released on another label." The same press release revealed that Livingston and Mel had reached an agreement for a "long-termed contract as a producer, writer and performer of comedy albums."

Mel the performer had saved Mel the writer. With no suitable creative outlet he had become his own mouthpiece, his own comic mask, and he wore his visibility well. Much of the frustration that had accompanied the anonymity of writing (he used to introduce himself: "Hello, I'm Mel Brooks. I write the Sid Caesar Show") evaporated with the first signs of celebrity. He gladly shed the vicariousness of watching others perform his material and found that performing was not only fun, it was second nature. Carl had once explained his own versatility in a phrase: "All comedians are writers." For Mel, the equation could be reversed. In contrast to other comedy writers who for reasons of shyness or simple preference choose to reveal their madness solely through entertainers (for many there is a real genius in this manner of escape), Mel actually found shelter in performance. As he later told a *Playboy* interviewer: "It's easier to hide behind accents. Once you're playing a character you have more mobility, more freedom. I suppose it's also cowardice on my part. I can say anything I want, and then if people question me, I say, "Don't blame me. Blame the old Jew. He's crazy!" Even so, Mel would later acquire the peculiar habit of introducing himself as "your obedient Jew."

There was no doubt that Mel would be able to parlay this latest success into other successes if not an entirely new career. He thrived on his new celebrity and the public was at least as charmed (and, judging by the skyrocketing record sales, hungry for more). For Carl, the recent success was just one of many. The greater triumph came by way of his seemingly stillborn situation comedy. Convinced that the basic premise was sound, Carl withdrew from the principal role, created a juicy peripheral role for himself, and then hired a superb light comedian, Dick Van Dyke. CBS approved the recasting and prepared to present the show in 1961 as "The Dick Van Dyke Show."

The late-blooming graduates of "Max Liebman University" were alive and well.

12

Two for the Seesaw closed on Halloween 1959, but without Anne Bancroft. She had opened in yet another Broadway play the week before, and was already assured a second success. The two openings spanned less than two years but for the changes wrought, it might have been a decade or a lifetime.

Despite its turbulent and troubled road tryout Seesaw prospered from the first. It played to packed houses, quickly paid off its investors and delivered a handsome return on investments, shattered attendance records at the Booth Theatre, and spawned a national company and over a dozen foreign productions. The gilt-edged particulars aside, Henry Fonda played out the season, departing after six months in New York and was replaced by Dana Andrews. Asked later why he stayed as long as he did, Fonda replied "because it was a good play," but went on to explain what many had taken as a saturnine attitude: "I was fighting as an actor to make my part even on the seesaw. There was never any jealousy about Annie, I adored her. I think she was and is one of our finest actresses. It was not a competitive thing at all, it was for the sake of the play. It was the hardest job I ever did to play that character that wasn't fully drawn and not just fall into the background of the scenery—it wouldn't have worked."

Anne was still the play's showpiece. Just as earlier she had taken the struggles and scrapes mostly in stride, she now accepted the adulation with poise. She was touted as the find of the current season and was left to endure all the scrutiny, fawning, and press agentry that endows. It was enough to swell the most sober head, but it scarcely turned hers. To begin with, Anne had, while in Hollywood, tried the route of fame for fame's sake and found it to be a dead end.

But if Anne seemed to take her stage success coolly, she did not do so dispassionately. Much of her calm was due to the simple fact that she had mentally rehearsed the advent of fame time and again, as early as her curb-side songstress days in the Bronx. When the actual moment arrived, it was really very much as she had expected, no more or less. Her reaction was not one of insouciance but of reaffirmation, a leap of faith that landed squarely where she hoped it would. Still, not all of Anne's self-possession was arrived at independently—she was getting a mighty boost from Gittel. It was only natural that the diligent research and transference that had animated the character on-stage would seep into Anne's offstage outlook. Viewed another way, the character had alerted the actress to certain kindred traits—individuality, quizzicalness, and a self-styled bohemianism. True, among local columnists Anne was known as "the kook." But as her good friend Marta Orbach later explained to John G. Mitchell: "Maybe Anne was a kook. But she's getting away from that now." To which Anne added: "I think of a beatnik and I think of a beard. I never had a beard."

It would have been out of character for Gittel or Anne to accept success at face value without reservations or a tinge of skepticism. In sum and in short, as Anne would much later point out in an interview with *Viva* magazine: "I was psychologically prepared for it, but not," she was careful to add, "for its possible consequences."

Anne's filmwork had been anything but fulfilling, but it had left her time and energy for public relations and flack work. On Broadway, and in a physically and mentally grueling role, acting seemed a complete outlet for her energies, but there was still pressure from the press. It was a standard paradox of the business that when the actress least wants attention, she most receives it. Anne's agent at William Morris, Bernard Seligman, did what he could to ration requests for interviews and guest appearances, but it was a losing battle. As a result, many of the interviews Anne accepted she accepted as a lark. In an effort to make them less repetitive and more interesting for her, she would try out new ideas and attitudes or, in a pinch, playfully adorn or even invent the facts. Despite the incidental camouflage, she cut a fascinating figure. Her dress was decidedly late-fifties beat—black skirts and stockings topped with black knit sweaters and turtlenecks. Her comments were often of a like dark nature, as when she concluded an interview with the Sunday *Times:* "My philosophy is that life is here only to be lived so that we can, through life, earn the right to death, which to me is paradise, really . . ." a kind of morbid existentialism which she was quick to qualify: "That's how it all looks to me today. Tomorrow?"—she shrugged and smiled.

Part of what Anne was avoiding was celebrity, a largely television-fed phenomenon by which the personality is known less for a given achievement than for being known for being known. It could be an enticing narcissism but Anne was having none of it. If anything, her drab beatnik pose was a backlash against the customary varnish of celebrityhood. It was at worst a reverse snobbery or an inverse vanity (some called it "pretentious unpretentiousness"). The fact remained that Anne refused to trivialize or two-dimensionalize her self-image for popular consumption.

Whatever else Anne's evasive maneuvers brought, they protected her growth as an actress. Widespread publicity might have worked to freeze her image as Gittel, and that was the last thing she wanted. She had viewed theatrical success as not so much a culmination as a certification of her acting ability. She continued to regularly attend classes at HB Studio, winning high praise from the master who at one point stated: "She is like a little daughter of Anna Magnani." It was an apt description, con-

sistent with Anne's own habit of comparing her mother's temperament to Magnani's, "hot as fire."

Anne's thirst for self-improvement was not confined to study
with Berghof. In the fall of the year, she applied to the Actors
Studio and like the least or most renowned applicant, had first to
audition. That done, Anne devised a weekly personal agenda
that would eventually include: two visits to the Actors Studio,
two lessons with her vocal coach, three sessions with her analyst,
and one stop at the hairdresser. In her spare time she carried a
Broadway play.

One by-product of success Anne chose not to dodge was
money. Her value to the show had been proportionately
reassessed and her pay upgraded from its modest early terms.
Anne had always been generous by nature, and her generosity
kept pace with her climbing income. While she was more than
willing to help out her family financially, they were proud working people and continued working, accepting little. Anne found
other ways to spend, and her looseness with a dollar reached
such proportions that even she admitted: "I'd have bought the
Central Park Zoo if it was up for sale." She ultimately rejected
the prodigal life and hired David Cogan to act as her business
manager. He immediately put her on an allowance of $50 per
week to cover meals, taxis, and oddments. All other income and
bills went directly to him, and through his shrewd management,
Anne became as eminently solvent as she was successful. It not
only left her enough to rent a Village brownstone apartment
(the modishness of which escaped Millie who insisted it was just
another "railroad flat" like the ones Anne grew up in), but enabled her in time to purchase one of her own.

Though Anne was doing quite well by *Seesaw*, other more lavish offers followed quickly on its heels. There was the usual talk
of spinoffs and sequels. There was a tempting offer for a nightclub tour which would give Anne the chance she had longed for
to sing and dance. There was also talk of playing Las Vegas at
pay into five figures per night. Each proposition seemed more
tempting than the last. Each might offer an interesting new direction to her career, or act as a buffer if she intended to return
to the stage. Likewise, each offer meant a chance for Anne to

cash in on her success which, though it was hard-won and deserved, was confined to the Broadway theatre world. Anne was still young and had little to lose by way of diversification, but her instincts told her "no." It was nothing she had logically worked out, and anyway logic might well have come down on the side of a brief, well-paid venture. Her refusal probably upheld some basic instinct for professional survival which insisted she stay in New York and continue to improve her craft. Or, not unrelatedly, it might have stemmed from a sense of unfinished business, a fear that without a prompt return to the stage in a role wholly divorced from Gittel, people might simply assume that Anne *was* Gittel. She seemed to want to meet any possible theatrical sophomore jinx head on. Besides, Anne had already tentatively charted her next career turn. The invitation had come months before, and the inspiration years before that.

In 1953, while rummaging through the town library in Stockbridge, Massachusetts, William Gibson chanced upon the autobiography of Helen Keller, *The Story of My Life*. Appended to the work was a series of letters written by Annie Sullivan, Miss Keller's teacher and lifelong friend. Gibson was deeply touched by the story and decided to dramatize it as a solo dance which he sketchily choreographed and to which he attached an original verse narrative of twelve pages, to be recited in accompaniment offstage. The dance was never produced but the incentive remained as Gibson went on to write a novel, *The Cobweb*. While completing the novel, the author hit upon the idea for *Two for the Seesaw*, and began the first act of that before the other was even finished. Then, the novel published and the early *Seesaw* agonies begun, Gibson repeated his pattern of subsidiary writing *in medias res*, and returned to the Keller story almost by accident. He had already offered the barely begun *Seesaw* to his friend, Arthur Penn, and the two men met regularly in Stockbridge to discuss casting and fantasize over a first Broadway production which both longed for. It was during one of these visits in 1956 that Gibson mentioned the Keller autobiography, and especially Annie Sullivan's letters, and suggested that the material might be dramatized as a teleplay. There was also a modest financial motive on the author's part. He was gleaning the last royalties from

his novel and would welcome any supplemental income an advance on a teleplay might bring. Penn sparked to the idea, Gibson roughed out a script and a summary, and Penn circulated
the script among network program executives with a nominal initial price tag of $500, which both men hoped would in turn help
underwrite the playwright's completion of *Seesaw*. Producer
after producer passed on the project, and when Penn had all but
exhausted his personal contacts, he submitted the presentation to
Martin Manulis at "Playhouse 90." Manulis was tremendously
impressed with the work, and promptly scheduled a production
for the early '57 season with a budget of close to $10,000 and
with Penn as director.

The story, a somewhat stylized account of the initial encounter between Annie Sullivan and Helen Keller and their first days
together, drew on the Keller volume as well as Nell Braddy's biography *Anne Sullivan Macy*. Gibson's teleplay was called *The
Miracle Worker* and starred Teresa Wright and Patty McCor-
mack. It was telecast February 7, 1957, over CBS and received
an overwhelming response, but Gibson who had come West for
rehearsals and broadcast, had no time to steep in the praise.
That same night, he caught a flight for New York, and, at the
request of Fred Coe, attended a noon meeting the next day with
a young actress. The script for *Two for the Seesaw* had been
kicking around for some time but, bogged down at the casting
stage, had gotten no further off the ground. At that meeting,
Anne captivated Gibson as she had Coe and would Penn. Still,
she was no more than a latecomer to a struggling project, and if
Gibson looked past the matter at hand to a remake of his teleplay with Anne, he made no mention of it that day.

Within months, Anne was inextricably tied to *Seesaw* and on
the road in Washington. Meantime, Gibson's teleplay had pock-
eted almost every imaginable television award and a pair of motion picture offers as well as bids to have him refit *The Miracle
Worker* for Broadway. The ongoing battles over *Seesaw* had
served somewhat to anneal the alliance of playwright, director,
and producer. Gibson invited Penn and Coe to share in the
teleplay's eventual rebirth and each gladly accepted (Coe's response was "bless you"). That left unanswered the casting of

Annie Sullivan, but following Anne's rave notices in Washington and her almost magical transformation from a passable actress in impossible films to a theatrical diamond in the rough, Gibson's choice was made easier. For a second opinion, he consulted a trusted friend who had witnessed Anne's opening night performance, and asked if he thought Anne might be able to portray Annie Sullivan. The friend's reply was "I think she can play anything." Gibson returned to Penn and Coe and announced: "There is only one girl to play *The Miracle Worker* and that girl is Anne Bancroft." With that, he arranged a Sunday brunch with Anne and Jessica Levy (*Seesaw*'s production secretary and resident confidante). Between pancakes, he offered the part to Anne who replied, with no false modesty: "You think I'm right for it?" He did, obviously, and the matter was nudged to a back burner in favor of the stewing current production.*

By the first of the year, *Seesaw* had mightily survived its New York opening and Anne had taken Broadway by storm. She was the show's chief drawing card, with or without Fonda, and since Gibson, Penn, and Coe each had a vested interest in the show, none was especially eager to hustle her out of a sure property into an unsure one, which would have meant taking from Peter to pay Paul. At the outside, Anne owed *Seesaw* two years at the producer's discretion. That eventually was discreetly trimmed back to just eighteen months so that Anne might begin to prepare in earnest for *The Miracle Worker*.

Penetrating, painstaking preparation had become embedded in the Bancroft technique. Anne began by reading every last page that had been written by or about Annie Sullivan. Secondary research completed, she moved on to the primary and subjective. One element which Anne quickly seized upon was Sullivan's childhood blindness. As a disability, it was all but dwarfed by Helen Keller's dual curse to be both blind and deaf. But Anne knew that the characters' visual impairments left them with a common vision. To understand one was to begin to understand the other.

* While in Philadelphia Anne had an opportunity to read the first act of *The Miracle Worker* and at first was unenamored of it, though she later chalked up her reaction to her own emotional immaturity at the time.

Anne arranged to spend three weeks as an observer at The Institute of Physical Medicine and Rehabilitation at Bellevue Hospital on East Thirty-fourth Street. Anticipating her arrival were
two of the Institute's teachers, Grace Kumar and Joan Chase. As
it happened, they were caught that day with no volunteer
workers and were not at all keen on having to further diffuse
their energies on some actress's offhand observation. Anne had
no sooner arrived and exchanged greetings, than she began to
mingle with the children with a skill that did not escape Joan's
notice: "She sat down on the floor and began to work with our
youngsters almost as if she were a trained teacher."

Anne's work at the Institute was limited by continued work in
Seesaw, which only afforded her time between midmorning and
early afternoon. That did not limit her engrossment with the
work and she soon began to concentrate her efforts on a seven-
year-old boy who had not yet mastered the art of eating with a
spoon. Anne's patience and persistence won out, and before she
left for other preproduction duties, she had the rare and "wonderful" opportunity to see him feed himself with a spoon. In the
course of her visits to the Institute, Anne and Joan became
close friends and later that summer flew to Chicago for a week
of seminars and workshops with the American Foundation for
the Blind at Northwestern University.

Anne was not content to stop at the objective which, while it
was enlightening and undeniably enriching, was still not directly
experiential. She arranged to be sightless for a day. Anne had
adhesive placed over her eyes which she then hid behind dark
glasses so as not to draw undue attention or be thought of as
anything other than blind, and set out in the company of an escort. Under the circumstances, navigating a hallway or a city
block might have been experience enough, but Anne demanded
more. With her escort she went to an amusement pier in Wild-
wood, New Jersey, and with no small trepidation took a ride on
the roller coaster—a kind of dramatic, capsule lesson and meta-
phor for blindness in the sighted world. Afterward, she visited a
nearby restaurant and struggled with a dish of ice cream, much
of which melted and ran off her spoon and onto her hand. Later,
she returned to her hotel room, removed the adhesive, squinted

at the light, focused, looked about, and said, "My God, I never knew this room was so beautiful."

To round out her preparation, Anne attended the Vacation Camp for the Blind in Spring Valley, New York, where she soon perfected the manual alphabet she had begun studying months earlier.

Although Anne was soon immersed in the character of Annie Sullivan, vestiges of Gittel still hovered about. The most palpable had come the year before with Anne's nomination for a Tony (Antoinette Perry) Award for her work in *Two for the Seesaw*. The ceremony took place at a Waldorf-Astoria dinner dance attended by some 885 invited guests. There was to be a telecast of the event but that was thwarted by a last minute strike by the International Brotherhood of Electrical Workers against WCBS-TV. The ceremony went ahead as planned, and of little surprise to anyone, *The Music Man* and *Sunrise at Campobello* divided most of the spoils. There was, however, at least one surprised winner—Anne Bancroft.

The Tony consecrated the popularity which had built steadily since opening night. Soon Anne's name alone carried a distinct familiarity and weight, and on the advice of her agent and business manager, she modestly exploited her success with a commercial endorsement. By fall, her picture could be seen in magazines in advertisements extolling the virtues of Rheingold Beer. But that was virtually the extent of her image-mongering.

As *The Miracle Worker* neared rehearsal, there was little time for such extracurriculars. In addition to Anne's other research there was the matter of dialect. Annie Sullivan spoke with a pronounced Irish-American brogue, whose mellifluous tones had little in common with the sharper crescendos of Anne's own Italian-American inflections. The cadences were in certain ways similar, and each dialect had its own peculiar lyrical quality, but phonetically they were quite different. Anne had never tackled a sustained, serious dialect role (not counting her halting Indian maidens) and she went about preparation as she did everything else, scrupulously and with no slight to authenticity.

But these concerns were really just trimmings and trappings.

Anne knew that the role as written would be the linchpin of her performance, and after *Seesaw*, her faith in Gibson's character conception was unshakable. Much of what she uncovered in research would ultimately be discarded. The essence of the role was in the script, and it was her job, with Penn's assistance, to extract the correct interpretation.

It was an exacting task yet made easier by Anne's vastly improved acting technique. Throughout her early television and filmwork, and carrying over into the first phases of *Seesaw*, was a purely intuitive, emotional approach to character. She had never wanted for creative passion or emotive sensibilities, only the right technical training to funnel them properly into character. Her experience with *Seesaw* was tremendously remedial in this regard. She was learning to think through a role, to draw her own interpolations, to temper the emotional with the intellectual. She was quick to credit her director with the change: "It was Arthur who taught me everything—not how to live my roles, because I always did that, but how to control it, how to turn it off." Anne deserved more of the credit than she admitted. By the time she began work on her second play, she did not have to turn constantly to her author and director for insights. She was better equipped to assay the character and the early signs were dazzling.

There could hardly have been two more different productions. *Seesaw* had tied an inexperienced but determined actress to a seasoned but disgruntled actor in a playwright's maiden stage work, and the road to Broadway was about what might have been expected—rocky. That struggle alone seemed to give Gibson, Penn, Coe, and Anne the wisdom of a dozen plays and made *The Miracle Worker* a more mature production from the outset. Casting helped immeasurably. The accomplished Torin Thatcher and Patricia Neal were expertly cast as Helen's parents, Captain and Mrs. Keller. James Congdon was a fine choice to play her brother, James. With Anne well on her way to an almost sublime understanding of Annie Sullivan, the only shadow of doubt was over the role of Helen, who was being depicted here in her tragically benighted youth.

It was an extremely physical role, and unflattering in its stark presentation of the girl's at times animal-like behavior. There was no dialogue as such to commit to memory, but that made expressiveness and timing just that much more difficult. The eventual choice for the part was a little-known youngster from Manhattan named Patty Duke.

It was no accident that brought Patty to the part. Her older brother, Raymond, was an actor and a client of agents John and Ethel Ross, whose specialty was child actors. The Rosses met Patty, signed her, and repeatedly found her work on television. By early 1958, word of a stage production of *The Miracle Worker* began to circulate and John Ross started to school Patty for the part of Helen, first with blindfolded grope sessions in his apartment, then, blindfold removed, with a conditioned sightless stare oblivious to visual movement. To simulate deafness, John Ross gradually untaught her the reflexive reaction to sudden sounds. As a result, Patty was singularly prepared for the audition, which she handily won.

Patty was petite, with an almost doll-like beauty that spliced with the character in a figure that was not merely pathetic or for that matter grotesque, but rather the image of a normal child disfigured by the rage of sense deprivation. In addition to these more visible qualities, Patty brought a native intelligence which helped her rapidly learn the manual alphabet necessary to the part.

While for William Gibson *The Miracle Worker* conjured none of the peculiar demons that had sprung from *Two for the Seesaw*, the play was not problem-free. For one, it was somewhat bound to its beginnings as a teleplay, and the televisual paraphernalia of close-ups, cuts, commercial cuts, camera movement, and fades had no exact equivalent onstage. Also there was the matter of Annie Sullivan's flashbacks which on television had been handled aurally and, by Penn's own ready admission, badly.

There were other less concrete considerations in translation from medium to medium, justification for instance. Critics, most of whom could be counted on to have seen the original television production, were likely to ask what had been gained in trans-

position. It would not do to simply turn out a stagebound carbon copy, no matter what the virtues and merits of the original.
Although teleplays were increasingly finding their way into other
media, movies were the usual outcome and movie critics seemed
to demand less in the way of originality. Movies could get by
dressing up the material with more expensive casting and
mounting, and without commercial interruption. The line between televised and filmed drama had been effectively blurred to
the benefit of both. Theatre was stodgier and more prescriptive,
and the play needed vindication beyond the fact that it had been
a successful teleplay.

There was however at least one auspicious sign beforehand
when a copy in Braille of the play was submitted for comment to
Helen Keller and returned with four pages of notes showing no
displeasure with the spirit of the writing and seeking only to correct minor factual errors.

As the show moved into rehearsal and then out-of-town tryout,
other problems emerged, but few were major and none were due
to the playwright's active intervention. Gibson had been chas-
tened by his *Seesaw* sojourn and as the new play took the road,
he stayed a safe distance away revising and rewriting in the
comfortable confines of his Stockbridge home.

The only persistent problem was one of overzealousness on the
part of the two leads in a key scene. The play's most physical
and forceful interaction between Helen and Annie had been
drawn from one of Sullivan's letters describing a "battle royal"
over the girl's dinner-table habits. The Kellers had indulged
Helen her practice of wandering from plate to plate, taking what
she wanted from anyone. The indulgence placated the child and
enabled the family to carry on at least a semblance of conversation. Annie Sullivan had been aghast at this practice, sensing
that it only worked against the discipline that would be necessary to free the child from her disabilities. In the play, over
breakfast, Annie refuses to share in the permissiveness, and after
hustling the family from the room proceeds with Helen's first object lesson in social conduct—but not without a fight. The
rough-and-tumble that ensues during the play's second act was
only loosely diagrammed by Penn, who resisted the temptation of

blocking and choreographing every last movement, leaving considerable room for improvisation so as not to sacrifice spontaneity. At first Patty was tentative but Anne used a little Bronx psychology and taunted, "Naw, you come on and hit me!"

After that the two went at it wholeheartedly. Anne and Patty were rigged with elaborate hidden padding but there were inevitable bumps and bruises. The better the scene, the worse the beating, and both actresses were taking a hell of a beating (before it was over Patty would have chipped a tooth). Still, the rewards were immediate and gratifying—the scene never failed to grip its audience and almost always ended in applause, with Annie victorious, and therefore Helen as well. In fact, during the successful September Philadelphia run at the New Locust Theatre, the fight, usually nine to ten minutes in length, ran a full twelve minutes and brought down the house. These were problems a director liked.

The play improved on the road and Anne's hold on her role tightened. By the time the company reached the Wilbur Theatre in Boston, her confidence was such that when she paid a visit to the Perkins Institute for the Blind (which Annie Sullivan had left to work with Helen) the memorabilia and simple fact that Sullivan had once walked the same halls, was of interest to Anne but otherwise not especially helpful. She had arrived at her understanding of the character using her talent and tools as an actress, and that as much as obviated any sort of mystical transference. The play was the thing, as was her place within it. And the road notices gave ample testimony to her work, which had been uniformly praised. As the production prepared to strike sets and move to Broadway, there was little question that this performance would muzzle those who had implied that Anne's stage achievements would go no further than Gittel Mosca. *The Miracle Worker* would banish any past specter of typecast.

On October 19, 1959, a month and two days after Anne's twenty-eighth birthday, *The Miracle Worker* opened at the Playhouse Theatre. For a Broadway opening night the backstage mood was unusually calm—serene next to that of *Seesaw*. There was none of the former edginess, and Anne experienced none of

the assorted psychosomatic ailments that had plagued her before.

The play's action covered roughly seven years, from 1882 to
1887, although the principal drama occurs in a few days of that
final year. There is a prologue in which the Kellers' infant
daughter Helen has just survived a severe fever which nonetheless leaves her deaf and blind. The lights fade, chimes sound,
and the drama resumes seven years later with Helen grown but
yet bereft. It is soon clear that the mother pities and coddles
Helen while the father is fast reaching an end of patience. Short
of institutionalizing her, arrangements are made for professional
live-in care. Annie Sullivan arrives from the Perkins Institute in
Boston; she is affable, forthright, and eager to meet her charge.
It is revealed that Annie herself was once blind, and that only a
series of nine operations was able to restore a measure of sight.
Annie and Helen slowly begin to test one another, but the acquaintance quickly turns to conflict as each finds in the other an
unbudging foe. Their relationship is set as adversary, mutually
obstinate, and not without a touch of humor. Helen prevails in
this first encounter, but a second battle of wills is only as far
away as breakfast, where, after dismissing the family and grap-
pling fiercely with the child, Annie files the beleaguered report:
"She ate from her own plate. She ate with a spoon. Herself. And
she folded her napkin."

Discipline is essential to unlocking Helen's mind. Annie foot-
notes each encounter and experience by spelling on the child's
palm using the standard manual alphabet. Language is the key.
But progress is slow because of the family's interference and
Annie all but extorts permission to live alone with Helen for two
weeks in the garden house. At fortnight's end, the child has become less unruly, more obedient, but the spelling remains no
more than a finger game for her, and Annie takes this lack of association as evidence of her failure to truly help the child. The
Kellers are more than satisfied with the child's domestication,
and their renewed indulgence causes her to regress. In the
course of a homecoming dinner, Helen is once again misbehav-
ing much as she did at that fateful breakfast some two weeks
ago. At one point, she douses Annie with a pitcher of water, but

Annie, in a last-ditch effort of reclamation, drags Helen bodily to the outside pump to refill the pitcher. It is there that Helen at last equates the manually spelled water with water itself, and the other lessons which have remained stubbornly in abeyance, begin to flow. Annie spells into Helen's hand: "I love Helen, forever, and—ever." Helen takes Annie's hand and leads her back into the house. Curtain.

The audience reaction was tumultuous. It had been a magnificent performance, but it was almost all Anne could do to stand for the curtain calls—ten in all. For her the show had been exhilarating and exhausting, for the audience riveting and unforgettable. The company had only to await the reviews.

They were well worth the wait. One of the first to file was the *Daily News*'s John Chapman, who had boundless praise for all, and even went so far as to call Anne "presently the best actress on Broadway." Frank Aston of the *World-Telegram and The Sun*, could not say enough about the play's two leading ladies: "Anne Bancroft and Patty Duke will shatter every crowd that gathers in The Playhouse for months to come." The *Post*'s Richard Watts, Jr., while raising questions as to some of the playwright's devices (viz. offstage voices) was yet quick to compliment Gibson for not succumbing to saccharine sentimentality. He described Patty's work as "wonderfully touching and real," Anne's as "nothing short of superb." Likewise, Robert Coleman of the *Mirror* reserved some doubt about the play's "literary merit," but went on to call it "magnificent theatre," and added that its author was "rapidly assuming the stature of a Tennessee Williams or a William Inge." Walter Kerr's *Herald Tribune* review had nothing but approbation for all and although the critic emeritus, the *Times*'s Brooks Atkinson, was specific about what he considered to be the play's primary deficiency ("It has the loose narrative technique of a TV script"), he, too, was generous with praise. But it was John McClain of the *Journal-American* who provided what was for Anne the definitive postscript: "If there was even the slightest question about Miss Bancroft's versatility it can now be answered. In *Seesaw* she was Jewish, now she is Irish; she is forthright, explicit, funny, and enormously endearing."

This time the wider media reaction which after *Seesaw* had

been enthusiastic but subtly conditional (as if Anne were a novelty or fad and likely to quickly pass out of fashion), now found fuller dimensions. That month Anne appeared on the cover of *Theatre Arts* magazine, after that the cover of *The Theatre*, and after that, the December 21 cover of *Time*, and with that came national recognition. The article, by Dick Seamon, traced the embattled course of Anne's still young career, and eagerly ranked her among the top stage actresses of the day (Julie Harris, Geraldine Page, and Kim Stanley). Such listing might have seemed unseemly or at least premature, but even so esteemed a Broadway denizen as producer Harold Prince added his personal endorsement: "We've come to the end of gracious ladies in the theatre. Why, I don't know. But this girl Bancroft is the greatest there is. She marks the beginning of an era." Not all comments were so unrestrained. Arthur Penn, recalling Anne's early work on *Seesaw*, pointed out that at first: "She couldn't stand. She couldn't turn. She'd play with her back to the audience. She was too broad and too vulgar." But he was quick to amend that: "She'll be a 'grand dame' of the theatre by the time she's forty, but today she's marvelously uncivilized. Just about the only thing she couldn't do is a comedy of manners—that's because she doesn't have them." Anne's self-assessment: "I'm still an ignorant slob."

The Miracle Worker settled in for a long run. It had cost $125,000 to mount, with $26,000 a week running costs, and it was more than earning its keep. Through the first year of performances, Dick Via, a member of the stage crew, kept a detailed log of memorable events, including a running tally of the number of chairs broken each week during the battle royal. (The average worked out to some 3 or 4 per week, which in the course of 408 performances worked out to 140 broken chairs—enough to necessitate purchasing the chairs wholesale from a Brooklyn supplier.) Other noteworthy items included the boosting of Patty Duke to co-star billing, making her Broadway's youngest star ever. And, perhaps most moving, was Helen Keller's eightieth birthday party on June 27, which Anne and Patty attended and at which

Miss Keller told Anne that her handshake was like that of Annie Sullivan's. In all there were amazingly few missed performances. Pat Neal left the show in March for some other work, and in April, Anne treated herself to a week's vacation with her understudy, Tresa Hughes, filling in while she was gone. Anne adhered to her rigid schedule of performance, acting class, voice lessons, and sessions with her analyst. And despite the fact that her income climbed rapidly to $150,000 a year, she abided by her $50 a week allowance and gave not the least impression of flaunting her wealth.

But it was not all work and no play. Anne gradually gave in to requests for television guest shots. She became a frequent visitor on Jack Paar's popular late-night talk show, and even opened the doors of her Village brownstone to the cameras of CBS for a visit with Edward R. Murrow on his celebrated interview program "Person to Person." Anne took the greatest delight in appearances on Perry Como's top-rated variety show, which gave her the chance to do publicly what she had long secretly most wanted to do—sing.

Somehow, she still found time to log occasional volunteer work at the Institute, and she was readily available for the seemingly ceaseless series of awards, banquets, and testimonials which came her way. There was a plaque from the New York Philanthropic League, an assortment of social service club awards, and even an honorary membership from the Hadassah. And, of course, there were the Antoinette Perry Awards, where Anne collected her second Tony for as many performances.

For all Anne's accomplishments, there was a nagging sense of failure about her personal life. Her recent success might have helped to relax many of her work obsessions, but that only magnified her longings for a stable relationship. As she explained to Dick Seamon: "I don't know why, but I can't make a mature relationship based on trust, respect and recognition. Most of Annie Sullivan is myself. It's my own blindness I draw on, my unawareness of myself." Anne had long since abandoned hopes of some knight on a white charger come to sweep her off her feet. But her fame (though she was unaffected by it) seemed to

184

intimidate most men, few of whom had the fortitude, let alone the chutzpah, to approach her. Anne was phenomenally successful, yet in many ways, lonely. Still, she was hopeful: "All of my love affairs have been flops. But that doesn't mean the next one will be."

13

Charles Strouse first met Mel Brooks when both were working for "Your Show of Shows." Mel was already fortified within the program's power elite, while Charles was an extremely talented if unsung young composer who wrote dance music and occasionally helped out playing rehearsal piano. Mel was always very friendly and the two were the best of passing acquaintances. Years passed and after composing music for a handful of minor Broadway shows, Charles hit paydirt with the tremendously popular *Bye Bye Birdie*. Meanwhile, the success of *The 2000 Year Old Man* album had consolidated Mel's reputation as a writer's writer become performer's performer. But with his continuing estrangement from movies and television, his reputation was busier than he was. In short, Mel was available, and Charles had an idea.

Charles had just read Vladimir Nabokov's *Pnin*, about an immigrant Russian professor who is charmed by America's indigenous gaucheries. Charles thought that it would make a "sensational" story for a musical, but when approached for rights, Nabokov refused. When it seemed as if the project might never materialize, Charles turned up a novel by Robert Lewis Taylor, *Professor Fodorski*, which treated much the same theme. Charles and Lee Adams (his lyricist from *Birdie*) agreed that this second book might serve their aims just as well, and found that the rights were virtually theirs for the asking. That left them to find someone who could turn a novel into a libretto. Mel's name came up, and although he had never tackled anything of quite this nature for theatre (*New Faces* was piecework, *Shinbone Alley* primarily patchwork) he was asked to write the adaptation and accepted.

Meanwhile, unknown to the others, director Josh Logan had recently returned from Europe and went with his wife Nedda to see *Bye Bye Birdie*. They were, in a word, "entranced." Afterward, Logan spoke with the show's producer, Ed Padula, and implored: "Please find a show like that for me someday." Within weeks, Padula paid a visit to Logan's Stamford, Connecticut, home. With him were Charles, Lee, and an uncharacteristically quiet Mel Brooks. The five of them started going over the story and Mel quickly snapped to, mixing keen and considered observations with his patented off-the-wall patter. By day's end, little more was known about the projected play except that it now had a director.

For Mel, the prospects of a musical of this sort must have seemed encouraging. True, it was hardly on a plane with the Russian novelists he had become so enamored of, but neither was it the random sampling which typified his early revue work for television and stage. Properly done, the libretto could split the difference—a popular, commercial work, yet with an unusual but sustained story line that might have something to say apart from grafting one production number to the next. It was more promising in theory than in practice. There were obvious rough spots from the start which required much attention and patience. Mel had little interest in repeated rewrites, and his largely untried skills as a constructionist now appeared somewhat lacking.

If anything, Mel was more absorbed in another idea he had hatched and was steadily nurturing. He arrived at work one day to announce: "I'm going to write a play called *Springtime for Hitler* as soon as this one's over." Everyone tried to laugh it off as just another *outré* Brooks gag, but Mel persisted and Logan, appalled, warned: "*Springtime for Hitler!* You can't *say* things like that, Mel—the audience will throw stones at you." Which was exactly what he had in mind, once removed. Mel had begun piecing together a story, actually a story within a story, about a pair of theatrical producers who concoct a plan to make a killing by oversubscribing backers for a play that is sure to fold. *Springtime for Hitler* was to be that play, and, according to plan, it would bomb, the angels would write off the loss, and the producers would repair to South America with the loot. That was the scenario that unfolded each day as Mel arrived with new scenes, twists, and scraps of dialogue for his next work. Charles understood what Mel was doing. Having been at one point a rather "blocked" composer, he saw this as the attempt of an almost blocked writer to try out ideas on a small but select audience. Whatever the deep-seated motives, the effects were apparent—little was being accomplished on the matter at hand while Mel auditioned new material for a project everybody was sure would never come to pass. And if Mel's attention was now divided, it was soon to be subdivided.

One work day, while the show was still taking shape, Charles was paid a brief visit by a good friend, Anne Bancroft. She stayed a short while, then left. Mel rushed up to Charles: "Wow, you know Anne Bancroft?" Charles explained that they had first gotten acquainted at the Actors Studio when Anne was still with *Seesaw.* She would sing while he accompanied her on piano. They'd kept in touch over the last few years, and for a short while, he'd even held out hope that they'd become something more than friends. Mel instantly had similar thoughts of his own. He asked Charles if he would introduce him to Anne. Charles knew the two of them well enough to know that nothing could possibly come of an introduction. He acquiesced.

It was the first week of February and the weather was frigid. Anne, soon due to depart *The Miracle Worker*, was busily about one of her favorite pastimes, preparing a guest shot for the "Perry Como Show." She was to appear on a show scheduled to air February 22, to be taped shortly before. Like all Como shows it clustered around a general theme, in this case, "Boy Meets Girl." Anne's principal contribution was a turn in a sketch opposite special guest Jimmy Durante as "Mrs. Durante," and a rendition of the standard "Married I Can Always Get." The show rehearsed at the Ziegfeld Theatre, then a converted NBC television studio at Sixth Avenue and Fifty-fourth Street. By four o'clock, rehearsal had gotten as far as Anne's song. The Ziegfeld was only a short distance from where Charles and Mel were working, and at Mel's urging they decided to knock off early and drop in. They arrived in time to see Anne onstage, in white, and in fine voice. The moment she finished, Mel was on his feet, applauding. He rushed the stage and before she knew what hit her, he was shaking her hand and introducing himself. She smiled, and laughed. The cast and crew broke up.

Afterward, Anne excused herself and said she had to pay a visit to her agent at William Morris. Eager to prolong the meeting, Mel did what anyone in his shoes might have—he lied: "Oh, I happen to be going there, too." They stepped outside and Mel hailed a taxi with a shattering whistle that might have roused whole flocks of Canadian geese. Anne and Mel shared the ride, then Mel followed Anne into the office of her agent. Just to break the ice, Mel said: "I haven't seen *The Miracle Worker* yet, but I hear it's great." Anne rose to the bait and offered to do the whole play for him, right there on the spot. Mel sat spellbound as Anne performed a comical condensed version of *The Miracle Worker* right down to the final epiphany with Helen at the water pump. Mel was weeping with laughter.

They parted. Mel went home, thought it all over, and then spent the better part of the night calling Anne. She wasn't home. He caught up with her the following day, and arranged to drop by her brownstone. Mel arrived with a copy of *The 2000 Year Old Man* album, a handy conversation piece since Mel was to make his network debut with Carl the following week on the Sullivan show. There was no shortage of conversation and they found that the professional admiration was mutual—Anne had been a Caesar devotee for years. Six hours later, Mel left. Anne had plans that evening to go to the Village Vanguard, a cellar jazz club on Seventh Avenue South in the Village. It was not a casual drop-in place but an atmospheric, out-of-the-way night spot for aficionados. That night, Mel just happened to drop in.

In the following weeks, when Mel reported for work on the

play, he brought with him a pair of prophecies. Naturally, there was mention of the glory-bound work-in-progress *Springtime for Hitler*, but appended to that was a second prediction: ". . . and then I'm going to marry Anne Bancroft." This stirred disbelief among his workmates who together compared his fantasies to the proverbial kid at the candy-store window.

Whatever Mel thought his chances were with Anne, he was clearly getting nowhere with the play, which now had benefit of title (*All American*), a smattering of songs, a moody director, and a shaky book with an elusive second act. The show had been well cast with Ray Bolger in the lead, and Eileen Herlie, Anita Gillette, Ron Hussman, and Fritz Weaver in supporting roles. But as the start of rehearsals neared, a viable second act was nowhere to be found. In conference, Mel was his usual, dazzling, impish, endearing, maddening self; yet when it came time for him to unriddle Act II, the magic was missing. Ultimately, with his back to the wall, Logan empaneled his creative staff, and working from Mel's basic outline arrived at a usable act. Mel was displeased with the results, but when asked to do better, returned empty-handed. And so *All American* limped into rehearsal.

Anne departed from *The Miracle Worker* on February 4, replaced in the role by Suzanne Pleshette. The next day, a Sunday, New York was buried under close to 17½ inches of snow, the largest accumulation since 1947. Floored and edged in white, Manhattan looked like some mythical storybook kingdom. The streets were impassable, the normal earful of horns, motors, tires, and sirens, gone. Impervious to all but the usual problems, subways continued to run, but their customary whoosh and rumble below street level was muffled by the acoustic covering of snow. It was New York in repose, in rare serenity, and it must have been indescribably soothing for Anne. Except for a few weeks' rest between her exit from *Seesaw* and the start of rehearsal for *The Miracle Worker*, Anne had been working nonstop for close to three years.

It would be a short-lived respite. There were now scripts to read, appearances to consider, and the continuing regimen of classes and professional appointments. At the outside, Anne knew there would be no greater pause than the start of shooting for the film version of *The Miracle Worker*, scheduled for that summer.

Manhattan was soon enough returned to its metronomic norm, and Mel was back to courting. In the past several months, Anne's well-deserved fame and not entirely deserved reputation as an eccentric had been a deterrent to most men. Mel was not most men. He hounded her and as Anne later confided: "No man had ever approached me with that kind of aggression." He repeatedly asked Anne out on dates which, were that not in itself novelty enough, were extraordinary for their relative ordinariness. Mel had been impressed from the start by Anne's intelligence, and to his mind that made her eligible for dates to assumedly weighty foreign films. That brought them repeatedly uptown to the Thalia where the 99 cents' admission was compatible with Mel's budget, despite the fact that Anne probably could have bought and sold the theatre. There were occasional thrifty dinners in Chinatown, but that already was a splurge. Real economy dates consisted of visits to recording studios, for which Mel's enhanced status with Capitol meant free entrance. Anne, aware of Mel's limited budget, often offered to cook dinner at home and that was a boon to both—to Anne, who was an excellent chef but seldom had the opportunity to cook, and to Mel, who could save money while enjoying some of the best eggplant parmigiana and lasagna south of the Bronx and west of Little Italy. Their time together was delightful for its sheer unpretentiousness. While other "personalities" were careful to be found in only the chic night spots and watering holes of café society, Anne and Mel took to the city as only two true New Yorkers could. They knew the grottoes and hideaways and the seclusion to be found simply strolling the sidewalks. They were spending more and more time together, but neither was eager to formalize the relationship. Both had married in haste before and had lived to regret it. In fact, Mel's divorce was yet to be finalized.

Besides, Mel more than had his hands full with a musical that was approaching an out-of-town run but refused to spring to life. The second act was still up in the air, and that was not to be taken lightly since this was to be a two-act musical. *All American* eventually took to the road and all but fell on its face. The show itself was often listless, the notices lackluster. And tempers were steadily on the rise! At one point, Charles and Mel nearly came to blows over a minor creative impasse. Charles was no scrapper, before or since, and he knew that Mel could probably have taken him apart, but the frustration of the play was fast turning into desperation which, with a New York opening closing quickly, was enough to turn the most mild-mannered composer into a would-be Dempsey. The two were restrained, no blows were exchanged, and all was soon forgiven. But the show was no better off for the truce.

The company pulled into Philadelphia with the production still at loose ends. For Charles, Philadelphia was "stale rye bread"— Broadway just up the pike, a show in need of polish, anxiety bordering on panic, and late-night rewrite sessions with undrinkable coffee and skimpy sandwiches with room-service rye curling slightly at the edges. It was in just such a setting at the Warwick Hotel that life momentarily surpassed art for sheer invention and absurdity.

Mel, Charles, Lee, and Josh had gathered in a room of the Logan suite for a wee-hour logistical meeting. They were joined by a young student, Joe Wishy, who had obtained a college grant for a thesis that would chronicle the making of a Broadway show, with emphasis on the director. The thesis might just as well have concerned the unmaking of a musical, with Act II still in disarray and the pervasive feeling that Ray Bolger was somehow being misused. The strategists sat grimly, the observer attentively, when the door of the room suddenly flew open, and a barefooted, bedraggled woman entered wearing the flimsiest of nighties that seemed in danger of slipping off entirely. Charles and Lee were the only ones there able to make sense of the hysterical entrance. They knew the woman was Rita Almaviva, one of the show's backers, and they knew that she had been suffering some severe psychological problems. The others stood by speechless, mouths agape, but before Charles could utter a word of explanation the woman fixed Mel with an accusing finger and shouted: "You have no talent!" Mel was nonplussed, the first

time anyone there could recall seeing him without a fast re-
joinder, let alone the least word of defense. The subsequent
scene was outrageous and confused, but Logan had the presence
of mind to make accurate mental notes. Her hysteria mounting,
Almaviva continued her tirade at Mel: "You can't write a line!
You can't tell a joke! You can't smell what an audience listens to
—you're a No Talent—you stink!"

Charles rose to Mel's defense addressing the woman by name,
but that only fanned her anger as she wheeled on her new victim: "And you can't write a tune!" The charge seemed a bit un-
founded for the man who had just composed the music for *Bye
Bye Birdie*, which had won four Tony Awards including one for
the season's best musical. She continued to rail against Charles:
"Nobody can whistle anything you put on paper! You're going to
end in the poorhouse—and you'll drag us all down there with
you! You're a No Talent too—you stink, you have stunk, and you
will go on stinking! And besides, you're Jewish!"

Lee was not about to stand by and watch his partner insulted,
and he tried to quiet the woman, offering to escort her back to
her room. That had the predictable result as she now turned on
him: "You snot-nosed poet that can't rhyme! You ass without a
hole! I always knew you were a vacuum," an uncharitable description of *Birdie*'s celebrated lyricist. With her next breath, she
commanded the student to stop taking notes. Aware that in matters of hysterical backers, discretion was the better part of schol-
arship, Wishy put down his pencil. Almaviva then resumed her
diatribe, leaving Logan mercifully or mistakenly unscathed,
when Nedda Logan appeared groggily from the bedroom and
offered to play peacemaker. She fared no better than the rest
and beat a hasty retreat back to the bedroom. Meanwhile
Charles and Lee were trying gently to steer their assailant toward the hall, but she recoiled and grabbed the nearest available
weapon—a pillow—and had at them. In the melee, one of her
breasts found its way out of the nightgown, completing the picture of some surreal Joan of Arc, menacingly brandishing her
trusty pillow. When it seemed as if nothing short of a fist to the
chops would subdue the woman, a friend of Logan's entered and
prevailed upon her to return to her room. She complied, but not

before permitting herself a vitriolic exit line: "Good night, you shits—you talentless shits."

With that benediction, the company moved on to New York. The structural problems had not all been ironed out, but the play was at least playable and presentable. On March 19, 1962, *All American* opened at the Winter Garden, a large theatre on Broadway in Times Square.

The curtain rose on a throng of immigrants just arrived at Idlewild customs. The slack-jawed head customs officer welcomes the newcomers: "Dis here's a democracy so we're gonna divide you into your own ethical groups. Now all you Krauts over dere . . . all you frogs dere . . . Limeys there and the rest of you gooks right here." While awaiting processing, they all burst into song, "The Old Immigration and Naturalization Rag," in the course of which enters a Professor Fodorski who has emigrated from Hungary to teach at a southern university. There follows a song by him celebrating his newly adopted country, "What a Country." The professor reports for work at the Southern Baptist Institute of Technology where he meets the woman dean, the stout-hearted but hapless football coach, the football-crazed president and his pert daughter, and assorted players and students including the disinterested members of his "Engineering Two" class. Fodorski is soon too bitten by the football bug, charmed by what he sees as an irresistible amalgam of colorful Americana and sound engineering principles. He realizes he can use football dynamics as a teaching model, which not only captures the attention of his nearly catatonic students but also turns the luckless football squad into an invincible team applying the professor's scientific formulae to sport. Fodorski becomes coach, then coach of the year. He falls in with a conniving promoter but uses the money to help bail out the financially faltering institute. He then takes the team to the Cotton Bowl, but is undermined by the dean who thinks the professor's obsession with winning is an unseemly token of his wish to out-American the Americans. The team loses the game and Fodorski nearly loses his faculty position, but the dean learns the error of her ways, Fodorski stays, and the curtain rings down on a blissful ending.

It was an unexceptional libretto, weak in spots, with some

painfully obvious moments. But the performance was strong, and the score helped buoy the show. One song in particular was a standout, a beautiful, wistful tune sung by Bolger and Eileen Herlie, "Once Upon a Time." By next morning, the reviews had all been posted and there was agreement on at least one point—the strength of Bolger's performance. Beyond that, opinion was mixed. The *Journal-American*'s John McClain thought the overall production winning, but found the story "labored and spotty," John Chapman in the *Daily News* sounded a far more positive note, complimenting all departments, including the book which he found to have "both solid humor and satirical wit." Norman Nadel of the *World-Telegram and The Sun* agreed, pointing out that Mel "had held the spirit and reproduced the color of Taylor's novel." The *Mirror*'s Robert Coleman thought the show "old-fashioned" and in some respects lacking in taste, but he was won over by its "enormous vitality." The *Post*'s Richard Watts, Jr., was less enthusiastic, saying that the production offered "some excellent satirical ideas, and then bounces back and forth between the agreeable and the embarrassing." Walter Kerr, for the *Herald Tribune*, was positively unenthusiastic: "The show then is schizoid, half-sentimental and half-desperate enough to send a squad up and down the aisles passing footballs over the customer's heads," summing up, "No beauty this, despite its stars." The *Times* review by Howard Taubman was by far the least enthralled. Taubman was enchanted by Bolger's performance but he found little else to like. His primary complaint, repeated again and again for emphasis, was the book's diffuseness: "With a rangeful of choice targets in its sights, 'All American' has managed the amazing feat of hitting none." He thought Mel's story heavy-handed, and at least one character "ponderously written." Taubman scarcely made mention of the score, except to refer snidely to the "songs, such as they are." There were bits and pieces of scenes, characters and numbers he found likeable, but that did not disguise the fact that, essentially, he was panning the show.

The reviews had run from generous to indifferent to disdainful, and whatever the consensus or median, the fact of the matter was that nothing less than an acknowledged hit would satis-

ANNE BANCROFT AND MEL BROOKS 195

factorily fill a theatre the size of the Winter Garden. *All American* endured for a total of eighty-six shows, and in late spring went under. None of the collaborators could quite pinpoint the show's Achilles' heel. Not one of them was a stranger to success; still their separate creative energies never really synergized and with no single department able to carry the rest, everything seemed to revert to the lowest common denominator. But of all the explanations and post mortems, Mel's was best able to put its finger on the crucial problem. Asked what had happened to the show, Mel explained: "We had an unfortunate stroke of luck, it opened in New York when there was no newspaper strike." Looking back, Charles had some insight into the Brooks working style which he compared to a street fighter, not a boxer but a brawler who "keeps swinging wildly and wildly and wildly, and when he connects he knocks you out." As it was, the libretto could have done with less punch and more finesse.

The rising sales of *The 2000 Year Old Man* record helped cushion Mel's latest fall from Broadway grace. Moreover, he was soon finding more pickup work writing for television specials, working his way to the front of the cameras for still other shows. The balance of his time was spent in pursuit of Anne, who had already begun to take some of the initiative away from her suitor. They enjoyed each other's company and were really all the entertainment either could want. A typical night might involve a board game, say "Careers," with Jerry Orbach and his wife Marta. Walking was a pursuit second only to talking, for which the Village, with its comfortable bistros and assuasive coffeehouse ambiance, seemed to have been made. Village soirees often took up where others left off, extending late into the night. For Anne and Mel, doing nothing in particular in the Village, among friends, and without curfew or curiosity seekers, was itself particularly something.

Although it had already been several months since Anne was last onstage, she still received a great deal of press attention. She retained much of her former interview sportiveness, but she was also taking the opportunities to go public with her relationship with Mel. It was usually phrased in rather noncommittal terms, almost girlish, such as "my boy friend" or "we're dating." But their affection for one another was apparent to the most casual observer as was their apparently separately arrived at habit of dodging any question about possible marriage. Besides, Anne had other topics to discuss with the press, for example, the start of shooting on the film version of *The Miracle Worker*.

It had not come about as automatically as hoped for. United Artists had agreed to back the project for $2 million, but as a precondition the studio felt it needed greater "star" insurance at the box office. In short, UA wanted Penn to dump Anne and hand over the role of Annie Sullivan to an Elizabeth Taylor or an Audrey Hepburn. Penn flatly refused: "It would have been absurd for somebody else to play it. Annie is marvelous—the way she 'feeds' Patty Duke." It was not the sort of reasoning Hollywood was in the habit of condoning. *Seesaw* had been a case in point. Gibson had sold the film rights for a tidy sum, which left him flush but powerless with regard to casting. Jerry Ryan was no problem since Fonda had long since washed his hands of the role and would have been the last person to object to the drafting of Robert Mitchum for the movie. When it came to the matter of Gittel however, the studio had little concern for the fact that Anne had virtually metabolized the role onstage and much concern over the fact that she had not proved particularly magnetic at the box office in her past filmwork. The film of *Two for the Seesaw* was released in 1962 with Shirley MacLaine as Gittel, and Anne was helpless to do a thing about it ("I'd have given anything to make the movie of that but it got away from me."). The movie had been released by United Artists.

The Miracle Worker was another matter entirely. The line producer was Playfilms, Incorporated, which as somebody pointed out, "was just another way of saying Penn and Coe." Given artistic control, they stuck to their guns and retained Anne, but not without a sacrifice. Reluctant to gamble the full $2 million on a "stage" actress, United Artists summarily chopped the budget by 75 per cent to half a million dollars. But for Penn, Coe, Gibson, and Anne, all of whom had serious reservations about the Hollywood way of thinking, it was a tolerable price to pay for independence, integrity, and creative license.

The third incarnation of *The Miracle Worker* was to most minds a case of a work finally finding its best medium. As a teleplay it had been considered by some to be too stagy, as a stage play too televisually choppy. A screenplay, properly handled, could accommodate both intense long-take dramatic moments and quick-cut narrative devices. Contrary to *Seesaw*, which came to the screen without any of those involved in its stage production, *The Miracle Worker* was transposed nearly intact. William Gibson was writing his own adaptation, Fred Coe was again the producer, Arthur Penn the director. Patty Duke, whom many feared would outgrow the role of Helen during the theatrical run (there was even a contractual height stipulation of fifty-four inches) was still within limits and was asked to repeat her performance for film. Also repeating were Beah Richards and Kathleen Comegys (who first had to be talked out of Florida retirement). The rest of the supporting parts changed hands: Inga Swenson replaced Patricia Neal in the role of Kate Keller, and Victor Jory became Captain Keller.

The show still belonged to Anne and Patty. What remained to be seen was whether or not their consummate stage work would suffer in transition to film. While it was not the first filmwork for Patty (she had three previous appearances, one a documentary), it was her first major featured role. There was also the fear in the back of some minds that the glancingly unappealing graphic depiction that had been so moving onstage might turn unsightly with the intimacy of the camera.

For Anne, it was a return to the medium that had so misused her, and there must have been at least a subliminal twinge at the prospects of again stepping in front of the cameras she had fled almost five years earlier. However, there were many salves for any open wounds. To begin with, the film was being shot on the East Coast, not in Hollywood. A suitable location had already been found in rural New Jersey, and the remaining studio work was set for a New York soundstage. Beyond locale, there was the added comfort of confidence and familiarity with the material and the director.

By June 11, two of three interior sets had been built and a pair of exteriors long since located and adapted. As a television production center, the New York/New Jersey area had already given ground to the West Coast and film production had all but abandoned the East. *The Miracle Worker* company was something of a rarity, and they savored their joint nonconformity. The simple fact that they were out from under Hollywood's thumb carried a distinct cachet and implied that these were creative mavericks, serious artists. In truth they were, and therefore were not obliged to take themselves overly seriously. There was a healthy, genial, but professional atmosphere about the production. As director Penn told reporters: "Things are a little raw-er here, but that's all to the good, it's freer." In addition to the obvious artistic amenities, Anne thrilled to the convenience of shooting virtually in her own backyard, and the relief of being able to return home after a day's work and not to the insufferable stucco of some Hollywood hotel.

The film had been many months in planning and preparation. There was for the director a dual incentive to the meticulous groundwork. One was the natural inclination to take a proven good work and try to perfect it. As Penn saw it, "Our main problem was not in expanding the action to fit the screen, but rather in compressing it for an elliptical, intimate medium." Which was another way of saying that he didn't merely want "filmed theatre," with its flatness and overprojection. Beyond a conceptual overview, there were specific structural flaws both he and Gibson were eager to patch over. Foremost was Annie Sullivan's flashbacks, which in the play were cued by offstage voices—the sort of narrative shortcut that had bothered Brooks Atkinson and which Gibson had come to call "cough time" because of the bored restlessness of the audience at these interludes. The flashbacks could not be dropped from the picture because they contained necessary information and insights into Sullivan's character. Aware that the attention span of average movie audiences was at best a fraction of that of theatre audiences, Penn knew that the flashbacks had to be carried off with a certain inventiveness without unnecessary concession to gimmickry. Ultimately, Penn settled on a stylized visual effect that would diffuse the past images into a grainy impression (as Brock Bowar astutely pointed out in his *Times* profile: "Dramatically, the scenes now become almost retinal memory, matching in their blurry texture the actual visual distortions of Anne Sullivan's half-blind childhood."). That way, Penn would be able to mingle his directorial styles, breaking up the film's basic traditional look with more modernistic touches.

But these decisions fell under the heading of stylistic judgments, and while of considerable gravity, they still did not speak directly to an underlying incentive shared by Penn and Coe. Three years before, the two had made their movie debut with a rehash of the Billy the Kid lore entitled *Left Handed Gun.* The film had starred Paul Newman, and it was a prime example of the heavily psychologized "Method Westerns" that had been infiltrating Hollywood's most beloved genre. Afterward, Penn realized the film had in many ways been misconceived and specifically misdirected at many points. *The Miracle Worker* would be Penn and Coe's first film since that disappointing first effort, and they were understandably eager to even the score.

Exterior shooting began on location at an old Victorian farmhouse in Middletown, New Jersey, and was completed by mid-July. The company then moved to Manhattan to shoot interiors at the production center on West Twenty-sixth Street, nestled in the city's garment district. The mood was contagiously optimistic, especially for Anne, who was within walking distance of her Village brownstone. She would rise early each morning, and at six o'clock set out for the studio, only a dozen blocks or so to the north. It was an invigorating way to begin the day, and it plainly showed in her work, which seemed even better than her nearly flawless stage performance.

In the back of everybody's mind was the upcoming shooting of the "battle royal," which in many ways would be the acid test for the film. In addition to the implicit dramatic demands was a host of technical worries. The scene's chaotic improvisational side which had never failed to work onstage, would be difficult to film unobtrusively. Penn decided to record the scene with three cameras, and after repadding Anne and Patty and getting them back into fighting shape, filming got under way. In all, it took five days to get what would amount to nine minutes in the film, but the results were electrifying. Penn recalled that by the completion of shooting on the fifth day, "Annie and Patty Duke were whipped, so were we all."

Principal photography concluded on schedule. Early signs were that Anne had tastefully scaled down her performance to fit the medium, and in the process had again earned the admiration of her peers. It was the sort of thing that prompted Penn to tell reporters: "You have to understand, you see, that Annie's a very gutsy girl. I swear I wouldn't hesitate to put her in at shortstop for the New York Yankees." She may have been gutsy but she was not invincible. Feeling unusually fatigued at the end of shooting, she finally visited her physician who informed her that she had pneumonia. Anne was hospitalized for two weeks and then ordered to Fire Island for a month's recuperation.

While Anne awaited what everyone assumed would be a triumphant movie homecoming, Mel was hardly marking time. The first 2000 *Year Old Man* album had already generated a pair of sequels—*2000 and One Years with Carl Reiner and Mel Brooks* and *Carl Reiner and Mel Brooks at the Cannes Film Festival.* Neither offshoot was quite up to the original, but neither was far off the mark. In addition to being a writer who also sometimes performed, Mel was moving into yet another category—celebrity. While the Old Man had a staunch following, Mel himself enjoyed what was essentially overgrown cult recognition, which was as much as might be expected from fame that was attached to a record album. But Mel, who had always indisputably been a personality, was fast becoming a television celebrity, the personality public and one better. Along with Rudy Vallee, Tony Bennett, and Joan Crawford, Mel appeared on the "Tonight Show" the night of Johnny Carson's debut, and all but stole the show. Mel was enjoying the limelight. It gave him the chance to do what he did best—talk and entertain, tossing off a kind of superitalicized world view.

By late April of '62, *The Miracle Worker* was ready for distribution. The advance review in *Variety* was complimentary though short of ecstatic, and it carried an odd caveat: ". . . Its appeal may be leveled somewhat by a curious reluctance on the part of some people to expose themselves to such a grim, emo-

tionally devastating experience." What was especially annoying
about the view was that it overlooked the fact that any unsettling realism was really just a long, dramatic prelude to the
uplifting, climactic scene. *Variety* typified the sort of misap-
prehension that led William Gibson to repeat a particular anec-
dote: "Somebody asked Anne Bancroft if it wasn't a sad play, all
that stuff about a deaf, dumb and blind child. To which Anne
replied, 'Yeah, sad like Christmas!'" In fact, what had struck *Variety* as a somewhat grim depiction had had just the opposite
concern for Penn, who feared that the play's final miraculous
breakthrough was too pat for film, and had prompted him with
Gibson to subtly shift emphasis at the end: "In the film, after
Helen's breakthrough, you're led to wonder: 'Will she hold it?'
. . . instead of Helen suddenly being in the promised land as in
the play."

At any rate, the theatrical release of the film brought a rush
of adulation and most reviewers found a great deal to like and
very little to be squeamish about. Anne's performance was
breathtaking. From the moment of her first entrance, she com-
mands the screen. There is a tacit sense of interior about her that
works in counterpoint to the character's forthright and volatile
exterior. Penn's direction is sensitive and always in service to the
film. The strictly narrative camerawork is virtually seamless, allowing the cast room in which to work and continuity with
which to sustain that work. Except for a rather baffling opening
montage which first brings Sullivan to the Keller home in Tus-
cumbia, Alabama, the more stylized directorial touches work
beautifully. The flashbacks, in particular, achieve precisely what
Penn had hoped for: establishing a factual, chronological backdrop; setting interpersonal parallels between Annie's childhood
and Helen's plight; and ultimately, integrating the past and present in a kind of narrative deep focus. The visual and optical
effects are all worked in integrally so that the flashbacks seem to
magnify the story's texture rather than disrupt it. Penn adds to
this effective use of somewhat more modern techniques, a
proficiency for more traditional direction as well. The camerawork is the agent of the shifting emphasis Penn was seeking in
this transposition. The final boom shot, beginning with Annie

and Helen's climactic revelation at the water pump, quickly recedes up and away as if to place this in some fuller cosmic perspective, raising the intended doubt as to whether the young girl
will now be able to find a meaningful place in the world.

One month after the movie's opening, there was a special
benefit screening of the film to raise money for the American
Foundation for the Blind and Research to Prevent Blindness. It
was a star-studded gathering, with such guests as Cary Grant,
Lauren Bacall, Margaret Leighton, Irene Dunne, Joan Fontaine,
William Bendix, Jane Powell, and Ray Bolger. But the crowd of
onlookers at the police barricades outside the Sutton Theatre
was more interested in catching a glimpse of Anne. She arrived
wearing a simple black gown and cape, and the applause was
overwhelming. Afterward the guests gathered at the nearby
MCA offices, and aside from raising some $40,000 for charity, the
evening seemed to validate what the theatregoing public had
already known for four years—that Anne Bancroft was an actress of powerful range and stature. She had returned to film on
her own terms, and while she was pleased with the film's success,
she gave no indication of being self-impressed. She had done a
job, done it well, and was already looking forward to the next
job.

But first, she had more obligations to *The Miracle Worker*.
The film was to be presented at Spain's San Sebastián Film
Festival and Anne was to accompany it. In August, she agreed
to an interview with Neil Hickey of *The American Weekly*, and
she admitted that a trip to Spain was less than appealing to her:
"When you're in love, it's no fun going away. I should be looking forward to this trip more than I am." Unsurprisingly, Hickey
asked about this love interest, and Anne enthusiastically replied:
"Mel is so wonderful. Most people, if you pinch them, they come
out with a conventional 'ouch.' But he never says anything ordinary, he's so alive to the fun of life." That said, the interview
swung to the topic of marriage: "All of my family is very religious. My grandmother is especially concerned about me, because to her I'm not Anne Bancroft, after all. I'm her grand-
daughter. She knows that next September 17th I'll be 31 years
old, and she feels that an unmarried woman at that age isn't safe,

so I have my grandmother's permission to marry again if I want to. That means a lot."

Permission or not, Anne and Mel were not falling over themselves to get married. They shared the trepidation of the not-so-distantly divorced, as well as serious apprehensions about the possibility of one marriage embracing two careers. Anne had already set the precondition that any mate would have to accept her as a "totally involved actress." Likewise, it was understood that Mel's approach to work could never be anything other than it had always been—totally involved. They first had somehow to resolve that polarity before seriously considering marriage.

Mel was without steady work, but he was still known as one of the better comedy writers in New York and the next job was only ever a phone call away. One call in late fall brought him down to Philadelphia, the scene of memorable wrangles with the late *All American*. Sidney Lumet had agreed to direct a three-act musical comedy about a pair of resourceful Prohibition agents who use disguises to undermine bootleggers. The show, *Nowhere to Go but Up*, featured a fine cast headed by Tom Bosley and Martin Balsam, with Dorothy Louden, Bert Convy, and everybody's favorite gangster character actor, Bruce Gordon. James Lipton had written the book and lyrics, Sol Berkowitz the music, and the show was being produced by Kermit Bloomgarden and Herbert Greene. There was only one problem—the show was in trouble and floundering in Philadelphia, with a November 10 New York première. Mel was asked to help get the show back on its feet, and he tried valiantly but in vain. *Nowhere to Go but Up* opened at the Shubert Theatre to what was at best a lukewarm critical reception, did only middling business, and then moved to the Winter Garden (site of *All American*'s last gasp) where it fared even worse. *Nowhere* went precisely nowhere and the producers decided to close the show. But the backers, who had helped pay the production's lavish price tag of $350,000, refused to let it die a quiet death. Closing notices were no sooner posted than pickets appeared outside the Winter Garden, insisting the show remain open and threatening to seek a court order to insure that no further steps be taken to close. The investors, some two hundred in all, were eventually convinced of the futility of the show's staying open at a sizable daily loss and finally let it go by the board.

It was just one of a run of recent letdowns for Mel. Far more lamentable was his failure to find a taker for a screenplay he had written, *Marriage Is a Dirty Rotten Fraud* (a subject close to his heart since that year, 1962, his breakup with Florence finally became official). If Mel's career had passed into the doldrums, at least his personal life was active. Mel had abandoned his Perry Street cubbyhole and moved in with his old friend Speed Vogel. The two of them became the nucleus of a conversation *cum* eating club with an imposing membership that would in time include Joseph Heller, Ngoot Lee, Mario Puzo, and Zero Mostel. Mindful of the once-renowned Algonquin Round Table, they took to calling their regular conclave the "Oblong Table." The high-powered company provided Mel with much of the intellectual stimulation that was singularly missing from his career. And, of course, there was Mel's relationship with Anne.

After the nationwide success of *The Miracle Worker*, Anne occupied herself reading and rejecting the scripts with which she was now swamped. If she had learned nothing else from her Hollywood odyssey, it was to be circumspect in selecting roles. When columnist Earl Wilson asked her if she wouldn't prefer some property that would allow her to play a more physically flattering part, she replied: "Sure, but I wouldn't do a play just to prove I'm attractive. If the script is great, I'd do Abraham Lincoln." In truth Anne had spent some six months looking at scripts that might allow her glamour as well as good acting, but finally despaired of finding what she referred to as a worthy "heels and hose" role. Afterward, when asked if she was avoiding work, she shot back: "No, just bad scripts."

The selective was inescapably subjective and Anne's judgment was hardly infallible. At one point she was approached by composer Jule Styne and asked if she would be interested in starring in a musical based on the life of Fanny Brice. Isobel Lennart had already written a libretto which Styne was to score, Ray Stark produce, and Jerome Robbins direct. It was a tempting offer.

Anne's first love had always been singing, and since resuming voice lessons she wanted very much to appear in a musical. She had even prepared a scene from *My Fair Lady* for the Actors Studio and reportedly done well by "Just You Wait, Henry Higgins." Anne was shown a draft of the Lennart play which she read and then declined. Later she confided to friends that she thought it not at all good. A young actress currently stealing the show in *I Can Get It for You Wholesale* thought better of it, and Barbra Streisand and *Funny Girl* became the best things ever to happen to each other.

If Anne lost the opportunity, she still got the director. After long deliberation, she decided to appear in a new translation of the Bertolt Brecht play, *Mother Courage and Her Children* to be staged by Jerome Robbins. She had already been offered the role once before by producer Cheryl Crawford, but refused. Later Anne attended Crawford's off-Broadway production *Brecht on Brecht* and was so impressed by what she saw that she soon read all the Brecht she could lay her hands on. When Crawford tendered a second offer, Anne accepted.

It seemed to some an odd choice. As Mother Courage, Anne would be playing a character many years her senior, and that would require heavy makeup and heavily padded costumes. And even though the play involved singing, the subject matter—the Thirty Years' War—and the Brechtian tone and practice of pre-announced didactic plotting stamped this as anything but the conventional Broadway musical showpiece. But then, Anne had been looking for something different.

The play had been written in 1939 and turned a bitter eye to the subject of war. It is set in the seventeenth century and concerns a woman referred to as Mother Courage who is a petty war profiteer, a camp follower peddling wares to whatever army is at hand. The war costs her her two sons and daughter, but she survives to continue as she has in the past, making her living from the fortunes of war. The play was being directed with an eye to its inherent symbolism, as Anne explained at the time: "Mr. Robbins feels that this is not so much a play about war as a play about business, about the cost of being in business. We have done some improvisation on business, on buying and selling."

Any way she looked at it, it was a far cry from "Don't Rain on My Parade."

The play was scheduled for a March opening at the Martin Beck Theatre. Although this was to be the first time the piece had been performed on Broadway, none of those involved expected a runaway hit. Anne's decision had been an artistic one, and she suffered no illusions, nor for that matter, did she spare the part any of the assiduous research which had become something of a trademark. She boned up on the pertinent history, examined the work of the seventeenth-century painter, Brueghel, and, in hopes of arriving at some sense of the desolation of the Thirty Years' War, toured New York's slums and even arranged to visit Hortense W. Gabel of the Mayor's Housing and Redevelopment Board.

The play was cast and the "who's who" brimmed with talented, young actors, among them: Zohra Lampert, Eugene Roche, Barbara Harris, and a mild-mannered, angelic-looking young man, Gene Wilder. The sets were designed by Ming Cho Lee and patterned after those used in Brecht's Berliner Ensemble production. Robbins' direction was likewise styled after the original. Everything was proceeding more or less on course for opening, when it seemed there might be a possible obstacle.

The Academy Award nominations had been released, and Anne was among those in the running for best actress for her work in *The Miracle Worker*. Ordinarily she might have gone, but the Awards ceremony took place on April 9, at which point the play would have been less than two weeks into its run. She decided to ask Mel's opinion. He took one look at the competition—Lee Remick for *Days of Wine and Roses*, Geraldine Page for *Sweet Bird of Youth*, Bette Davis for *What Ever Happened to Baby Jane?*, and Katharine Hepburn for *Long Day's Journey Into Night*—and essentially told her to save the airfare, adding later: "I didn't think she had a chance in the world and I told her so. We felt that with Hepburn and Davis in it, that Hollywood would salute them for thirty years . . . that Bancroft was a theatre personality and that Hollywood would honor its own." Mel was not in the habit of sugarcoating reality.

Convinced that her Oscar nomination was likely to be the ex-

The newlyweds, one week after their August 1964 wedding.
(WIDE WORLD PHOTOS)

Anne as a suicidal housewife in *The Slender Thread,* 1965.
(FROM THE PENGUIN COLLECTION)

On the set of *7 Women,* 1965, Anne stands between Margaret Leighton and director John Ford. (WIDE WORLD PHOTOS)

Mel in song with Dom DeLuise on location in Yugoslavia for *The Twelve Chairs*, 1970. (WIDE WORLD PHOTOS)

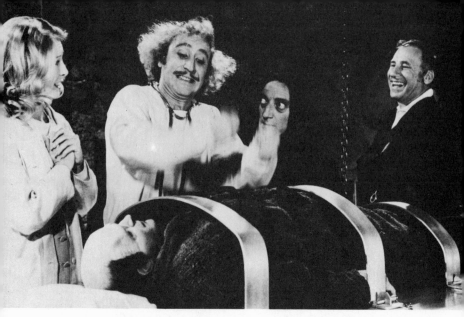

On the set of *Young Frankenstein*, 1974, with left to right: Teri Garr, Gene Wilder, Marty Feldman, and (supine) Peter Boyle. (WIDE WORLD PHOTOS)

Mel on the set of the short-lived television series "When Things Were Rotten," 1975. (WIDE WORLD PHOTOS)

A street-corner candid, from left to right: Ron Clark, Mel, and Will Jordan. (COURTESY WILL JORDAN)

Preparing *Golda*, Anne seated between her favorite playwright, William Gibson, and her favorite director, Arthur Penn.

(PHOTOGRAPH HELEN MARCUS)

Between shots on *Silent Movie*, 1976, Mel with Dom DeLuise and Marty Feldman. (COURTESY WILL JORDAN)

Anne with Golda Meir en route to a reception following the gala preview of *Golda,* 1977. (WIDE WORLD PHOTOS)

Mel with Alfred Hitchcock discussing the "Hitchcockian" *High Anxiety,* 1977. (WIDE WORLD PHOTOS)

The Turning Point, 1978. (WIDE WORLD PHOTOS)

tent of the compliment paid her by the Hollywood establishment, Anne turned her full attention to the play. However,
while Anne was preparing a serious theatre role, there was out
West some perfectly ridiculous Hollywood maneuvering going
on around her nomination. Joan Crawford had been passed over
in the best actress category for her co-star from *Baby Jane*, Bette
Davis. Determined to have a share of the spotlight, if only by
proxy, Crawford arranged to stand in for any absent nominee,
which meant, that if Anne somehow won, she would have a
rather illustrious Oscar caddy.

Nothing could have been further from Anne's mind than Hollywood vanities. Not only was her preparation for *Mother Courage* arduous, but the role itself was grueling. The show opened
on March 30 and was well received, that is, by all but Millie,
who had certain motherly reservations about the part. She was
alarmed to see her little girl trudging around in heavy padding,
pulling a wooden cart, and said so in no uncertain terms afterward backstage: "Listen, miss, you take your vitamins every day
and get plenty of sleep or else!" Anne couldn't resist asking: "Or
else what, Ma?" But Millie was unfazed: "Or else . . . or else
you can't work here! That's what else." Reflecting on the exchange later, Anne reflected with some irony: "She was going to
put me out of the play. Maybe I ought to tell her I'm a goddess."
The incident was typical of how unchanged Anne's family was
by her success. They were terribly proud and thoroughly accepting of her work, but as Anne pointed out they never pretended
to advise or criticize her: "When they come to see me, if I don't
forget my lines, that's good enough for them."

The notices for *Mother Courage* were approving, thoughtfully
written, and intellectually piqued as befits Brecht. There was
praise for the staging and sets, and some mention of the supporting work, but predictably most of the critical attention gravi-
tated toward Anne. The fact that she would follow a celebrated
film role with an unusual and unflattering stage role provoked a
great deal of curiosity as well as admiration for her decision not
to capitalize on screen success with some lightweight role. The
Daily News's John Chapman readily pointed out that she had, as
expected, sustained her penchant for the unexpected: "Anne

Bancroft has added a powerful characterization to her little string of notable performances," adding, "It is a brilliant portrayal and diamond-hard." The *Post*'s Richard Watts, Jr., also attested to her brilliance, explaining: "Miss Bancroft . . . achieves a lovely magnificence in her final moments." Howard Taubman, writing for the *Times*, welcomed this departure from ordinary Broadway productions and found the play well executed at every level. Of Anne's performance, he wrote: "Anne Bancroft plays Mother Courage with surface impassivity through which gleam heartiness and cunning and, at the right rare moments, emotion." He was equally struck by her detectably modern conception of the character, as well as by her singing: "She speaks with a marked New York accent which, though odd for the Thirty Years' War, conveys the sense of a toughened working woman, and she sings creditably in a pleasant voice."

Critical endorsements notwithstanding, attendance quickly tapered off as the play began its run. Without Anne, it's doubtful the material would even have reached Broadway. With her, it was still failing to draw well enough to meet expenses. However, Anne had signed on through January and was even willing to go off-Broadway in order to honor that commitment. The show's press agent did what he could to stir interest, but nothing seemed to work. What he needed was a minor miracle, for instance the leading lady turning up with an Academy Award.

On April 9, Anne left the Martin Beck Theatre and hurried home to catch the tail end of the televised Awards ceremony. Mel was there to greet her, and the two of them were joined by Anne's press agent, Lillian Pickard. Anne arrived to discover that William Gibson had lost to Horton Foote (*To Kill a Mockingbird*) in the category of Best Screenplay Based on Material from Another Medium, and that Arthur Penn had been passed over for David Lean (*Lawrence of Arabia*) for best director. While in the taxi coming home she had heard over the radio that Patty Duke had survived stiff competition (Shirley Knight, Angela Lansbury, Thelma Ritter, and Mary Badham) and had come up with an Oscar for Best Supporting Actress, thus becoming the youngest woman to receive that award.

Patty's award seemed to further weaken Anne's chances. But

she and Mel sat glued to her color television set and watched
Maximilian Schell recite the list of Best Actress nominees, fum-
ble with the envelope, and announce the winner: "Anne Bancroft."

Anne buried her face in her hands, then looked up to see a
beaming and ultra-glamorized Joan Crawford holding the stat-
uette, and shouted laughingly: "My God! Joan Crawford looks
like me!" She gave Mel a big kiss, collected herself, and called
her family to celebrate the news, while Mel smugly told reporters that he felt Hollywood had vindicated itself: "It's a
tribute to them that they dug two unusual performances—Patty's
and Anne's."

Anne shared the cover of the next morning's *News* with Best
Actor winner, Gregory Peck, and the *Mother Courage* publicist
quickly shifted into gear with an ad reading: "Annie Won It,
and We've Got Her." A few days later, Joan Crawford paid a
surprise visit to the Martin Beck Theatre and presented the Oscar to Anne during curtain calls, and the two women were
caught in an almost surreal photograph—the aging Crawford,
glittering, made-up, and doing her level best to look half her
age; Anne, in costume and looking like some weathered washer-
woman twice her age. Despite Anne's newfound fame, the press
attention she generated failed to revive her play, and *Mother
Courage* closed on May 11 after only fifty-two performances.
Anne took the closing philosophically: "I didn't expect 'Courage'
to be a popular play, but I wanted to do it anyway." She went on
to compare the decision to a Hollywood marriage: "They know
it won't last, but they want the experience anyway."

The Oscar had catapulted Anne into headlines and the press
attention quickly encircled those around her, in particular Mel.
Reporters repeatedly asked him if the two of them had any plans
for marriage, but he would only put them off coyly: "It's up in
the air, but we might bring it down to earth." When the *Post*'s
Ralph Blumenfeld asked point-blank: "Is it love?" Mel was a
little more candid: "Well, let's just say we have an affection for
each other and we like each other . . . and I'm crazy about her
and I'd kill for her!"

14

April 1964. The Santa Monica Civic Auditorium was filled to overflowing with some 2,500 celebrities, smiling, bejeweled, and dressed to the teeth. Among them were Mel Brooks, and a terribly nervous Anne Bancroft. It was Academy Awards night, the first not only for Mel but for Anne as well. This year however, Anne's name was not among the nominees, since her most recent film had been completed much too late to even be in the running for the current Oscars. Her reason for being there was Mel.

Two years before, Mel had gone to see a movie which was preceded by a brief animated work by Norman McLaren. Behind Mel sat an elderly man who was clearly unimpressed with the abstract piece and muttered as much to himself throughout. It was a priceless slice-of-life vignette and afterward Mel asked his friend Ernest Pintoff to help him recreate it all as a satirical short. Pintoff became producer-director, Bob Heath designer-animator, Mel writer-reciter, and the result was just over three minutes of animated film with a running improvised commentary by Mel, called *The Critic*. The film had been nominated for best short subject in the cartoon category, and Anne was more excited over this than her own nomination the year before.

The Critic is a small gem, perfect in every facet. It opens
with a succession of animated geometrical shapes changing form
and color in time to baroque music. It seems the very sort of art
film for which McLaren was known. However, the elevated
mood of it all is soon broken by the sound of shuffling feet and
an intrusive voice—unmistakably that of some elderly Jewish
man—asking no one in particular: "Vhat d'ell is this?" Soon the
satire is apparent, an old man who has come to see a movie and
is trying to make sense of the prefeature short subject. His running commentary is our "critic." The next image is of some fore-
ground pink configuration which recedes into the distance:
"This is cute, this is cute, this is nice. Vat da hell is it?" He then
tries to answer his own question: "It must be some symbolism
. . . I think it's symbolic of junk." The images flow, and the
man's patience ebbs. "That fella that made this . . . Vat does he
vaste his time with this? A fella like that, he probably could
drive a truck, do something constructive. Make a shoe." And
finally, his critique: "I don't know much about psych-analysis,
but I'd say this was a dirty picture." Music up, fade, credits. It
was a masterpiece in miniature. More than just further mileage
out of the 2,000 Year Old Man persona, *The Critic* was a tightly
made satire which worked beautifully.

When it came time for Award presentation, *An Occurrence at
Owl Creek* was named Best Short Subject, live action, *The Critic*,
Best Short Subject, animation. Mel and Anne now had matching
Oscars. They might have made nice bookends except that Kitty,
like Millie before her, would be the statue's curator. Before Anne
and Mel could leave town, Anne was buttonholed by Louella
Parsons, an acquaintance from the Fox days, and Parsons was
itching to know of any marital plans. The most Anne would say
was: "I'm at that time in my life where you stop looking for the
man on the white horse and settle for another human being."

The ill-fated *Mother Courage* may have momentarily damp-
ened Anne's enthusiasm for the stage, but with movie offers
constantly pouring in, there was no scarcity of work. Unchanged
in her thinking by her Oscar, Anne still exercised the utmost discretion in her professional commitments. If it was a matter of
months between jobs, that was a luxury she could well afford, as

well as something she could now better deal with emotionally. Only three years before, Anne had felt a constant urgency to be working, to step from one project to the next. As she explained at the time in a published conversation with her Actors Studio instructor, Paula Strasberg: "When I'm not working, I sometimes feel if I don't get a job soon, I'll probably ruin everybody around me. You know, I feel sorry for what my poor boy friend has had to listen to and put up with sometimes." Anne admitted she had been thinking of marriage but was afraid of the potential conflicts between her career and a home life, to say nothing of the complications of motherhood.

Career won out, for the moment anyway. At the suggestion of her agent, Anne had read Penelope Mortimer's novel, *The Pumpkin Eater,* which director Jack Clayton was planning to turn into a motion picture from an adaptation by Harold Pinter. She promptly told her agent that she "desperately" wanted the lead role of Jo, only to learn that she was being considered for it along with a dozen other actresses. Anne was not about to give up without a fight, and figuring that the shortest distance between an actress and a part was a straight line, fired off a cable to Jack Clayton which said succinctly: "Only I can play this role." She received a return cable: "Please send stills." Anne promptly sent several production stills from *The Miracle Worker,* but these mostly showed her in various states of dishevelment following the battle royal and Clayton cabled back asking for more, insisting that he still didn't know what Anne looked like. Tiring of the continued confusion by cable, Anne caught a flight to London. It was a gamble, but it paid off, as Clayton pointed out: "The first time I set eyes on her, I agreed with her. No one but Anne can play this role. You'd never know it from *The Miracle Worker,* but she's beautiful."

Filming was to begin in early autumn at England's Shepperton Studios. But Anne left for London in late summer in order to spend some five weeks researching her British accent. She was to have such superior company as Peter Finch, James Mason, Cedric Hardwicke, Eric Porter, and Maggie Smith (to say nothing of periodic visits from Mel). But what had really attracted her was the role itself.

Jo is a complicated, even convoluted personality, with an odd proclivity for procreation bordering on compulsion. She has been widowed once, divorced once, and is now married to a writer whose sudden success leaves her in a state of advanced bourgeois *anomie* which deepens into melancholy and depression, and eventually leads to a breakdown. Jo visits a psychiatrist who intimates rather frostily: "Perhaps sex is something you feel you must sanctify, as it were, with incessant reproduction." She no sooner comes around to his way of thinking than she discovers she is pregnant. Afraid that another child will ruin the marriage, she chooses an abortion, and with some dubious persuasion from a doctor, agrees to a hysterectomy in the process. That supreme sacrifice made in the interest of her marriage, she discovers that her husband has been having an affair, and, after beating the hell out of him in a fit of rage, walks out. Ultimately, the two are reconciled in a sensitively played scene conducted mostly visually, and, which although it holds out hope for the future, registers the hurt that has gone on before.

It was a modern if enigmatic role, precisely the sort Anne had been looking for and she wore it like a second skin. She prepared a soft but precise British accent, and neither favored nor upstaged her imposing cast but met them on an equal footing in scenes that were often acted better than they were written or directed. Anne not only won considerable respect as an American portraying a Briton in a British production, but also managed on one occasion to scare the wits out of her leading man, Peter Finch. The script called for a confrontation between Jo and her husband Jake (Finch) once she has discovered his philandering. The scene was to end in a fight, which Anne went about tooth and nail. In all it took two and a half days to arrive at what amounted to forty-five seconds of screen time, and when it was over Finch emerged much the worse for the wear: "I had to remind myself she was only acting. Thank heavens she was only acting. I thought she was going to kill me." Anne was understanding if short of sympathetic: "I was the aggressor—I enjoyed that—it's harder to be the receiver."

The Pumpkin Eater wrapped in mid-December 1963 and Anne returned to England the following July for its première at

London's Columbia Theatre. The film was well received, certainly more so than in its November opening in New York, where critics differed. Some thought the film held up well, given the oppressive subject matter. Others thought it deliberate and overdirected, with a brooding quality that permeated the writing, direction, and even the score. All seemed to agree that, whatever the various imperfections, Anne's was a gutsy performance and a sensitive handling of a difficult and unique woman's role. That view was born out by Anne's Oscar nomination for best actress (which she lost, ironically, to Julie Andrews for *Mary Poppins*) and a nomination for best actress at the Cannes Film Festival, which she won.

Nineteen sixty-four had been a winning year in more ways than one. After several years of little more than flirtation with television, Mel was again trying his hand at the network shell game. A year earlier, Sean Connery had made his debut as Ian Fleming's consummate secret agent, James Bond in *Dr. No*. Since that time, another Bond film was in the can, another was on the way, and the mid-sixties spy rage was off, running, and ripe for parody. Danny Melnick had talked it over with David Susskind (both of them television producers), and Susskind went off to have a look at this character, Bond. He was so inspired by the idea of a secret-agent parody that he returned to his office at the Newsweek Building on Madison Avenue prepared to talk it over with the first willing listeners. At the time, the Susskind office was a hangout for actors and writers "between jobs." In fact, there was a pool table in one room where Peter Falk's sharpshooting had already become legend. The day Susskind returned to his elite pool hall, he was greeted by a pair of comedy writers—Buck Henry and Mel Brooks. The two had already been in touch with Melnick, and Susskind's enthusiasm sealed the deal.

ABC anted up the "development" money—a network's way of speculating before deciding whether to commit time and resources to an actual pilot and series—and Mel and Buck went to work. They had in mind a protagonist who would be well-meaning, self-confident, and incompetent; a bungling anti-hero who would clumsily capsize the Connery-Bond chic. Mel and Buck refused to pad the character with some play-safe affability that might place him more in the mainstream of likable situation-comedy buffoons. If anything, they were working against the grain of rampant television blandness. Their character would be pedantic, officious, above all maladroit, with no blatant pitch for audience sympathy. The last thing they wanted was Ozzie Nelson *à la* CIA. What they came up with after several weeks' work was "Maxwell Smart," a.k.a. Secret Agent 86 working for CONTROL and combating the combined forces of evil, that is, a diabolical rival organization, KAOS.

"Get Smart" was, from its inception, a different comedy. Unlike so many other sixties situation comedies—whose chief aim was to be inoffensive, an ode to demographics for the broadest appeal to the largest number of people, television's answer to Tupperware—the pilot upheld the primacy of comedy. In that sense, both Mel and Buck were purists who agreed that it was not the job of television comedy to perpetuate some middle-class ideal. Good comedy was its own best argument, and they went about their work patiently and painstakingly. Most comedy concepts (as the prepilot "premises" are known) were tossed off quickly, the facile blend of formula and a few bright lines. Mel and Buck created from scratch, using the Bond mold as a vague reverse reference point but not as a literal negative model, since the character (as conceived by Ian Fleming and personified by Connery) contained a good deal of its own self-parody. They not only wrote the pilot but improvised it, using a practical-minded trial-and-error method which helped them weed out lines which read funny but didn't play. In the end, they had synthesized a half-hour pilot not one line of which was untested or ill-considered. Maxwell Smart's supporting cast consisted of Agent 99, a woman, capable as he was inept; the Chief, deadpan and long-suffering, ever amazed at Smart's knack for snatching defeat from the jaws of triumph (and vice versa); and an assortment of minor agents and distinctively wrought villains. The first episode pitted Smart against a notorious Mr. Big (to be played, of course, by a midget) who having kidnaped a certain Professor Dante and his doomsday melting machine "the Inthermo," demands a ransom of $100 million.

The pilot was ingenious, grouping elements of low comedy with a certain comic sophistication, yet not straying from a sustained if obviously strained plot. The script was prepared, polished, and submitted to ABC. The network wavered for nearly three months before rejecting it. Program executives called it "too wild." What was meant was "too different," and Mel and Buck set about implementing changes that might make the script more acceptable to the bland network palate. They even went so far as adding a dog, but that failed to win them any points, since in keeping with the show's general irreverence, the dog was cowardly and asthmatic.

ABC wrote off the nominal seed money and passed on the pilot. That left Mel and Buck with a script without a home. "Get Smart" seemed destined for some pilot graveyard when Mel chanced upon an acquaintance in a hotel lobby, producer Grant Tinker. The two made conversation, and according to the protocol of such show business meetings, Tinker asked Mel what he was currently doing. Mel promptly answered: "Well, Buck and I wrote this script," and before it was all over, Tinker had offered to take the pilot to NBC. Within ten days, word returned—"Get Smart" had found a home. Production quickly shifted into gear, with a scheduled September '65 debut. Barbara Feldon, a model then popular for a scintillating cologne commercial in which she purred atop a tiger-skin rug, was hired to play Agent 99. Ed Platt, an excellent character actor, became the Chief. The diminutive Michael Dunn was cast as Mr. Big. And the title role was handed to a young comedian who seemed tailor-made for the part—Don Adams. For a director, they turned to Mel's close friend dating back to "Your Show of Shows," Howie Morris, who had effectively turned his expertise from acting to directing and already had a pair of films to his credit, including the successful *40 Pounds of Trouble*.

Mel was anticipating his first real financial stability since parting with Sid. That meant an entirely new complexion for his life, particularly his love life. In some three years together, Anne and Mel had worked out many of the problems that had, at one time or other, seemed insurmountable. She had dispelled many of her compulsions for constant work while Mel, at the same time, had come to accept her continued devotion to her career. Anne had long since been accorded the unsolicited family sanctions for remarriage, and Kitty Kaminsky was ever willing to abide by whatever her Melvin chose. That had left Mel's employment uncertainty as the lone stated stumbling block, although it was probably more of a blind for their lingering mutual ambivalence toward marriage.

Mel and Anne had taken a house on Fire Island for the summer of '64, repairing to separate rooms for family visits. When NBC picked up the pilot, the promise of Mel's solvency seemed to throw a new light on the topic of matrimony, but no one was immediately saying anything. Finally, Anne approached Mel and broke the ice: "Why don't we get married? It'll be so much easier for the folks to deal with our relationship." Mel said, "Fine," and Anne nearly fainted. She instinctively recoiled: "Well, I don't know if I want to do this—really get *married*." Though she had been talking about remarriage for years, the sudden reality of it was unsettling. They talked about it, and thought about it.

On August 5, 1964 at lunchtime, Deputy City Clerk Thomas F. McLaughlin was greeted by a man and woman asking to be married in a civil ceremony. They presented him with a marriage license which read "Mel Brooks" and "Anne Italiano." On the way into the Clerk's office, Mel had stopped a young black man, Andrew Boone, and asked him to serve as witness. Everything seemed in order except for one small matter—the ring. There was none. Caught up in the spirit of the moment, Anne offered one of the thin silver earrings she was wearing, and with that, the ceremony was performed. The newlyweds left City Hall and went their separate ways, Mel back to work, Anne back to her brownstone to prepare a sumptuous wedding night spaghetti supper. Asked some time later whether there had been any parental opposition to the choice of husbands, Anne explained: "I was single for a long time. I was divorced and single and living a very wild life. My mother was so happy I got married, it could have been to an orangutan." Actually, the parents were thrilled with the news.

The marriage was an open secret for a week, then it became official with a captioned picture in the *News*. Some friends and acquaintances sent congratulations, others laid odds against the marriage lasting the year, others did both. Outsiders were mystified by the union, but insiders knew there were any number of similarities in background, temperament, professional ups and downs. Though their lives had different starting points, they seemed to approach the same midpoint at roughly the same time, like facing sides of an isosceles triangle. At least one friend and colleague understood one reason why they enjoyed one another's company: Anne loved to laugh, Mel loved to make people laugh, it was as simple as that. But of course, relationships never are. In any case, the newlyweds were too busy to notice the speculation. Mel was still involved with "Get Smart," and Anne, true to her vow to wed marriage and acting, soon packed her bags and headed for Seattle and a movie entitled *The Slender Thread*. They kept in touch by phone.

The Slender Thread was written by Stirling Silliphant (whose first screenplay, *Nightfall*, Anne co-starred in) based on a feature story by *Life* magazine staff writer, Shana Alexander. The original story had documented the role of a recently opened crisis clinic in preventing a single would-be suicide. Using that as his point of departure, Silliphant constructed a story about a young student volunteer at a Seattle crisis clinic who receives a suicide call from a housewife who has just taken an overdose of sleeping pills. The volunteer must summon all his resources to keep the woman conscious until she can be found and medically treated. Where most dramas telescope real time, this one must protract time in order to expand what is really a relatively brief incident. The script resorts to digressions in the form of chronological flashbacks which lay the groundwork for the present predicament. These, then, are intercut with the ongoing telephone conversation and glimpses of a police detective trying and ultimately succeeding in locating the woman. There were good performances by Sidney Poitier, Telly Savalas, and Ed Asner. Anne's frazzled, superrealistic portrayal is essentially sound, but its quiet authenticity is disturbed by the structural devices of flash-back and narration which work at cross purposes with the central story and bleed it of dramatic urgency.

Later, while again on the Coast, Anne agreed to an interview with Hedda Hopper and suffered the questions of Hollywood's leading gossip with surprising good nature. Hopper was especially curious about Anne's marriage to Mel, which she said was rumored to be unhappy, adding that stories had also circulated to the effect that Anne was expecting a baby. Anne mildly teased her: "You shouldn't believe everything you read," adding, "Mel is basically a writer who acts once in a while to get the energy out of his system." Hopper, not content to leave the topic at that, pressed on and was rewarded with a candid reply: "I'm a moody person. When I'm in a bad mood, anything can make me angry; if I'm in a good mood, nothing bothers me. I'm hard to live with; Mel is hard to live with, too. I don't know how we did it but we've been together a year. My husband is one of the funniest men who ever lived; sometimes I laugh at him until tears roll out of my eyes." As Carl Reiner would later add: "Annie and Mel are as well mated as any couple I've ever seen . . . quick to anger, quick to forgive."

Anne would have been content to take temporary leave of film-making and tend to married life, but she had received an offer she ordinarily would have refused and now could not. John Ford, the peerless but aging director, had been preparing a film which, though in all likelihood his last, would represent a radical departure from his classic he-man romantic epics; 7 Women, written by Janet Green and John McCormick, concerned a collection of proper ladies operating a Chinese mission that is suddenly overrun by Mongolian bandits. The pivotal role of a tough-minded, tough-talking woman doctor whose frank modernism at first offends the prim missionaries but later saves them from the hedonistic roughnecks, was to be played by Pat Neal, Anne's friend from the stage production of The Miracle Worker. Miss Neal had already worked three days on the film when she suffered the first of a series of strokes which left her hospitalized and critically ill. Anne was asked to take her place, and although it was not a role she would normally have sought, accepted the offer as a tribute to Pat.

There was actually a good deal to like about the assignment. The cast included Margaret Leighton, Mildred Dunnock, and Dame Flora Robson, as well as Betty Field, Eddie Albert, and the young Sue Lyon. There was the added attraction of working with one of the singular masters of American film, John Ford, who was like no other personality Anne had ever encountered in her acting career. Certainly his reputation for autocratic and at times intimidating rule of his casts was a far cry from the considerate, confidential approach of an Arthur Penn. It would have been hard to imagine two more outwardly opposite personalities than Anne and Ford: the one, urbane, modern bordering on beat, a woman; the other rustic, traditional bordering on antique, and a man's man. There was, however, at least some common ground—both were unflinching professionals, and that was as good a starting point as any. The shooting got under way and there was a far homier mood than anyone might have expected. It was an anomalous scene: a grizzled John Ford with his ominous eyepatch, wearing a faded blue Los Angeles Dodgers baseball cap, chewing an omnipresent cigar and prefacing remarks politely, if solicitously, with "Dear." In the early going, there was some threat of antagonism, as Flora Robson recalled: "He ticked me off a time or two when I'd done something wrong, but I turned him away by accusing him of teasing." But, for the most part, the customarily regimental Ford was the soul of civility, even to the point of scheduling a daily afternoon teatime over which he posted one stern rule—no shop talk. On the table beside him sat a small box of change, and the fine for any lapse into talk about the work at hand was a stiff two bits.

Anne managed from the start to impress the wizened old pro with her rock-hard characterization as well as her high threshold for physical action. In truth, the rough and tumble she'd endured from a dramatic cuffing from Jerry Ryan in *Seesaw*, through the battle royal in *The Miracle Worker*, to the marital roughhousing in *Out on the Outskirts of Town* (which she'd done for ABC) and *The Pumpkin Eater*, had brought her more bruising than a dozen John Wayne barroom brawls. There was a scene in 7

Women which called for Anne to struggle with one of the Mongols before pasting him with a firm swat to the jaw. Her assailant was played by Woody Strode, the muscular former all-American from UCLA. The scene had required a number of retakes since, in the fracas, Strode was inadvertently obscuring Anne's face from view of the camera. When Ford finally got a printable take, he hollered: "Cut, print!" chuckled, and said to Strode: "Okay, Woody, count your teeth."

All things considered, the shooting went smoothly and wrapped in early April, but the finished product fell short of all expectations. The culprit was the script. It was a familiar enough setting—mid-thirties China in the last throes of the feudal war lords and bandit armies. Although the notion of populating the mission with women under a stiff, iron-willed director (Margaret Leighton) who encounters the fresh, equally tough doctor (Anne) was novel in conception, it was drab in execution. As written, the characters were mostly stereotyped, which caused the action to sour into melodrama. Anne's performance is one of the few salvageable parts. Wearing jodhpurs and riding boots, she looks lean and tough. Her short, tousled hair hints of a one-time free spirit now belied by a womanly creased face and set jaw. Contrasting the starchy, Victorian Leighton, she is natural and modern, swaggering, cigarette-wielding, hand-shaking. Inevitably, the character succumbs to the poor writing and veers repeatedly into hokum, with only Anne's presence to keep it from utter cliché. For all the hopeless dialogue she is handed, she is still afforded a memorable exit line. Having exchanged her freedom for that of the missionaries, she sits with the bandit chieftain, Tunga Khan, his unwilling queen. Satisfied that the others are safely away, she proposes a toast, but first slips a dose of poison into both glasses. In a sardonic farewell to Khan, who understands not the least word of English, she says in a conspicuous Bronx accent: "So long, ya basta'd." He drinks and drops off at once. She drinks and smashes the glass to the floor. Up music, fade.

On Saturday, September 18, 1965, "Get Smart" made its television debut and was an instant hit. It was unlike any other comedy then on the air, and its combination of occasional high wit and a generous helping of low humor won an immense following. On the preshow credit crawl, Mel had seen to it that his name loomed large—for the "created by" credit, Mel not only got top billing over Buck, but his name was in lettering nearly twice the size of his collaborator's (it was to be an eternal sore point with Buck and Susskind). As the popularity of "Get Smart" continued to gain momentum, it was, considering the billing, small wonder that most reporters turned to Mel for interviews. He was more than ready for them, with capsule histories of his life as a writer, as well as lofty exegetics on the show's appeal. He told a reporter with the *Herald Tribune*: "It's a show in which you can comment, too. I don't mean we're in the broken-wing business. We're not social workers, but we can do some comment such as you can't inject in, say, "My Three Sons." Later, in an interview with *Playboy* magazine, Mel made it clear that "comments" were not to be confused with "sermons": "For years, 'The Danny Thomas Show' was doing the Ten Commandments." It was a point well taken, although apparently Mel was not above a little pontificating himself. In an interview with Joanne Stang for the *Times*, Mel elaborated on his views of television writing:

> Right now there are guys sitting at typewriters in rooms all over Los Angeles, trying to find sure-fire formulas for what might become wildly successful TV shows. Is this an aggregate waste of talent? I'm not sure. Most of them are probably poor writers, poor thinkers and poor craftsmen, who would do very well to turn out some dopey show every week. It's just that writing has become a business and a lot of people have gone into that business who are not really writers. For that matter, I don't know if I'm a writer. O'Casey is a writer, *that* I'm sure of.

Mel went on to defend the fact that, aside from his work with Buck in creating "Get Smart" and collaborating on the pilot, he chose not to stay on with the show: "I'd run dry very soon." He then took a few swipes at the network practice of development or step deals, reasoning *ad absurdum* that great writers would never submit to such crass commercialism and rallying no less a personage than Tolstoy to his point. Mel's piety appeared misplaced and raised a few eyebrows. He not only seemed to bite the hand that fed him, but further implied that most television writing was little more than slumming. He expounded upon his own higher aims, also to Joanne Stang:

> The closer I get to my own goals, the more I realize what impalpable stuff they're made of. I like what I do—getting ideas and writing about them—and one day I'd like to be better at it. I'd like to write more screenplays, or a Broadway play, or a book, which—hopefully—would note people's tears and joys, and say something about the human condition. Some day I'd like to grow up and be Sean O'Brooks.

Meantime, he was Mel Brooks and still plotting how to foist "Springtime for Hitler" on an unsuspecting public.

But first there were other more pressing concerns. The "Old Man" was about to come back into Mel's life. The recent rebirth could be traced to WNEW's William B. Williams, who sometimes featured segments of *The 2000 Year Old Man* album on his much listened to radio show. An executive with the Young and Rubicam Advertising Agency heard one of the routines and hatched the idea of lending the character to one of the agency's clients. After some negotiation, the Old Man was aged another 500 years, given a markedly more Teutonic accent, and loaned out to Ballantine Beer as the "2500-year-old Brewmaster." It was an inspired pitch. Mel was granted complete script approval, and he proceeded to tape a series of radio spots with a young comedy writer/comic, Dick Cavett. The two worked well together. Although Cavett could not really rival Carl Reiner's awesome instincts as an interviewer and straight man, he did have going for him a deep voice, an unflappable manner, and the fact that he was unmistakably gentile. That added a new dimension to the Old Man's patter which, with the expanded scope of another 500 years of history, made life more enjoyable for Mel, Dick, and, of course, Ballantine.

As Mel's career got securely on track, Anne's seemed somehow to have derailed. Back in May '65, it was announced that Anne would star with Jason Robards in a play by John Whiting entitled *The Devils,* based on Aldous Huxley's *The Devils of Loudun.* The play originally had been commissioned by the Royal Shakespeare Company, and had opened in early 1961 at the Aldwych Theatre in London. Following its American première at Washington's Arena Theatre, producer Alexander H. Cohen arranged to bring the production to Broadway.

Anne was to play Sister Jeanne of the Angels, a deeply disturbed prioress who, feeling scorned by the libertine vicar, Father Urbain Grandier, becomes hysterical and accuses Grandier of having caused her spiritual possession. The drama spins a complicated tale involving political subterfuge and emotional blackmail, and concludes with the Vicar's condemnation and execution. It was a difficult play set in the early seventeenth century, designedly Elizabethan in tone and structure. Anne's role was extremely demanding. Sister Jeanne was physically grotesque, a hunchback (which would require of Anne a sustained body contortion) which was nothing beside the character's emotional contortions. It was an exotic role, to say the least, perhaps one that should have recalled Arthur Penn's admonishment of a few years before, that Anne should: ". . . resist the temptation to exercise her range with a good part in a bad play."

Meanwhile, Anne, as was often her habit, was already thinking ahead to her next project. During the summer of '65, she had read a novel by one of Mel's former "Show of Shows" co-writers, Lucille Kallen. *Outside There, Somewhere* was about a housewife turned successful television writer, and the rewards and traumas of a woman's venture into a man's world. The story was essentially autobiographical, the style distinctly Lucille—a wry, puckish, and sometimes self-effacing world view; a central character that is unarguably talented but by turns hesitant, vulnerable, and cynical; peripheral characters who tend to misperceive and misuse the protagonist; and a knowing point of view that incisively examines sexism in the home and the workplace—all told trimly and briskly, with dialogue that was concise, clever, and crisply phrased. Topically, the book was unlike anything else then in publication, something of a feminist treatise expertly submerged in an entertaining and commercial work. It was, in short, years ahead of its time.

Anne had no sooner read the book than she invited Lucille to come and discuss the possibilities of turning it into a play, with Anne to star. Though Lucille and Mel had been friendly while working together on "Your Show of Shows," they had drifted since the debacle of the Coca show, which meant that chance meetings aside, Lucille had never spent time with both Anne and Mel. She didn't quite know what to expect when she came to town from her home in Ardsley, New York. She entered the Eleventh Street brownstone and was immediately impressed with Anne's warmth and informality, but surprised at what seemed to be Mel's rather imperious attitude, even allowing for the fact that he was feeling somewhat under the weather that day. Lucille was a tremendous admirer of Anne's work, and remembered thinking afterward that it was: "Sort of as though a younger brother of mine had married the Queen of England."

The two women discussed the possibilities of turning the novel into a play, and although nothing final was decided, a squib soon appeared in the *Times* announcing that Anne expected to begin work on the project once she was done with *The Devils*, and that Arthur Penn was being asked to direct. As it turned out, Lucille found herself unable to adapt the book for the stage. Obviously it was not for want of ability or experience (through three Broadway plays, several summers at Tamiment, and years with "Your Show of Shows," she had worked under the most pressurized and difficult circumstances). The truth was, she was simply still too close to the subject at the time and would first have to get some distance on it before attempting an adaptation. The project would have to wait.

As for Anne, she was soon to be finished with *The Devils*, in fact much sooner than expected and under anything but the best circumstances. During the Boston tryout, Anne missed eleven performances for what was given as health reasons. She was back for the November 17 Broadway opening, which went well and received a rave review from the *Times*'s Howard Taubman, who found Anne's performance both chilling and "affecting," and roundly praised Robards along with the rest of the cast and production staff. Unfortunately, Taubman's was the minority opinion amid other reviews that considered the "spectacle" spectacularly hollow, while indicating that Anne had not only been cast in an impossible play, but that she had been miscast.

Attendance at the Broadway Theatre declined and Anne continued to miss performances, sometimes by prior arrangement as with her days off for Christmas holidays. While the repeated absences might have compromised marquee strength to say nothing of cast morale, the actual performances suffered not at all since the role was filled by Zoë Caldwell who as a favor had agreed to serve as standby. The decision had already been made to cut short the show's run when Anne returned after the holidays. In addition to the production's chronic internal problems, the entire theatre district was feeling the effects of a city-wide transit strike. Then, as if there were not already enough problems, during an evening performance on Wednesday, December 29, Anne accidentally fell from a ladder onstage and injured her back. She was whisked off to Lenox Hill Hospital, while Zoë was wrenched away from dinner with a friend and transported to the theatre in time to don both hump and habit for the second act.

Anne's injury was not permanent but it was painful enough to keep her away from the show for another ten days. She returned, at length, to play the last performance, but, as a spokesman for the show later disclosed to Douglas Watt, Jr., she "played her role in such low key that she infuriated the rest of the cast." The show mercifully closed, requiring the refund of an estimated $300,000 in advance ticket sales. The show's producer, Alexander Cohen, took it all with equanimity and saintly grace, expressing only mild displeasure with Anne. The entire project went into the books as a costly mistake.

It had been a sobering experience. Except for some spot work on television, Anne took a self-imposed sabbatical. Come summer, she planned to appear in a Berkshire Festival revival of *The Skin of Our Teeth* which Arthur Penn was to direct and which Anne looked forward to for "rejuvenation." If the balance of 1966 had been a breather for her, 1967 anticipated nearly noth-

ing at all. Aside from a television musical due for March, Anne
had no other plans to work that year, certainly none for filmwork. At least that was the case until she received a telephone
call from Mike Nichols about a movie he was going to direct
from an adaptation of a Charles Webb novel. With Anne's permission, Nichols sent along a script, and after one reading, she
signed for the production.

That year also found Mel conspiring to make good his claim to
higher literary pursuits. After years of talking, and recent months
of writing, Mel's fabled work-in-progress, "Springtime for
Hitler," was at last about to take shape as a movie.

15

In the predawn hours of Saturday, July 15, 1967, a film crew
stood off to the southeast side of the Revson Fountain at Lincoln
Center in New York City. They were shooting a scene that was
simple in concept but intricate in execution. The sequence called
for dialogue between two actors perched on the lip of the bub-
bling fountain. There was to be a pause, and then a phrase of as-
sent, cuing the fountain which was to burst into shimmering col-
umns of water. It was a prodigious task—working out the
technical kinks and gremlins of the fountain mechanism while at
the same time obtaining the correct visual quality and dramatic
timing. By 5:30 A.M., it was done. With that, the principal photography concluded on *The Producers*.

At first it seemed like little more than a gag, a story entitled
"Springtime for Hitler" (a twist on the old light comedy
Springtime for Henry). But Mel was taking it more seriously
than he was being taken himself, and as early as 1961, he had
begun accumulating scenes, segments, and scraps of dialogue.
The parts were slow in fusing. There had been distractions and
detours, but once "Get Smart" was safely on its way (and both
Brooks the writer and Brooks the comic had declined other tel-

evision offers), Mel was free to flesh out "Springtime" in earnest.

There remained the question of form. Initially, he had thought of expansion in terms of a novel, which, of course, could at some future point be resurrected as a play or movie. And yet as the story evolved so much of the action relied so heavily on dialogue that Mel rejected the more deliberate exposition of a novel and thought of shortcutting directly to a play. It then became apparent that while much of the emphasis was verbal, it was the sort of dialogue that would play best over more and quicker scene changes than the theatre might engineer (besides, Mel had repeatedly found Broadway inhospitable). Which meant that, if only by default, the form would be film.

A catchy premise had been one thing, but amplifying it into a story, paring that down to a script, and then parsing that as comedy would be quite another matter. Mel, who neither typed nor worked well alone, needed a hand. He called on a young woman who had sat in on a number of the "Get Smart" pilot brainstorming sessions, jotting down notes and generally kibbitzing. Her name was Alfa-Betty Olsen and her skills ranged from the clerical to the highly sophisticated comical. She and Mel entered into a somewhat loosely defined working relationship, and went to work on the material. In time, they came up with a "treatment," a kind of underfed scenario, which they then plumped into a 150-page outline. Already, they had begun to embroider the original idea. After bouncing conceptually from medium to medium, the story was finally to be something of a hybrid, a play within a film. That, in and of itself, was hardly unique, but the handling (and especially the intra-plot subject matter) was. At center was an old chestnut about the proverbial (if not apocryphal) shady theatrical producer who makes his living off of flops (an area of some expertise for Mel). This rendition went the proverb one better by having its producer and raw recruit actively draft the most abysmal cast, director, and, of course, property—which is where the original notion came into play, since the sure-fire failure was to be something called "Springtime for Hitler—A Gay Romp with Adolph and Eva at Berchtesgaden." In a not altogether unexpected plot reversal, with implicit jabs at the caprices of Broadway, the show becomes a huge success as some popular monstrosity between high camp and kitsch, leaving the conspirators in a jam to make good the oversold investments. There is a failed attempt to sabotage the theatre and a closing courtroom scene that is just this side of maudlin, redeemed in large part by a brief postscript before the closing titles. The script—distended at one point to 400 pages before being reduced by half and finally trimmed to a 122-page shooting script—drew on many familiar themes but fashioned them into a screenplay that was, to put it mildly, without precedent or peer.*

And no studio wanted to touch it. Mel walked the script around to all the majors and, short of being thrown bodily from the inner sancta, was told that perhaps not all America would find Nazis to be the marvelously wry comic foils he found them to be. Unfaltering, Mel circulated the script among independent producers but received much the same reaction. It started to look as though "Springtime" might go the way of "Marriage Is a Dirty Rotten Fraud," when a good friend, Barry Levinson, offered to introduce Mel to a friend and independent producer, Sidney Glazier. Glazier had, just a few years before, produced a film about Eleanor Roosevelt for American International Pictures (*The Eleanor Roosevelt Story*) which won the 1965 Oscar for best documentary feature. He was successful, well-heeled, and well-connected, and Mel jumped at the chance to meet him.

The meeting took place at the Hello Coffee Shop, on the ground floor of a large office building. Introductions were exchanged and Glazier sat quietly sipping black coffee as Mel rendered the story. He gradually built up to the crucial opening night, and no sooner mentioned the curtain-raising production number (and title song) "Springtime for Hitler," than Glazier started to choke on his coffee and fell to the floor laughing. Once he resumed normal breathing, he extended his hand and said: "Kid, we got a picture. And you're going to direct."

That was barely half the battle won. The film was budgeted at roughly a million dollars, but it was all Glazier could do to raise half that. Between the unlikely title—at that point, still "Spring-

* Although the Hitler-musical bit had been a staple of Lenny Bruce, who lifted the idea from Will Jordan, neither man had dared expand it to motion-picture scale.

time for Hitler"—and an aspiring director known more for an aberrant comic imagination than direction, the project seemed dealt a double dose of poison. With options rapidly narrowing, Glazier contacted yet another producer, Joseph E. Levine, who despite a number of stage and screen successes, was currently tied up with a picture to be directed by Mike Nichols. Nonetheless, Levine, a frank and fair man, gave the proposition a hearing over lunch, and afterward turned to Mel and asked: "Listen, kid, do you really think you can direct a movie?" Without pause or the least sign of doubt, Mel replied: "I know I can." Levine shook his hand and told him: "O.K., kid, go to it." The deal was sealed on the condition that the title be changed, and Mel was in no position to argue the point. For his various contributions to the production, he was to receive $35,000. Mel went home a happy man, went to sleep a hopeful man, and woke up in the middle of the night a haunted man, telling himself: "You had to open your big mouth."

Actually, Mel was not a total stranger to direction. In the first place, he had, in his years with Caesar, taken careful note of directors, often cursing them under his breath for what he considered a lack of comic sensibility, a tendency to cut away from a joke or, worse, to anticipate a joke with a premature cut to the speaker. Mel's first hands-on work, however, was a trailer he wrote, directed, and enacted for promotion of a United Artists release, *My Son, the Hero*. The film itself was originally an Italo-French co-production called *The Titans*, a banal beefcake epic directed by Duccio Tessari, starring Mexican heartthrob Pedro Armendariz, and released by Vides-Les Films Ariane. Working with UA, Carl Reiner had prepared the film for domestic reissue not with the usual poorly synchronized English dubbing, but with a comic dialogue meant to parody that very sort of film. Mel was asked to create a promotional trailer intended for the television campaign and movie house coming attractions. The trailer was better than the film, and the two were distributed together for the theatrical run. As *Variety* correctly predicted, ". . . all things considered, audiences will be better entertained by the trailers and spots than by the picture itself." This sort of spoof of tacky foreign movies was carried off much better two years later by another Caesar alumnus, Woody Allen, whose *What's Up, Tiger Lily?* turned a cheaply made Japanese James Bond-like spy movie into a breezy parody. The shortcomings of *My Son, the Hero* were given dramatic emphasis when, one day after the picture's reissue, the original star, Pedro Armendariz, committed suicide.

For all intents and purposes, "Springtime" was still a maiden directorial effort and production personnel could be pivotal. Alfa-Betty was immediately made casting supervisor since she and Mel had worked closely from the start and knew precisely which roles were tailored to a specific type, which to a specific actor. The balance of the staff and crew positions were filled by some of the best in the business. Joe Coffey became director of photography, Ralph Rosenbloom (who would later work on several Woody Allen films) the editor, and Charles Rosen the production designer. John Morris (Mel's friend from *Shinbone Alley*) would score the picture, and the resourceful and infinitely patient Michael Hertzberg would serve as assistant director. Mel, who was determined from the start not only to make an exceptional movie but to bring it in on time and under budget, was helped immeasurably by Hertzberg in attending to details and cutting corners without compromising quality.†

Casting had already begun. The lead role of Max Bialystock, the small-time producer looking to avenge his many theatrical failures with a profitable calculatedly colossal failure, was as much as automatic. The part had been written with Mel's Oblong Table companion Zero Mostel in mind and after some persuasion by Mostel's wife Kate, he agreed to play it. Then there was the key supporting role of Leo Bloom, the bashful, neurotic accountant who begins by auditing Bialystock's books and ends by becoming his partner in crime. That too was as good as cinched. Years before, following the closing of *Mother Courage*, Gene Wilder was invited for a visit with Anne and Mel on Fire Island. There Mel told Gene: "I've got a great idea for a movie and you're the only one I want for the part." Except for intermittent reminders, little more was said until one afternoon nearly

† The production assistant was Robert Arthur Miller, son of the playwright Arthur Miller.

three years later. Gene was appearing in *Luv* on Broadway and had just finished a matinee when there was a knock at his dressing room door and Mel poked his head in and said: "You didn't think I forgot, did you?"

That still left the all-important character roles. Here again, Anne was of great help. She had recently worked with Dick Shawn in the original Comden-Green-Styne musical, *I'm Getting Married,* presented in January on ABC's "Stage '67." Shawn, an imaginative and tremendously versatile comedian and comic actor was also familiar to Mel through his successful nightclub act which numbered among its characterizations a burnt-out rock star. Based on that last bit alone, Shawn was signed to play Lorenzo St. DuBois (a.k.a. LSD) the hipster whom Bialystock designates to play his stage Hitler.

As for the part of Roger DeBris, the prissy and egregriously effeminate director of the musical, Alfa-Betty went the conventional route of asking agents to submit suitable clients, but the search quickly ended with Christopher Hewett, an actor (whose credits included *My Fair Lady* and *Sound of Music*) and sometimes Broadway director who delivered the deadpan parody the part demanded. Anne again lent a helping hand in the casting of DeBris's otherworldly "valet," Carmen Giya, suggesting an old Actors Studio friend, Andreas Voutsinas, who had little trouble nailing down the part. Lee Meredith won for obvious reasons the role of Bialystock's ultra-endowed non-English speaking secretary, Ulla. But the part of Franz Liebkind, the blithering former Nazi whose play Bialystock marks for certain failure, was something more of a problem. Mel considered taking the part himself, but ultimately gave it to Kenny Mars, an excellent comic actor whom Mel had first come across in 1966 while working briefly as a play doctor on Hillard Elkin's *The Best Laid Plans.* Another young actor (an Eleventh Street neighbor of Mel's) who had earlier been suggested to play Bloom, dearly wanted to play the lunatic playwright and very nearly walked off with the part, but had opted for a better offer which came just before Mel moved into production. It was a quirk of timing that kept Dustin Hoffman out of *The Producers,* and free to enter *The Graduate.*

Hoffman came to *The Graduate* as an afterthought, although
the project had been in the works for some time. The first adaptation of the popular Charles Webb novel had been written by
William Hanley. But Mike Nichols and Hanley disagreed as to
how faithful to the book the screenplay ought to be. Hanley
wanted a literal translation, Nichols more latitude, and Hanley
was discharged. Calder Willingham was then hired to try his
hand at the script, but he fared little better than his predecessor
and was soon too dropped from the project (although his co-
credit was to remain by Writers Guild insistence). Nichols then
approached Buck Henry, whom he knew through their mutual
friend, George Segal. For the next six months, the two of them
worked on the screenplay each day for six hours—of which
roughly three hours daily was spent clowning—and finally came
up with the completed script (because the writing budget had
been drained by the earlier failed attempts, Buck received only
$35,000 for his trouble). Of the many revisions made in Buck's
adaptation, two were most prominent—he changed the protagonist, Ben, from the tall Aryan of the original into a young man of
more modest height and looks, and he restructured the story's
climactic scene.

The Ben of the screenplay was a unique variation on an
identifiable type, and Nichols, and his producer, Lawrence Tur-
man, could think of no one to play the part. In desperation, they
resorted to a bit of Hollywood atavism and staged a nationwide
talent search aimed at "discovering" the best possible Ben. Appli-
cants had to be between nineteen and twenty-three years old,
and were invited to send photo-résumés to casting director Michael Shurtleff in New York. Ingenuous or not, it was redolent
of old-style go-for-broke press agentry. And it worked no more
miracles this time than it had in the past. *The Graduate*'s talent
hunt had come a cropper.

Meanwhile, the supporting roles were distributed among William Daniels, Murray Hamilton, Elizabeth Wilson, and Katharine Ross. The more minor character parts were delivered to
Norman Fell, Alice Ghostley, Marion Lorne, and Buck Henry, no
less. It was inspired casting across the board but it still left

unanswered the two pivotal roles of Ben, and Ben's middle-aged paramour, Mrs. Robinson.

With few exceptions Anne had been professionally inactive, and in fact had been absent from the screen since the ill-fated *7 Women*. In retrospect, it was obvious that she had exercised other than purely professional judgment in accepting that last film, and possibly no judgment at all in entering *The Devils*. She had not by any means stopped looking at scripts ("I'm always looking for a script that excites me and inspires me to return to work") but she was looking for a very specific sort of character. After a string of roles which had demanded one or another physical or emotional handicap (or both), Anne not only wanted a good role, she wanted one that would allow her to look good as well. When Mike Nichols first phoned about *The Graduate*, Anne was as yet unconvinced that this was the vehicle she was looking for, but the moment she read the script she knew that Mrs. Robinson was for her—an elegant and attractive woman on the near side of middle-age, by turns glacial and passionate, intelligent, and not without a certain brittle wit. Granted, the character was also coldly calculating, ruthless, vindictive, and potentially savage—but then, Anne wasn't looking to play Mary Poppins. Besides, she'd had her fill of saintly and martyred characters. It would be a challenge to give the character shading and dimension, to take Mrs. Robinson beyond the colossal bitch role it had every possibility of becoming. What's more, it would be an opportunity to work with a fine young director whose background, like hers, was tied to theatre. All things considered, there was little not to like. On February 1, Anne was announced for *The Graduate*.

That still left Nichols without a Ben with production rapidly closing. The talent hunt had been a fiasco, and Nichols was forced to jog his memory for obscure but able actors, when Dustin Hoffman came to mind. Hoffman, after a number of dry years as an actor in New York, had, of late, found success off-Broadway. Just the year before, he had won an Obie award as best off-Broadway actor for his work in *The Journey of the Fifth Horse*. He was currently appearing with Elizabeth Wilson at The Amer-

ican Place Theatre in a farce by Henry Livings entitled *Eh?*
Nichols was familiar with his work, just as he was aware that at
5'7" and a spare 135 pounds, with a handsome hangdog expression, a tentative smile, and youthful athletic looks, Hoffman was
the very image of Buck Henry's innocent virginal Ben (even if
he was much nearer thirty than twenty). Nichols brought
Hoffman to Hollywood for a screen test opposite Katharine Ross,
but the actor was unaccustomed to film and the test showed it.
Nichols was undismayed. He was convinced that Hoffman projected the image he was after: "A kind of pole-axed quality with
life, but great vitality underneath." The on-camera awkwardness
was nothing a good actor and director could not correct or even
put to good use. On February 13, Dustin Hoffman was announced for the role of Ben.

Anne traveled West for the start of shooting. Her performance
occupied little more than the first third of the picture, before the
story opened up on what was at heart a bourgeois picaresque. Of
her many early scenes, most took place in various states of undress. But that was more than clear in the script and Anne had
hardly paid it a second thought—until actual shooting: "The first
time I had to take off my dress and stand in my bra and slip I
thought I'd die. I chased everyone off the set." Thereafter Nichols was sensitive to his star's sense of modesty and, apart from
restricting scantily clad scenes to all but essential personnel, he
also erected partition screens for an added measure of privacy.
Once any early qualms were assuaged, Anne and Dustin got
down to the business of acting, and did so beautifully. Anne was
patient and instructive, eminently unselfish in helping extract
the exact dramatic tension between Mrs. Robinson and Ben.
Hoffman, in turn, quickly rose to the occasion and the result was
a series of scenes with Anne that were uncannily natural yet
unerringly set in the high relief (short of caricature) Nichols was
seeking. Their consummate work gave the script's thematic-
stylistic flourishes credibility at the character-narrative level: In
the course of an affair with Mrs. Robinson, Ben finally comes to
see the ultimate emptiness of the life he is instinctively avoiding.
She is the antithesis of his addled idealism—vain, acquisitive, aggressive, cynical, hollow. Mrs. Robinson supplies the moral re-

pulsion essential to Ben's delayed assertion of will. That accomplished, she virtually drops from sight. With that, Anne's contribution all but ended.

The Graduate finished shooting on August 5, just three days before Dustin Hoffman's thirtieth birthday. The production was brought in at just over $3 million. Nichols and Sam O'Steen set diligently about editing and adding a score by Simon and Garfunkel, hoping to distribute the film before year's end, thereby making it a late entry for the 1967 Academy Awards. It was already obvious to everyone associated with the project that the film had succeeded mightily in achieving what it had set out to do, and, of equal importance, promised to be an unforgettable screen debut for Hoffman. Anne, already so helpful to the young actor, added more concrete endorsement to his work by amending her initial contractual billing privileges, and insisting that he be accorded credit commensurate with his work. Hoffman was elevated to co-star status, meaning that on all ads, posters, and marquees, his name would appear beside hers in like-sized letters.

A coast away, life was proceeding less swimmingly. *The Producers*, which at one point had been set for a Thanksgiving release, had had to revise its schedule. In view of the fact that this was Mel's directorial baptism, there was much that was going right. There was also much that was going wrong. A great deal of the trouble was of Mel's own making. Apart from sheer newcomer's jitters (the first day on the set Mel dramatically barked "Cut" instead of "Roll 'em") he was under tremendous stress (personal and external) and his normally volatile temper had become volcanic.

Some of that energy fed what was ultimately a useful creative tension. It rudely banished any trace of the complacency or mere journeywork that can creep into a film, particularly a comedy, and leave it oddly de-energized. As Dick Shawn noted, this was an intentional and effective directorial device: "He keeps you on edge while you're working so you're always doing your best . . . that's the kind of people I like to work with." This technique was

a natural outgrowth of Mel's habit of goosing any given gathering, a talent which had after all been his entree into big-time
show business. It now served a double purpose—first, maintaining a supercharged if perceptibly dangerous air of spontaneity,
and, second, and perhaps more important, allowing Mel to venti-
late his ample anxiety. Spontaneity was also promoted by Mel's
practice of permitting his players something of a running start as
well as a running stop by sometimes shooting a little before and
after the precise scene at hand. This practice stopped short of
wastefulness while supplying that extra inch of space and freedom conducive to good comic acting. Then too, the pervasive
sense that any moment the ceiling might cave in gave the acting
an added note of urgency essential to a script which relied heavily on exposition and which needed to generate much of its momentum at the performance level.

Not everyone responded equally well to Mel's methods. Gene
Wilder was at first put off by his brusqueness, as he recalled:
"Mel said to me, 'You don't have to act at all, because I got all
the people who are just right for the parts.'" Wilder consulted
Anne, who told him: "Just go along with him." Zero Mostel was
less inclined to humor Mel. By temperament and by virtue of
success, Zero was in many ways as self-directed, dogmatic, and
tempestuous as Mel, if not more so. Their sessions were often
overheated and contentious, but both men were professional
enough to know that what mattered was the final product, and
so long as their collaboration yielded good work, the rest was tol-
erable. Zero had liked the script from the start, and, as he told
reporter Joan Barthel, he had a comic's admiration for his director: ". . . Mel has great craziness, which is the greatest praise I
can have for anybody." But he went on to qualify his remarks:
"My nature is not to take anything too heavily; I make a few
jokes here and there and I bear with it, because it's better than
working with a sweet ass who has no talent at all." "Talent," was
the operative term, and whatever Mel was lacking in patience or
discretion, he more than made up for with creative fervor. That,
nonetheless, did not deny Zero a wistful parting remark: "But
someday—someday I'll work with somebody who is both talented
and sweet, and I'll die in his arms."

SEESAW: A DUAL BIOGRAPHY OF

Mel was quick to counter that directing Zero was no bed of roses either, as he later recalled: "Working with Zero was like working with no protection. He was a violent force, and we had some stormy sessions. But he was a good man." The problem was that Mel's ferocity could be expansive. *The Producers* had been declared a closed set and as such was off limits to curiosity seekers, well-wishers, and reporters. Practically the only outsiders admitted regularly without prior appointment were Anne, Carl Reiner, and Joe Stein. At length, *Life* magazine offered to do a picture spread—the sort of *pro forma* puff piece that meant free advance publicity—to which Mel agreed, but only under duress. Joan Barthel was assigned the story and she had the misfortune to encounter Mel after a particularly emotional flare-up, falling victim to the spillover of his anger. Mel began flippantly, "What do you want to know, honey?" But he soon dropped the least shred of geniality: "I don't know how these lying interviews go. I don't know how to do this. . . . But I hate to lie and sound jolly, and I wouldn't tell the truth except to people I have known and loved for years." Casting caution to the winds, she asked him if he had encountered any problems so far, and he retorted: "No problems at all. I know everything and that's my problem." Then he again went on the attack, "Anyway, what good does it do us *now*, this story? Save this and give it to me when the picture comes out. If the story came out in November, it could be valuable to the film company. What good does it do us now?" The reporter weathered the outburst and then overheard Sidney Glazier (whose cigarette intake had increased threefold since giving Mel full creative control) say: "They call me the producer. Pray for me."

Later that day, as Barthel was leaving, Mel confronted her again and asked why she had come in the first place. When she explained that she had had no "preconceived notions," Mel fumed: "That's too vague, that's too general. You must have had some idea. Or are you just a big blob of cotton?" Having had her fill of invective, the reporter moved to exit, but Mel hurled one last insult, a cheap shot: "Do you fool around?" The story proved too ornery for the pages of Middle America's favorite picture magazine, but was picked up by the Sunday New York

Times which ran it virtually uncut and with a picture of Mel wildly ranting. It was as handy a piece of promotional suicide as anyone could remember having seen in quite some time.

As far as public relations went, Mel might have been his own worst enemy, but he was still getting the job of directing done and surmounting the many logistical nightmares of shooting in New York City. While exterior footage presented problem enough, there was at least one interior sequence that rivaled the worst the outdoors had to offer—the play within the film. In story sequence this follows the careful creation of the most disastrous musical imaginable. That step-by-step process occupies better than half of the film, after which the company must retire to the theatre for auditions and, finally, opening and closing night (which according to design were to be one and the same).

The audition scene was to be typically informal and unfussy, requiring only a bare stage, a piano, and the extras. For its simplicity, it was still a riotously funny setup, a stage full of brush-mustachioed would-be Hitlers, of all shapes, sizes, and sexes. Visually, it was marvelously bizarre. As written and directed, it was underplayed with a business-as-usual manner, as if this were merely a revival of *The Sound of Music*. The play's director, De-Bris, assigns the singing Hitlers and dancing Hitlers to separate wings and the audition gets under way. It is a brilliant satire on Broadway auditions, with the oddball and the inept giving their all only to be dismissed by the director with a curt "thank you." The scene was shot efficiently and effectively, but that was mere child's play.

The same stage which had housed the audition had to be set up for what was to be the opening-night overture and production number, and that was as complicated as the other had been simple. To begin with, Mel had selected a theatre primarily for its exterior (which was to be used in a later scene). The options narrowed and eventually pared down to the Playhouse Theatre on West Forty-eighth (the same theatre where *The Miracle Worker* had run and where now *The Impossible Years* was near to closing). The Playhouse Theatre fulfilled the exterior requirements but inside was less than ideal. To begin with, it was not a musical house, which meant a relatively diminutive stage and fly

242 SEESAW: A DUAL BIOGRAPHY OF

and no orchestra pit. Production designer Charles Rosen did what he could to work around the first two, and improvised the last by removing the first three rows of seats. But even the most straightforward production details were somewhat encumbered by the fact that this was a motion picture operating in a Broadway house, meaning that the technical work fell simultaneously within the jurisdiction of two distinct families of unions, theatrical and motion picture. Aside from the additional cost, there was the greater worry of squabbles and infringements and slights—the sort of thing that upsets unions and has been known to close down more than one production. As it turned out, the assorted locals co-operated well, and considering the fact that this had swelled the customary crew ranks by another thirty men (all working in close quarters) the air of good spirit was nothing short of wondrous.

The shooting began with an out-of-continuity overhead shot which had to be staged before the unwieldy sets were brought into place. Sequentially, the shot would be a cut-away from the opening production number in which a chorus of storm troopers lock arms in a formation which when seen from above, turns out to be a rotating swastika—a kitsch masterstroke that would fly in the face of every ultrapatriotic Busby Berkeley overhead ever perpetrated, making it, in fact, kitsch on kitsch. The scene, shot the day after the auditions segment, was the first of the day, and it was brought off without mishap. The fact that an aerial view was a visual non-sequitur from the play's otherwise authentic look (that is, an actual theatre audience would not be in a position to appreciate the formation) was an inconsistency worth the effect.

Mel next readied the production number. With his cameraman, Joe Coffey, he had decided to shoot synchronously from three angles—balcony, aisle, and finally an eye-level straight-on close-up. The entire action was to cover just under three minutes. The sets were moved into position, and the heavy lights (powerful enough to accommodate color stock) were arranged. There had already been a dress rehearsal on the third day at the theatre and the blocking and choreography were in order. It came time to shoot. The overture was cued and the curtain rang up on a bucolic scrim fronted by a line of chorines dressed as prim Bavarian milkmaids. They sing an introduction which concludes with the scrim rising on a set that is equal parts Ziegfeld and late-thirties Nuremberg—a symmetrical section of stairs flanked by large urns, tapering toward a raised platform and then fanning out into two smaller flights, one on either side of a quartet of pillars, hung in colored fabric and crowned with separate wreathed swastikas. Positioned about the staircase are assorted showgirls, Ziegfeldesque in their majesty, immobility, and voluptuousness. But instead of the familiar plumage and sequined décolletage, their skimpy outfits and massive headgear consist mostly of variations on beer and pretzels. A golden-throated tenor enters in SS blacks (complete with epaulets and riding boots) and jauntily launches into the verse of the title song, "Springtime for Hitler" (words and music by Mel Brooks). At that, the showgirls begin descending the stairs and are joined onstage by more storm troopers, males in traditional jodhpurs, females in abbreviated skirts. The showgirls exit and the troopers supply a handy time step with stop-time rhymed-couplets patter (one of which was recited by Mel in post-synchronized voice-over). The company then launches into an andante reprise of the chorus as the fabrics and swastikas fall away and the pillars swing into horizontal position to reveal themselves as the cannon of a common turret and fire toward the audience with white puffs of smoke. Simultaneously, an outsized poster of the Führer descends into view as the company picks up the tempo and, amid other accoutrements of war, go into a classic Broadway big finish. Curtain.

That left the audience reaction shots, and some four hundred extras were mustered for the occasion. In gowns and tuxedos they made an elegant opening-night crowd. There was still the exterior footage to be gotten. In context, this scene was to take place after the producers, fearing ruin by success, decide to mine the theatre. A plunger has been placed out front but the charges refuse to detonate, and while the saboteurs are within tracing the problem, a drunk ambles up and thinking the plunger a shoeshine box, lifts his foot and says to no one in particular "Shine 'em up." The theatre goes up in smoke as the drunk sidles away. The scene was finally wrapped shortly before daybreak. It was, however, eventually edited from the completed film.

The Producers completed principal photography in July roughly eight weeks after starting. But what little sense of relief that might have brought was eclipsed by the enormous task of editing yet to come. Even at this early juncture, Mel could point to at least two accomplishments with undiminished pride. He had ultimately concluded shooting on schedule and had brought the production in under budget at $941,000. If nothing else, Mel's directorial hyperkinesis paid off in dollars and cents. What remained to be seen was whether the edited final product would in fact stand up, since, as no one had to tell Mel, a bad film on time and under budget was no less a bad film. With Ralph Rosenbloom, Mel went about editing as he had directing, zealously.

Were it not for the accelerated completion of *The Graduate*, its release might well have coincided with that of *The Producers*. As it was, Nichols' film opened in late December just under the wire for Oscar nominations, and it caught the moviegoing public and the critical establishment entirely by surprise. The film was immediately championed as a social satire which, while owing something to the Preston Sturges tradition, was its own category of late-sixties screwball comedy, comedy with a conscience. The spate of adulation even swept along many of the stingier critics, and soon inspired the sort of scholarly inspection ordinarily reserved for "serious" foreign films. More amazing yet was the fact that the press reception was more than reflected at the box office. There was an instant public groundswell which, instead of subsiding, turned into that ultimate producer's fantasy—repeat attendance. People were not only going to see the film, they were going two and three times. Then too, the release strategy turned out to be the icing on the cake with seven Academy Award nominations matched by another seven for the Golden Globe to feed the extraordinary momentum.

Much was made of the film's thematic content, but while Nichols' direction was ingenious and Buck Henry's screenplay expertly crafted, this was still essentially an establishment motion picture with certain anti-establishment rumblings. The net effect was a film that had it both ways. It took a protagonist who verged on the anti-hero, and by villainizing those around him, turned him into something of a counterfeit hero (which lends itself to the Sturges comparison). But the greatest sleight of hand was to pit that protagonist against highly stylized bourgeois mores and make him nominally victorious though not appreciably less bourgeois.

In all fairness to Nichols, these apparent contradictions were primarily the result of a press which insisted on reading more into the film than was actually there. In fairness to the press, the late sixties was a time of social unrest and disillusionment with traditional values, and if critics were groping for some trenchant correlation between that and the massive youth audience the film had attracted, it was forgivable. Whatever the film's intellectual rewards, its theatrical rewards were for those connected with it, many and real. Dustin Hoffman was at once elevated to star stature, Katharine Ross's standing likewise improved, and Mike Nichols established himself as an exceptional and original director of film.

As for Anne, *The Graduate* broadened her already impressive range as an actress. More than just superlative film acting, her performance as Mrs. Robinson practically became a sixties archetype—the personification of the upper middle class as some comely but jaded vamp. The potency and detail she gave the character had saved it from any risk of stock bitchiness while at the same time allowing it to serve as the textual antithesis necessary to Ben's character synthesis. Unarguably brilliant within the film's context, the role was also a stunning addition to Anne's repertoire. It played directly against the virtuous afterglow of many of the other roles. But more, it enabled Anne to exercise her gift for comedy and to play the "heels and hose" role she had so long fancied.

With *The Graduate*, Anne clearly demonstrated there was little she could not do as an actress. She had another pair of award nominations (Oscar and Golden Globe) to drive home the point.

While *The Graduate* was being credited with everything short of having reinvented film comedy, *The Producers* was being preened for a March release. The early screenings had already caused some sweaty palms amid worries that the film would earn either regional approval or universal dislike. During the filming of *The Producers*, somebody had referred to it as a "home movie," meaning the cozy manner in which it had been cast. The finished product—technically polished and visually handsome— was anything but amateur work.

The film opens on a closed door labeled "Max Bialystock The- atrical Producer." There is mischievous laughter within—the once-mighty Max is now only mighty of girth, having sunk to tit- illating little old ladies for financial backing. The interlude is ac- cidentally overheard by Leo Bloom (borrowed in name at least from Joyce's *Ulysses*) a morbidly shy accountant come to audit Bialystock's books. All this is established in the course of the opening titles, handled in periodic freeze-frame over which plays an orchestrated medley of the tunes that will follow in the course of the film.

The film proper begins with Max motioning Leo into his office with the rhetorical challenge: "So you're an accountant, huh? . . . Then account for yourself. Do you believe in God? Do you believe in gold?" Leo explains that he is just there to go over the books and does so as Max spins his tale of woe, noting that he was once Broadway's most prosperous producer: "Look at me now, I'm wearing a cardboard belt." (No doubt recalling the age-old adage of Mel's Uncle Harry.) Leo turns up some incon- sistencies in the ledger, which Max at length persuades him to overlook. It is while making the adjustments that Leo poses the mathematical theory that: "under the right circumstances, a pro- ducer could make more money with a flop than he could with a hit," circumstances being monumental overbooking. Max takes this as an actual proposition, but Leo recoils. Max persists, enu- merating six easy steps to a dishonest fortune, concluding with a hasty retreat to Rio de Janeiro, after which he embraces the ac- countant in a brief comic tango (reminiscent of Joe E. Brown and Jack Lemmon in one of Mel's favorite movies, *Some Like It Hot*). It is soon apparent that Leo is as neurotically introverted as Max is grotesquely extroverted. The two make a skewed Laurel and Hardy, with a dose of Groucho Marx in Max's comic asides to the camera. Still, Leo is unpersuaded, as Max takes him for a walk through Central Park while doing his best to entice him into complicity.

The exterior sequence is a pleasant contrast to the office scene which Mel shot in close-ups and occasional wide-angle which lent a sense of caricature, particularly with Mostel who, mammoth to begin with, was made to look like some grinning, overweening zeppelin. The park scenes are playful and innocent as Leo reveals that beneath the neurotic surface is really something of a trusting little boy. The walk ends that night, at the fountain in Lincoln Center.

As originally scripted, this scene was to take place at the Coney Island parachute ride, but the ride had fallen into disrepair and would have been too costly to revive for shooting. The production needed an alternative location when Alfa-Betty Olsen, visiting the Lincoln Center Library for research reasons, hit upon the idea of using the fountain. With Mel's approval, that became the setting for Leo's conversion. In the film, Max has all but spent his guile on Leo, and finally confronts him, pointing out what a drab life he leads. That, at last, fires Leo's imagination: "That's right. I'm a nothing. I spend my life counting other people's money. People I'm smarter than, better than. Where's my share? Where's Leo Bloom's share? I want, I want everything I've ever seen in the movies." Leo agrees to throw in with Max and the fountain bursts into spray as Leo ecstatically circles the water and Max, his bulging figure silhouetted against the near-white of the water, throws back his arms and head in gales of joyful laughter.

The partners now go about the methodical business of finding a likely property, which brings them to the apartment of an unreconstructed Nazi, Franz Liebkind. The play secured, Max then goes about his specialty which is wheedling little old ladies into investing in his play. Once he has successfully sold 25,000 per cent of the play, he takes Leo to pay a visit to the one director who will all but guarantee failure, the outrageously effeminate Roger DeBris. The two are escorted in by the valet, Carmen Giya, and come upon DeBris, gloved and gowned, he explains, for the upcoming choreographer's ball. Max succeeds in interesting DeBris in the project, and as the director starts rapturously to imagine chorus girls clad in black patent leather boots, Carmen Giya hisses: "S-M! Love it."

With the production particulars squared away, Max has only to find the perfectly "wrong" lead. Auditions turn up the hippie minstrel LSD, which brings matters quickly to opening night. As Max and Leo look on, the curtain rises on the devastatingly tasteless opening number, and after one glimpse of their audience's outrage, they retreat to a nearby bar to celebrate what seems to be an irretrievable flop. Meanwhile, at the theatre, the play's second scene continues as the patrons begin filing out in disgust. LSD serves up his beat rendition of Hitler and there are nervous titters among the remaining theatregoers, and soon giggles that build into laughs. The audience quickly returns to its seats for what it now assumes is an intentionally campy comedy. Max and Leo then return to catch a fleeting glimpse of their flop, only to find that it's become a shambles, which is to say a success. The play ends and the audience exultantly exits proclaiming this the hit of the season.

Max and Leo return to their office to contemplate their imminent doom. Liebkind enters, presumably to kill them for turning Hitler into a laughingstock, only to be convinced by Max to help demolish the theatre, and thereby destroy the play which has refused to self-destruct. The three succeed in blowing themselves up along with the theatre and are next seen bruised and bandaged in court. There is a guilty verdict and the judge begins sentencing when Leo asks to say a few words. He rises to Max's defense, explaining that, subterfuge aside, Max had succeeded in bringing a little excitement into the lives of others. Max adds that he has learned his lesson and will never repeat the offense. The film cuts to the interior of a penitentiary, where Max in prison grays rehearses a convict chorus line for what is obviously a coming musical production. Outside the rehearsal hall, Leo sells shares of the production, and it is soon clear that he is again drastically overselling. The chorus launches into an uptempo "Prisoners of Love." The camera recedes, the music swells, and the closing credits roll backed by a reprise of the Lincoln Center fountain shot.

44

The notices for *The Producers* were virtually split down the middle, collectively and individually. Almost to a review, they agreed that the picture opened on a high note of comedy. *Newsday* pegged it well as "a high class low comedy" and "thinking man's slapstick." Most were willing to take certain excesses as a sign of vitality, and surprisingly few hackles were raised at the Nazi japing, "fag-baiting," or even the inimitable "Springtime for Hitler" number. There was, however, the widespread feeling that Mel had let the picture slip away from him after that very number, what one critic saw as Mel Brooks the writer having failed Mel Brooks the director. The remaining reviews generally divided according to readership—the mass publications holding that the good moments outweighed the bad, the highbrow periodicals maintaining the reverse. At points it seemed as if critics were reviewing two different movies, and, in a sense they were.

Through the theatre sequence, *The Producers* is wonderfully integrated and motivated. Even the more jagged narrative pieces find companion pieces in a kind of screwy sensibleness. By the time the play opens, we sufficiently identify with Bialystock and Bloom to share in their lopsided opening-night jitters and pull for them to get the failure they so want. However, the play within the film, in all its repellent finery, is both the film's high point and undoing. It is so monstrously outrageous that there is simply no way to top it, beyond a rapid denouement. Bloom, in his post-show delirium, keeps repeating: "No way out, no way out," and that would seem to speak for the film at this juncture. Unfortunately, were the film to end here it would be little more than an overdressed short subject. So the script, in something of a throwback to Mel's old habit of topping the untoppable, attempts to go the play one better with the failed sabotage and courtroom scene. The action descends into a crude burlesque, and, with the explosion, veers off suddenly into cartoonland. The movie comes unglued.

There was no fault to be found with the acting. Shawn, Mars, Hewett, and Voutsinas had all worked well in their supporting roles. Mostel essentially had done nothing different than he had elsewhere, and that was plenty. Gene Wilder, on the other hand, was the film's find. He skillfully cushioned both Mostel's and the film's occasional harshness, while giving depth to a character that might otherwise have seemed a neurotic stooge. His impassive expression not only served the film, but even had that rare quality of playing straight to his own humor. Wilder played Bloom to perfection.

The Producers proved that Mel Brooks the director was no mere upstart to be passed over lightly. Still, the box office was less than had been expected, and while the film did not lose money, it did not make much either. In an attempt to boost business, an ad was taken out in the trades quoting the "unsolicited" testimony of Peter Sellers, who screened the film and announced: ". . . Brilliantly written and directed by Mel Brooks, it is the essence of all great comedy combined in a single motion picture." It was a generous sentiment, but it gave no perceptible lift to receipts.

In their separate ways, *The Graduate* and *The Producers* were quintessential sixties movies. Both were somewhat fatalistic, both moderately iconoclastic, both cheeky, and both cynical in their questioning of social values, in particular the terms of success. And yet, despite thematic overlapping the two films are virtual opposites. They differ in tone (*The Graduate* is romantic-idealism, *The Producers* borderline nihilism), they differ in technique (the former more cinematic, the latter more theatrical), and they differ in their comic tools (the Henry-Nichols text and the Nichols direction is satire that sometimes strays near farce, the Brooks-Olsen text and the Brooks direction is essentially farce that at times settles into satire). Each was in its own way emblematic of the turmoil going on at the time in America. Neither offered weighty social comment, although *The Graduate*, unobsessed as it was with laughter, uncovered more small truths and perceptions than the much louder and laugh-obsessed *The Producers*. Practically speaking, the greatest disparity was at the box office, where *The Graduate* was threatening to overtake the then all-time high-grossing *Sound of Music*, while *The Producers* did only moderate business. Buck Henry must have felt avenged for his credit hassles with Mel over "Get Smart."

For her work in *The Graduate*, Anne received a Golden Globe Award but was passed over for the Oscar, which went to Katharine Hepburn. Any hurt Mel might have felt at his film's relative obscurity was somewhat soothed after the first of the year when he learned that the screenplay for *The Producers* had been nominated for an Oscar, although one look at the competition— *The Battle of Algiers* and *2001: A Space Odyssey*—would have placed its chances between slim and none. When Oscar night arrived that spring, Gene Wilder (who had received a nomination as best supporting actor) was passed over for Jack Albertson. However, in the category of best story and screenplay written directly for the screen, *The Producers* was the surprise winner and Mel cited as its sole author.‡ Whatever satisfaction and clout might have been lost at the box office was at least partially recovered through the Oscar.

With Mel now a filmmaker of some repute and Anne currently doing better by film than by theatre, it was only a matter of time before someone asked them publicly whether they had any intention of working together. It was Earl Wilson who finally asked: "Will you ever produce and direct a film with your wife?" And Mel who answered: "My wife is my best friend, and I want to keep it that way."

‡ In a somewhat belated acknowledgment of Alfa-Betty's input, Mel took out ads in the trade dailies *Daily Variety* and *The Hollywood Reporter* which read: "My heartfelt thanks to Alfa-Betty Olsen for both her creative contribution to the script and brilliant casting. Mel Brooks."

16

Making a movie in Yugoslavia was Mel's idea. Commuting between Belgrade and New York was Anne's.

Since marrying Mel, Anne had consciously reordered her work habits, as she explained to one reporter: "After each role, I always take a rest—six months to a year. It takes a month to adjust back to being a homemaker." By her own ready admission, she was no firebreathing feminist, but an "old-fashioned woman." Actually Anne did very little homemaking in 1967. She had not long completed her work for *The Graduate* when Mike Nichols invited her to accompany him in a revival of Lillian Hellman's *The Little Foxes*, to be performed in repertory at Lincoln Center's Vivian Beaumont Theater. The would-be homemaker joined a cast of theatrical elite such as Beah Richards, Margaret Leighton, Austin Pendleton, E. G. Marshall, and George C. Scott. Nichols had decided to stage the play in more traditional proscenium fashion despite the fact that the Beaumont's was a thrust stage, that is, a proscenium with a floor-level performance area that juts forward into a horseshoe shaped seating area.

The Little Foxes opened on October 27, and notwithstanding the nattering of a handful of critics who felt the play was outmoded or ill suited to repertory, the notices were almost all friendly and some (notably those of the *Times*, the *News*, and the *Post*) adoring. In fact, the *News*'s John Chapman had seen the 1939 original production and preferred the revival. There was consistent praise for all involved, and particular praise for Anne in her performance as Regina Giddens (originated by Tallulah Bankhead). Inasmuch as this was repertory, the show ran successfully for only one hundred performances before yielding the stage to the next production.

By summer, Anne was back onstage at the Berkshire Festival in Stockbridge, in a new play by her favorite playwright, William Gibson. *A Cry of Players* was a period piece about a young man who is, in all but name, a prefamous William Shakespeare, with Frank Langella as young Will and Anne as his wife, Anne. The play shortly found its way to New York, and little more than a year after her opening in *The Little Foxes*, Anne was back at the Vivian Beaumont Theater. The reception was noticeably cooler than the last. Critics cited problems with the play ranging from a topical coyness to a creeping contemporaneity in dialogue and staging despite many considered Elizabethan touches. Few found any fault with the level of performance between Anne and Langella, and though the two of them developed a close and lasting friendship the play was considerably less durable. Most considered it less a tribute to the bard and more just dramaturgical hubris on Gibson's part. *A Cry of Players* closed after only fifty-eight performances.

With that, Anne finally permitted herself the rest she had wanted, but her career no sooner decelerated than Mel's gathered speed. Oscar firmly in hand, Mel readied another project which was unlike *The Producers* in any regard except that it too was a comedy. In the wake of *The Producers*' uninspired critical and popular reception, Mel was eager to even the score, as he told Albert Goldman: "My comedy is based on rage. I'll show those cockamamie *Cahier*'s critics. I'll make a movie that'll bend their bagels. . . ." continuing, "We Jews have upward mobility, you know. We're short people but we know how to grow." Rhetorical flourishes aside, what Mel had in the works was something called *The Twelve Chairs*.

Beginning with what Lucille Kallen had once recognized in

Mel as "an ancient Jewish respect for literature" in general and fortified by his Tolkin-spawned passion for Russian literature in particular, Mel had written a screenplay based on a story by a late team of popular Russian writers. Ilf and Petrov were *noms de plume* for two Russian journalists, Fainzilberg and Katayev, who wrote satires of Russian life. Their best-known works were *Little Golden Calf* and *One-Story High America,* but Mel's personal favorite, a story he had heard as a child and read as a teenager, was a brief novel, *Diamonds to Sit On* (to which *Little Golden Calf* is a sequel), which told of three men in search of a treasure trove secreted within one of a set of twelve dining room chairs. Set in 1927 Russia, the story was technically picaresque and therefore broadly satiric, but its subject matter of avarice and unscrupulousness redeemed by fraternal love, shared a certain thematic outlook with *The Producers.* Granted, the material was not as literate or lofty as the nineteenth-century Russian novels Mel revered (much later he would in inimitable fashion tell *Time:* "My God, I'd love to smash into the casket of Dostoyevsky, grab that bony hand and scream at the remains, 'Well done, you goddam genius!'") but it was a unique setting and it did carry the aura of serious comedy he was after. Mel took his script to Sidney Glazier, who agreed to raise the $1.5 million it would take to bankroll the production.

Although the budget was half again what Mel had managed with on *The Producers,* this was a more ambitious production and it was clear from the start that some economizing would be necessary. Mel got in touch with Michael Hertzberg, his assistant director from *The Producers* and the man whose planning and ingenuity had been instrumental in bringing that picture in on time and under budget, and made him his producer. The decision was then made to shoot the film in Yugoslavia which not only provided the appropriate terrain but also freed the production of having to meet the high union scale of American technical crews. The movie was cast. The leads went to Frank Langella, Ron Moody, and Dom DeLuise, with help from André Voutsinas (the incomparable Carmen Giya). For the supporting role of Tikon, the unkempt, un-communized caretaker of a geriatric home, Mel hired a character actor with some expertise in dialect—himself. Following preproduction in England, shooting was to begin on location in late August 1969.

Allowing for preproduction, filming, and postproduction, Mel estimated his time away from home at between eight and nine months. That was of immediate concern to Anne, for whom Yugoslavia seemed no likely home away from home. But if she was opposed to wasting away in some foreign capital, she was just as averse to undertaking a film or play, either of which might preclude visits abroad. She was puzzling over the predicament when she realized that the solution had already been long at hand. For some time, Martin Charnin had wanted Anne to star in her own television special. She had repeatedly declined the offer, but when he next offered, she gladly accepted. The blueprint for the special was for Anne to portray, through sketches, vignettes, and songs the various types of women in the life of a man. Beyond the subject matter, Anne knew that the special would be flexible enough to allow her to rehearse in installments, leaving time for expeditions to Yugoslavia.

The plan worked better than imagined. *The Twelve Chairs* started shooting on August 25. Meanwhile Martin Charnin began piecing together the special which was to be called: "Annie, The Woman in the Life of a Man." The writing was farmed out to an impressive list of writers that included: Peter Bellwood, Thomas Meehan, Herb Sargent, Judith Viorst, Gary Belkin, William Gibson, Reginald Rose, Jacqueline Susann, and one absent friend, Mel Brooks. As it worked out, Anne would gather a batch of new material, fly to Belgrade, rehearse days at the Hotel Yugoslavia while Mel worked at the Studios Kosjutnat, return home for a fresh batch of material, and begin all over again. All things considered, it was one hell of a commute, but as Anne later told *Viva* magazine: "It was absolutely perfect. It worked out fine and it kept my marriage together. I was very happy."

The Twelve Chairs completed principal photography in December. The production had been notably less squally than *The Producers* and far from alienating his actors, Mel succeeded in winning their admiration. Ron Moody told *Show* magazine: "I think he's the only person living today who's a direct link, an active, direct link with the golden age of comedy," adding that he considered Mel more of a humorist than a satirist. Frank Langella said simply, "He's one of the few men in the world I would trust with my life." The more casual air was again apparent when during one of Anne's visits, Mel insinuated her into a take of a scene with Moody and Langella as a practical joke on his editor, Alan Heim. Later, also speaking to *Show* magazine, Mel reflected briefly on the film's theme, which, as he pointed out, was like *The Producers* in that it forged a conspiratorial but fraternal bond between male characters, wisecracking: "Maybe I'm a fag—I don't know. Two guys are always winding up together, you know. I better go back to my analyst and have a talk."

It had been a long haul, with foreign crews (British and Yugoslav), the vagaries of a totalitarian government, and such remote locations as Dubrovnik, Subotica, and Petrovaradin. Added to these hardships was a risky indigenous cuisine and highly suspect water. Mel survived on Kisela Voda, a bottled mineral water somewhere between Perrier and two cents' plain but with certain laxative powers. Mel was considerably grayer at the temples and narrower at the waist when he returned to England for post-production editing and scoring (actually, Mel had written the film's theme, "Hope for the Best, Expect the Worst"—music by Brahms—John Morris its score). Mel allowed himself a brief respite when he joined Jack Cassidy, Lee J. Cobb, John McGiver, Robert Merrill, Arthur Murray, Dick Shawn, Dick Smothers, and David Susskind, in an acting turn on Anne's special. Anne and Mel performed a delightful sketch (Mel's work) in which he plays a psychiatrist, she a patient. That was just one of many fine moments in the special which aired on CBS on February 18, 1970, and eventually won an Emmy for Anne to add to her burgeoning collection of awards.

So far, all Mel had to show for his work on *The Twelve Chairs* was a rather svelte and distinguished look, and $50,000 which covered his work as writer, director, and co-producer, and which, after taxes, was just enough money to leave him immoderately in debt. The fond hope that the film would reverse Mel's financial reversals faded with its October release. The *Variety* review was prophetic, declaring it: ". . . Funny and well-handled but doubtful mass appeal," adding that, "Brooks further distinguishes himself in the brief but important role. . . ." Cynics might have whispered that it was a measure of the film that Mel's acting could be the best thing about it. The fact of the matter is that *The Twelve Chairs* was good, the performance better. Cinematically, the film was, with the camera work of Djorde Nilolic, more sophisticated and visually fine than *The Producers*. True, to some extent the stylistic refinement was at odds with the comedy (there is a tension between scenic beauty which is composed and almost diagrammatic, and good low comedy which is calculatedly uncomposed and virtually anagrammatic). But more to the point was the sense that while the film worked well at the slapstick level, the intended satire didn't wash, as *The New Yorker*'s Pauline Kael lamented: "It's a bit forlorn, this attempt to make comedy out of old comedy that has lost its satirical bite,"—qualifying her remarks slightly—"When Brooks is onscreen, he brings a fervid enthusiasm to his own nonsense; when he isn't around, there's no comic tension." It was a funny and at times touching performance with only the barest traces of *The 2000 Year Old Man*, and a good deal more by way of original and sure-footed comic acting. The only problem with Mel's performance was that there was too little of it and the film suffered for his absence. Mel might have won at least a portion of the critical acceptance he had craved, but that did little to soften the blow of an eventual lackluster national showing.

It would have been wrong to say that Mel's film career was in a tailspin, but not far from right. He had made two films which, allowing for beginner's mistakes, had been no less than respectable. But even if Mel were the darling of the critics (which he was not) he was a commercial filmmaker and there the bottom line was, as it always has been, profit, of which *The Producers* had shown little and *The Twelve Chairs* even less. For a presumably up-and-coming director, Mel had nothing coming up in the foreseeable future. He was struggling and knew it.

So did David Begelman, then with Freddie Fields at the theatrical agency CMA. At Begelman's suggestion, he and Mel met for lunch and lunch promptly turned into an afternoon-long marathon seminar. The two of them raked over Mel's filmwork to date, analyzing it and trying to augur from it some career direction. First Begelman signed Mel as a client. Then, seeing that Mel was terribly crestfallen not only with the disappointment of *The Twelve Chairs* but with a recent failure to sell a screen adaptation he had written of Goldsmith's *She Stoops to Conquer,* he mentioned a new project. Judy Feiffer (former wife of cartoonist Jules Feiffer) was a story editor at Warner Brothers and had come across a treatment by a young man named Andrew Bergman who was, at the time, something more of a film scholar than a film writer. Still, the basic premise of the story (entitled *Tex X*) was not without possibilities—it worked a shrewd anachronism by taking a cliché-ridden late-nineteenth-century cowboy setting and placing in it a black sheriff who was strictly late-twentieth-century hip. Out of deference to his new agent, Mel agreed to have a look at the treatment, and slowly the juices began to flow.

There had already been some studio interest in Mel directing the material, but first the material had to be expanded and enlivened. Begelman worked out a deal with Warners which would pay Mel $50,000 to assemble and head a group of writers (who would be paid significantly less) to kick around the idea and come up with a script. Mel, who wanted personally to recover the lost vitality of his "Caesar's Hour" days, started to draft the members of his *ad hoc* pitch session, starting with a writing team whom he knew and liked, Norman Steinberg and Alan Uger. In a departure from the Hollywood norm, Mel also summoned the original author, Andrew Bergman. And in yet another departure from studio norm (which, when it came to comedy, liked its employees zany but docile) Mel hired a brilliant young comic whose genius was only exceeded by his reputation for erratic behavior, Richard Pryor. For close to four months (Pryor was a latecomer arriving roughly midway) they sat in a room and were ultimately able to wring from the premise a 412-page rough draft, which in script terms would have been long-winded even for Von Stroheim in his prime. A second draft reduction resulted in a slightly more wieldy if still bulky 275 pages.

Warners was sufficiently impressed to authorize another reduction into a shooting script. That meant that the project was officially "on," with Mel as its director at a wage of around $100,000. In truth, Mel was somewhat taken aback by the studio's willingness. The script was achingly funny, but it was also unconventional in the extreme, controversial, and adult (well, at least nominally adult) in a way that made *The Producers* look tame by comparison. Nevertheless, Warners was willing to take a flyer on it, and Mel, figuring he had nothing to lose, matched the go-for-broke writing with a free-spirited go-for-broke approach to directing that was devoid of the filmic self-consciousness that had tinged *The Producers* and infused *The Twelve Chairs*. If his filmmaking career was going to continue its backslide, at least he would have fun in the process.

The production was given the working title of *Black Bart*, and Mel went about casting the lead. There was no question in his mind who would be ideally suited to the part, but when Warners was asked to approve Richard Pryor in the starring role, it refused, citing his lack of box-office stature. The studio then turned around and approved Cleavon Little, a fine stage actor with even less national currency than Pryor. Warners had made its message crystal clear—it had been willing to gamble on Pryor, but only up to a point.

The remaining casting came more easily. One of the picture's plum roles was a devastating twist on Destry-vintage Dietrich (Lili von Shtupp) which not only made much of her Germanic speech impediment but made explicit what had always been implied in her whore-with-a-heart-of-gold character. In this case, before Mel could find the right actress for the role, the right actress found him. Madeline Kahn, late of what was to be an Oscar-nominated performance in *Paper Moon*, and long a fan of Mel Brooks, knew of *Black Bart*, knew of the Lili von Shtupp role, and knew she could act it in spades. The trick was convincing Mel. Madeline, who at one point had worked as a singing waitress at a brauhaus in Yorkville (Manhattan's German section), had acquired an ear for German. Beyond that, she possessed all the equipment for a superb comic actress, had also trained as an opera singer, and could easily handle the torch songs the role called for. Madeline arranged an audition: "It lasted two hours. I felt like I was at the Mayo Clinic. For a funny man, he's very serious." She made her own adjustments and embellishments, and won the part going away.

Harvey Korman, whom Mel had seen on Carol Burnett's television variety show, became archvillain Hedley Lamarr. Ex-football player Alex Karras played the lovable lout, Mongo, and other parts were handed to such topflight character actors as David Huddleston and Liam Dunn. Dom DeLuise (whose wife also took a minor role) agreed to a closing cameo, and for that one essential bit of western authenticity and orientation, Slim Pickens was recruited to play Lamarr's factotum, Taggart. That still left a pair of roles, one a minor character, the other a walk-on (actually a "ride-on"), and these Mel appropriated. He would play the wretched, lecherous, and addlepated Governor Lepetomane, as well as a linguistically peculiar Indian chief.

As for the second lead, Bart's besodden sidekick and onetime legendary gunman, the Waco Kid, Mel had wanted and had gotten Dan Dailey. But at the last minute, Dailey got cold feet and, after one failed substitute and with the production a weekend away, Mel turned to Gene Wilder, who postponed other acting obligations to help out his friend and mentor.

The shooting was scheduled to start in January, to be confined primarily to the back lot, but moving to the Palmdale Desert for several scenes. Some of the players, who knew Mel only in passing but knew of his marriage, had hoped for an opportunity to meet Anne. At length, Anne did start visiting the set, but seldom alone. She brought with her the infant son she had given birth to in June 1972. He bore both grandfathers' names, and was christened Maximilian Michael Brooks. The baptism had been at Anne's insistence. Neither she nor Mel had been "terribly religious" in recent years, but when little Max was born, she admitted: "I had to baptize my child." Mel was very understanding. He and Anne struck a bargain—he'd let Max be baptized if she'd let him be bar-mitzvahed.

Black Bart went smoothly. Mel was more relaxed than in either of his two previous films. He was luxuriating in the convenience of his first Hollywood movie. There were no urban locations or union complications to wrestle with as in *The Producers,*

no foreign government, homesickness, or plain sickness to con-
tend with as in *The Twelve Chairs*. Mel was still hardly one to
approach directing as a nine-to-five job, but at least when the
work day was over, he could come home to Anne and Max, and
not some bleak Belgrade hotel suite.

The good spirit showed at once in the dailies (the printed,
uncut daily footage). The comedy was there, rowdy and raunchy
as ever, but the former comic virulence and at times unsavory intensity were diffused to good advantage. With that went a degree of film technique and the stylistic and textual panache of
The Twelve Chairs but, as is so often the case in film farce, with
no scenic precociousness to upstage the material, the comedy
quickly moved center stage—with a vengeance. Mel continued
his method of not only challenging his cast to perform well, but
allowing them the freedom and space in which to do it, repeatedly exhorting his cast: "Go bananas!" There was probably an
even greater air of improvisation about this Mel Brooks set than
the others, epitomized by his own acting bitwork, as well as a
third turn as an extra.* Consistent with the now standard Brooks
approach, the script was the all-important springboard (as he
saw it, 90 per cent of any film), but the acting implemented it
handily by playing off the spirit and abiding by the letter of it. It
is an old axiom of comic acting that the funniest moments often
come with the straightest playing. Allowing for a measure of
broadness or archness, the comic actor cannot tip his hand by
telegraphing the material (except in the rare cases of such classic actors as W. C. Fields or the Marx Brothers). Contrary to amateur beliefs, a dead pan doesn't dampen the comedy, it
heightens it. And given the scripted madness, a straight face was
nothing less than valiant.

As usual, Mel brought the production in on time and at cost,
and having already written and composed a memorable torch
song for Lili von Shtupp, he added a title song sung by Frankie
Laine, which bore the film's final title, *Blazing Saddles*. After
Mel set about cutting the film, a minor flap developed over the
writing credits. When the completed script was finally submitted

---

* As further proof of the cozy atmosphere, Anne was included as an extra
in a church scene.

to the Screenwriters Guild, an employee there noticed something peculiar about it. Recalling an old Richard Pryor script he had once read, he noticed the similarities to the *Blazing Saddles* style, but also noted that there was not the least mention of Pryor's name. The employee (thinking to himself as Pryor later recalled: "This shit's like what Richard writes!") played a hunch and gave Pryor a call. Pryor was angry to find that his name had been dropped from the script, but simply said that if that was the way Mel chose to do it, let him. The Guild didn't see it that way, and through its intervention Pryor's credit was restored to the film.

There were other unsettling moments in store for Mel, as a final cut was readied and set for a screening before a stern jury of Warner brass.

Blazing Saddles was a mélange, grouping shards of satire, parody, farce, and lavatory burlesque, all owing something more to television (albeit with license) than film. The nominal plot— about a dimwit governor and his conniving attorney general (Hedley Lamarr) who conspire to defraud a town of the benefits of a railroad right of way by installing a black sheriff who, they figure, will make a shambles of things—is little more than a rack on which to hang assorted funny hats. It opens on a track gang, which, when taunted, and ordered by its cornpone foreman to liven things up with a "good ole nigger work song," launches into a perfectly harmonized rendition of Cole Porter's "I Get a Kick Out of You," with a savoir faire worthy of the Mills Brothers. That is the film in capsule—role reversal, racism turned on its head, gag humor, all rooted in the presiding anachronism.

Through a series of intrigues, one of the workers, Bart, is set up as sheriff of Rock Ridge as part of Lamarr's fiendish plan to destroy the town. Bart, dressed to the teeth in leather and suede by Gucci, prepares to ride in to town with rousing big band jazz playing in the background (the source of the music turns out to be the Count Basie Orchestra in full splendor, playing "April in Paris" in the middle of the desert). Bart rides on to what is at best a tepid reception—the townsmen want to hang him. He narrowly (if absurdly) escapes and befriends the Waco Kid, once the most feared gunman in the West: "I musta killed more men than Cecil B. DeMille." The Kid asks Bart the question of the hour: "What's a dazzling urbanite like you doing in a rustic setting like this?" The answer comprises a gratuitous flashback to Bart's youth in a wagon train hit by an Indian raiding party with Mel on horseback and in warpaint as a Yiddish-speaking Indian chief who takes one look at Bart's family, remarks "shvartzes" and then spares them, saying, "*Abei gezunt*, take off."

Bart and the Kid team to protect the town from Lamarr's treachery, and succeed in winning over the bigoted townsmen, whom the Kid describes as "The common clay of the West, you know, morons." Lamarr resorts to his secret weapon, the heretofore indefatigable Lili von Shtupp, whose job it is to seduce Bart into submission. That succeeds only in enamoring Lili of her intended victim, and forces Lamarr's hand as he puts out a general call for villains to help him destroy the town—he gets quite a turn out, including Nazis, Klansmen, banditos (reminiscent of *The Treasure of the Sierra Madre*), and one motion picture director wearing sunglasses, a leather flight jacket and white silk scarf, a broad-brimmed hat, and even broader grin. Bart gets wind of the impending raid and asks the townsmen's help in implementing an unlikely plan of defense. They hesitate, but he insists: "You'd do it for Randolph Scott," after which they relent, as the minister prays for guidance from above: "Oh Lord, do we have the strength to carry on this mighty task in one night, or are we just jerking off." Evidently, a little of both, as the villains fall into the trap, and are then set upon by the townspeople as the brawl swells, and the camera crane recedes as the roughhouse tumbles onto another set where Buddy Bizarre (Dom DeLuise) is rehearsing a musical with what appears to be a male chorus line full of "Carmen Giyas." Bizarre objects only to be told by Taggart: "Piss on you, I'm working for Mel Brooks." The pandemonium inevitably finds its way to the studio commissary where there is an obligatory (almost mechanical) pie fight as Lamarr escapes to Grauman's Theatre where the fare is none other than *Blazing Saddles,* and where, trying once more to escape, he is shot down by Bart. The film cuts to Bart and the Kid ultimately riding out of town together, not into a sunset but a waiting limousine in which they are spirited away.

The film had many high spots, not the least of which was the title song, punctuated as it was with whipcracks. Little's work as Bart was nicely underplayed, as was Wilder's Kid. Together they achieve much of the fraternal tenderness (short of the homo-erotic) that had typified *The Producers* and *The Twelve Chairs*. Korman's Lamarr was entertaining, if the archest of archvillains. Karras' Mongo was suitably subliterate. The townspeople were collectively effective in their abbreviated character work. And Slim Pickens, as Lamarr's eager assistant, showed a fine comic flair in what was to be one of his last film roles. Mel was Mel.

But the real showstopper was Madeline Kahn, whose Lili was a marvel of parody. Her oversexed, speech-impeded siren was masterful, and her rendition of Mel's bawdy send-up of Die-trich's "Falling in Love Again," "I'm Tired," was done to perfec-tion (Mel's voice sneaks onto the sound track as one of her Ger-man male chorus members).

That was the best of it. The worst of it was virtually the rest of it. Much of the comedy is overdrawn, much of it two-dimen-sional, and much of it shamelessly scatological (especially a campfire bean repast in full flatulence). The direction, while ade-quate, consists mostly of dispirited camerawork, labored reaction shots, belabored visual puns, and static dialogue two-shots that might have picked up some needed tempo with cutting. On the whole, the best that could be said of the direction was that it did not distract from the comedy, and that is actually saying a great deal. The one inescapable indulgence (for which the director must be held accountable) is the addendum in which the action surges out of its setting. So much of comedy, even farce, relies on a modicum of credibility, which *Blazing Saddles* surprisingly re-tains until the crane pulls back and opens the way to extraneous mayhem (some eight hundred feet of film). If Mel had in mind some comic comment on the filmmaking process itself, it was misplaced here, miscalculated and self-defeating (and besides, it had already been done with dubious results in *The Patsy*, which Jerry Lewis starred in and directed). The digression has the effect of breaking the thread of believability upon which the film's comic anachronism dangles. Mel was back to topping him-self, or trying to.

Self-indulgent finales were the furthest thing from Mel's mind when *Blazing Saddles* was previewed for the executives. It was one thing when the emblazoned opening credits and theme failed to get a rise, but when the Cole Porter gag (the picture in microcosm) fared as poorly, Mel whispered under his breath: "We have just entered cabin 4C on the *Titanic!*" The pained silence persisted throughout, and afterward, Mel repaired to the editing room where he tried to mentally assimilate what seemed like the largest single mistake of his life. His producer and friend, Mike Hertzberg, mentioned a public screening which had been booked for that night, but Mel told him to cancel it. Hertzberg persisted: "No! Invite more people. Let normal people see it. Then we'll know." That night at a Westwood theatre packed to overflowing, the film started rolling at eight o'clock, and with it waves of laughter which scarcely stopped until the final fade out. That was the exact response *Blazing Saddles* received with its general release (and premeditated "R" rating) that February. The reviewers were alternately thrilled and repelled (some were both at once), some proclaiming it a classic, others calling it a disgrace. But while the critics were searching for the right words to express their general bewilderment, the public was turning out in droves, and Mel, who before had made certain critical inroads, now settled for second best—massive popular success (as he called it a "megahit"). And with that, the Bancroft-Brooks became transplanted Californians.

Essentially, Mel had done nothing different than he had always done. True, he had taken his backstage chutzpah and vulgarity and plopped it directly center stage, something no popular filmmaker had had the drive, nerve, or indelicacy to do before. But the film's real success had as much to do with timing as anything else. America in the post-Vietnam mid-seventies wanted to put the war years quickly behind it, and the utter frivolity and escapism of *Blazing Saddles* seemed made to order. Culturally there was a degree of iconoclasm carried over from the activist sixties, but that had more to do with mores that were social and sexual and all but divorced from the political and intellectual. That too played perfectly into the hands of the film.

Mel, who accepted his sudden success and the press attention it entailed not with self-effacing modesty or even an excusable delirious self-congratulation but with an almost pedantic aplomb, tried to tack on a vindicating self-importance by insisting the film was intended as a comedic comment on bigotry and racism. It was a tenuous contention that smacked of afterthought. Racial humor can in fact have both a cathartic and defusing effect, but it can also cut both ways, exploiting and pandering to existing racism. And besides, as Richard Pryor would later point out, artistically Mel had done nothing before or since to support his pose as the comic foe of bigotry.

Good comedy needs no vindication or apologetics. Farce needn't be defended as parody nor parody as satire. Mel no sooner found laughter on a grand scale than he seemed to want more, as if to divine something in his comedy that would outlive the laugh. At surface it might have been a hedge against such ephemera as popular success. But the impulse for survival probably went deeper. Although Mel had matured in many ways since his early days in television, his comic outlook had changed little. He still seemed to work best in opposition to an existing framework, logic, style, or protocol. He was less the social critic than the social vandal, his comedy less commentary than graffiti (often highly literate, but graffiti just the same). In that sense, Mel not so much caught up with seventies America as seventies America caught up with him. As one early mentor put it: "Mel Brooks stood on the corner, and the world turned." He seemed anxious that it not turn again.

The net effect of *Blazing Saddles* was that in Hollywood, where money talks and as Mel was quick to sloganize "funny is money," Mel had earned instant credibility as a filmmaker, with all the clout and creative license that implied. Actually, though, the start of his second Hollywood film preceded the notoriety of his first. Before *Blazing Saddles* had even been completed, Gene Wilder came to Mel with an idea for a Frankenstein spoof about the famous mad scientist's normal doctor great-grandson who unwittingly falls heir to his father's monster-ridden legacy. Mel said he would be interested in working on it with him, and while *Blazing Saddles* was in postproduction, Wilder roughed out a first draft. He was soon joined by Mel, and the two of them started rewriting at Gene's room at the Bel Air Motel. There were differences, of course; Wilder fighting to prevent this from becoming "*Blazing Frankenstein*," Mel insisting that they not make an obscure little "art film." It was, finally, something in between.

When they were through, Mel estimated production costs at $2.2 million and showed the script to Columbia, which in turn showed some interest but offered only $1.7 million. When Columbia rejected a compromise bid of $2 million, Mel took the script to Twentieth Century–Fox where it was read overnight by no less a personage than the company president, Gordon Stulberg. Fox was not only willing to produce the film for $2.8 million but bestowed upon Mel the rare privilege of final cut. With the subsequent release and resounding success of *Blazing Saddles*, *Young Frankenstein* became for Mel the first of a three picture pact with Fox, and the key to a spacious suite of offices at the executive building in West Los Angeles.

The script was shown to Peter Boyle and Marty Feldman, who agreed respectively to play the monster and Igor. Wilder was to play the title role, Madeline Kahn his prissy girl friend, Cloris Leachman a sneering castle caretaker (a hilarious travesty on Dame Judith Anderson). Teri Garr (daughter of vaudevillian and actor Eddie Garr) was cast as a vacuous blond lab assistant, and Kenny Mars as the autocratic head of the Transylvanian constabulary. They were all, as Wilder pointed out, "self-starters," which was just what Mel wanted.

As designed, the story would be the perfect antidote to the dizzyness and delirium of *Blazing Saddles*. *Young Frankenstein* would trace the descent of a presumably sane lecturer on neurosurgery into the musty madness of his notorious ancestor's monster obsession. It would operate essentially by parody, in that it would utilize the plot twists of the original (Igor's inadvertent selection of an abnormal brain, the monster's "reanimation," and general running amok) but use it to its own comic ends. There would be the inevitable Brooks-Wilder touches: the young scientist's comic eccentricities such as insisting on pronouncing his name "Fron-ken-shteen," Igor's stark denial of a bulging spinal abnormality (with wall-eyed wonder "What hump?"), and the fact that the monster's physical massiveness evidently extends proportionately to his sexual anatomy. However, while the material could be made to accommodate a range of comic invention, digression, and hyperbole, it could not afford the unruliness of the nearly amorphous *Blazing Saddles*. This was to be parody, and parody demanded a certain imitative authenticity and literalness, which, as it happened, was precisely what Mel was after at that point.

Mel, like so many other comics, has a strong desire to be taken seriously as an artist. *Blazing Saddles* had in certain circles incited a degree of antipathy toward Mel, not so much for the subject matter or even the envious prosperity it brought, as for what many considered to be his slipshod direction. It was a moot point whether or not the direction had been suited to the subject matter, but it was nonetheless a charge Mel wanted to shake. *Young Frankenstein* was just the film to do it. Mel paid meticulous attention to detail, and in the interest of authenticity, he shot in a back-lit carefully toned black and white. As a "thirties" film in the James Whale style (i.e. an elegant Gothic) he used the scene-to-scene transitional devices of horizontal and vertical wipes (the next image sliding in behind the last), and iris outs (the image as a receding circle on a black background) as well as visual stings (sudden close-ups and cuts) to accompany the stings of the score. Further homage was paid to nostalgia when Mel dusted off and used the actual laboratory set that had been designed for *The Bride of Frankenstein*, a premodern masterpiece of highly stylized gadgetry.

For it all, there is still Mel's weakness for the bad pun, the running gag, the usual knee-to-the-groin subtlety. However, in the film's larger, more serene context, the cheap jokes seem less tawdry. Part of the reason is the tempering influence of Wilder's writing and acting, both geared more to nuance, the dead pan, the throwaway, and one of the better slow burns since Edgar Kennedy. Then again, Mel and Gene do betray a certain weakness for juvenilia, as when the eminent Dr. Frankenstein is asked by a student about his great-grandfather's experiments with reanimation, and the good doctor replies: "My grandfather's work was do-do." It was not the sort of repartee liable to show up in a Lubitsch, a Billy Wilder, a Marx Brothers, or Woody Allen feature. Thankfully, those moments are in the minority and more than balanced by the bright spots, resulting primarily from the beneficial mingling of styles—Mel's, which is hyperbolic, aggressive, and voluble (what Wilder once described as a scatter-gun approach) and Wilder's, which is measured, passive, and selective (what Wilder once compared to a single, well-aimed bullet).†

One of the film's high spots occurs when Dr. Frankenstein, apparently having succeeded in his reanimation work, presents "the creature" to the Bucharest Academy of Science. The two of them, in white tie, top hat, and cane, join in a natty rendition of "Puttin' on the Ritz" which is, incidentally, the only line of dialogue spoken by Peter Boyle in the entire film, the rest being grunts, groans, and hums.

A later superlative scene, arguably the finest sustained Brooks-directed scene, involves Boyle's monster and a blind man played by Gene Hackman. It begins with the monster on the loose and the blind man alone in his home praying for company. The monster arrives, and the blind man assumes his prayers have been answered, passing off the muffled silence as that of a mute. The two sit down to sup, and the blind man heedlessly ladles scalding hot broth onto the monster's lap. At length, they top the meal with a cigar, as the blind man unwittingly lights the monster's thumb instead. Unable to endure more, the overmatched monster departs as the blind man calls after: "Wait, where you going? I was gonna make espresso."

Hackman had requested and even auditioned for the part, and the scene was a full four days in the making for what ultimately amounted to approximately four minutes of film. It was well worth the effort, tastefully written, impeccably played, skillfully directed. In concept, it works much the same way as W. C. Fields's blind Mr. Muckle in *It's A Gift*. In both cases, the blind

† Later, for *The New Yorker*, Wilder would compare Mel's technique to Woody Allen's (Wilder had worked with both men): "The way Woody makes a movie, it's as if he were lighting ten thousand safety matches to illuminate a city. Each one of them a little epiphany, topical, ethnic, or political. What Mel wants to do is set off atom bombs of laughter."

man is the comic perpetrator, the other his victim and stooge. In this case, transforming the monster into straight man is a masterstroke, since his sheer size and wordlessness are wonderfully suited to the classic slow burn (here, finally, literally). Boyle's heavenward takes are priceless, and Hackman's impassive delivery flawless. Mel, meanwhile, plays against his usual directorial instinct of comic enlargement, choosing instead a directorial style whose essence is its unobtrusiveness.

Far more brief, but more to Mel's spirit is what can safely be called the film's comic zenith. It comes after the monster has spirited away the doctor's ironclad fiancée, Elizabeth (Madeline Kahn). When she is next seen her hair is coiffed à la Elsa Lanchester in *The Bride of Frankenstein,* with towering streaked tresses piled on top of her head. The original script had called for the monster to paw her, make lustful sounds, and then mount her as in a polite cutaway, we hear her cries of resistance turn into cries of passion and then segue into song. The problem was the song—a Cole Porter tune had been suggested and rejected, then another, but that failed too. Madeline then suggested that given the pitch of the cry as well as its obvious implication, the song "Ah! Sweet Mystery of Life" might serve the purpose. Mel gave it a try—Boyle rolled over onto Madeline, who let out a sonic crescendo of "ah" 's which peaked and segued into "Ah! Sweet mystery of life, at last I've found you." It was priceless.

In sharp contrast to *Blazing Saddles, Young Frankenstein* was designed to build steadily to a dramatic ending, accomplished in large part through effective cross-cutting between the onrushing enraged villagers and the doctor's final procedure intended to exchange his brain with the monster's. The procedure is disrupted midway, as we cut to the respective marital beds of the monster and Elizabeth, and the doctor and Inga. The former is a passionless scene, the monster is aloof, perusing his *Wall Street Journal* through hornrims. The latter begins with Inga asking what the doctor has gotten in exchange for having given the monster part of his brain. There is a close-up of the leering doctor and then a quick, coy cutaway to the crackling fireplace as we hear Inga's amazed cries of passion trail into yet another chorus of "Ah! Sweet Mystery of Life." It might not have been a genteel coda, but it was a good sight better than dyspeptic cow-pokes.

In all, the shooting lasted fifty-four days and involved location work at the USC Medical School, and Santa Monica's Mayfair Music Hall. Exteriors came by way of an M-G-M back lot, with the balance of interiors shot in an elaborate castle set designed by Dale Hennesy on Stage 5 at Fox. Principal photography was completed on May 15, 1974, editing followed (with Wilder, the protégé, at Mel's side) and *Young Frankenstein* was released that December, in time for year-end Oscar nominations and a planned reissue of *Blazing Saddles*.

Hoping to further capitalize on the earlier film's success, Fox (with Mel's approval) brandished Mel's name at every opportunity, beginning with the *Young Frankenstein*'s closing credits, which reprised "Mel Brooks" with no mention of co-writer Gene Wilder; continuing with the general advertising, including the studio's pressbook which excerpted one review referring to this as "Mel Brooks' Comic Masterpiece"; and ending with the *coup de grâce*, an enormous billboard (at 82 by 61 feet and lighted by fourteen kleig lights, the largest ever) painted on the side of the Playboy Building on Sunset Strip, and touting *Young Franken-stein* as a "Mel Brooks Film" with, again, no mention of writing credits—all in flagrant violation of contractual arrangements and Writers Guild rules.

The Guild's West Coast office went to bat for Wilder, contending that the omission ran afoul of its "minimum basic agreement" requirements stipulating that a writing credit appear wherever a "directed by" credit was given, in the same style and size type as the presentation credit. Walter Bruington acted as arbitrator, hoping to nip in the bud any trend tending to belittle writers' contributions to films. By March, the Guild had won a $10,000 award from Fox ($7,000 of which went to Wilder, the remaining $3,000 to the Guild), with an agreement to clear future advertisements with the Guild, as well as to circulate some two thousand corrective stickers to be plastered about Los Angeles.

The short-lived infighting did nothing to hurt *Young Franken-stein* at the box office. After a respectable round of reviews with several raves, and generally the best notices of Mel's career, the

film did tremendous business, jockeying at times in receipts with
Blazing Saddles. For the first time in his short but stormy film
career, Mel was enjoying the best of both worlds—critical praise
and popular success (although exasperatingly for him, this film,
like *Blazing Saddles* and *The Twelve Chairs* before it, would not
earn a single Oscar nomination).

Mel seemed more than ready for the increased press attention:
expounding for *Newsweek* on Mary Shelley's original intent in
writing Frankenstein: "She was writing about womb envy. Why
else should a man be literally creating a child? Like Freud, she
didn't fool around, she went right to it—man makes a baby"; expanding on his success for the New York *Post*: "I maintain there
is nothing you cannot deal with in comic terms and make a
point. I proved that by spoofing Hitler in *The Producers*. It was
the same thing that was done by Henry Fielding, Jonathan Swift
and Nikolai Gogol—applying humor to serious matters"; or explaining to Hollis Alpert the difference between himself and the
other major contemporary comedy filmmaker, Woody Allen:
"Woody and I don't get in each other's way—we do different
things. His comedy takes a more cerebral tack than mine does.
I've always been very broad. There are critics who regard me as
just a vulgar primitive. I never quarrel." For it all, Mel was
magnified under the lens of adoration, and if he disagreed with
those who openly regarded him as a genius, he seldom publicly
said so. It was this very air of noblesse oblige that finally
prompted Mel's former collaborator Buck Henry to comment:
"Hollywood writers take themselves too seriously. It's the only
place where someone like Mel Brooks could be called a genius."

What with the birth of Max, and Mel's professional second
coming, Anne had herself been comparatively inactive professionally. It had been a conscious decision, but one which demanded that she temporarily set aside her career. As she put it:
"Those two guys really took up my time." (She would later
describe Max as "Mel in miniature.") With the exception of a
performance as Lady Churchill for Richard Attenborough's
Young Winston (Anne first had to submit recordings of her voice
to Churchill's widow for endorsement before landing the part,

and finished her work for the production in midsummer of 1971),
she had done no filmwork since *The Graduate*. Her performance
in *Young Winston* was polished (a youngish grande dame) but
generally lost in the film's bloated epic running length of 145
minutes. The domestic opening in late fall 1972 brought mixed
reviews that expressed some surprise at seeing Anne as Lady
Churchill, some admiration for her handling of a generally
poorly drawn character, and much relief that the film ran no
longer than it did.

In late 1973 Anne signed for a more promising project, the film
version of Neil Simon's popular play, *The Prisoner of Second Avenue*. She would be playing opposite Jack Lemmon, and the production seemed blessed from the outset—a first teaming of two
extremely talented actors with a script that was as literate and
complex as it was entertaining. It is the story of Mel and Edna, a
middle-class, middle-aged, middle-happy couple living in a non-
descript, honeycomb apartment building on Manhattan's Upper
East Side. Their life, which is something between benumbed
contentment and mere complacency but above all secure in routine, is undecorously disrupted as Simon puts the couple through
a series of ordeals worthy of Job. Mel loses his job, the apartment is robbed, Edna gets a job, Mel loses his mind, Edna loses
her job . . . to say nothing of the more minor tribulations of
noisy neighbors, nosey relatives, and exact bus fare. The couple
suffers indignity after indignity (some self-inflicted), and when
they seem on the verge of surrender, they thumb their noses
defiantly and dig the trenches for battle. It is a cruel theme of
endurance, couched in the roughhouse humor of urban battle fatigue. At the comic level, Simon plays off the couple as if they
were both straight men, like some two-headed perplexed George
Burns opposite the city's wildly capricious Gracie Allen. But
rather than let them become chumps or patsies to the city's
mounting inhospitableness, Simon retrenches slightly and rear-
rays them as a new American Gothic—liberated, neurotic, and invincible.

Anne was splendid. This was her first sustained film performance in years, and the first role since *Seesaw* that partook so actively of comedy. There was not the least sign of her technique

having stiffened with disuse—if anything, just the reverse. As Edna, her worried and sometimes pained expression and slender build contrast a tough, indomitable spirit. Anne not so much delivers her lines as chews them in a mint-condition Bronx jawbone. If, under the concrete and asphalt, New York has any common clay, we are convinced it must be she. Edna is the story's chassis, accepting the burdens (especially of Mel's breakdown) while keeping things rolling. As a sinewy, independent woman, who not only has the fortitude to work and support her husband but the grace not to emasculate him with her strength, Anne is eminently believable. And, despite the occasional heavy hand Simon has applied to the plotting, Anne manages the comedy exceptionally well with a personal comic style that seems to come honestly by humor and wisecracks as a hedge against the injustices of life, and not as some glib, gratuitous banter.

As Mel, Lemmon is mercurial, mixing neurosis, moroseness, and melancholy and yet keeping the character short of obnoxiousness. Stylistically, he is the perfect foil for Anne. His frenetic, kinetic, slightly befuddled Mel contrasts her patient, enduring, somewhat bemused Edna. Interestingly enough, both play comedy primarily as straight men (Jack, an accredited master at this, and Anne, who gives nothing away in this regard) but that plays perfectly into the Simon design.

Jack had long admired Anne from afar, and with this film the admiration became personal and mutual, as Anne told his biographer, Don Widener: ". . . just the nicest man I've ever worked with; nice to a point where he's crazy." She was specifically referring to the penultimate scene in which Mel's long-awaited resolution to fight back against life was symbolized by a snow shovel which figured in a plan of vengeance. The scene was shot on a Friday in a tight two-shot, in the course of which Jack accidentally thumped Anne on the leg, raising a large bruise and interrupting the shooting. The scene was resumed the following Monday, with Jack playing as energetically as ever, but protecting Anne by, as it turned out, battering his own leg. The moral of the story was for Anne: "He is so kind he hurt himself rather than injure someone else. That's a little crazy! It's the *nicest* crazy I know, and I know a lot of crazy people."

For his part, Jack was immensely enjoying working with Anne, having been a fan of hers as far back as fifties television when he too was making the rounds of live series. What most impressed Jack about Anne's acting was her directness and her concentrated ability to truly listen as she acted—a quality rare among all but the finest actors.

The Prisoner of Second Avenue was released in March of '75 and received what were at best charitable reviews, though most complaints concerned the film and not the actors. Anne's next two film appearances fared no better. The first featured her as a disinherited German countess who ships aboard a fated zeppelin in *The Hindenburg*. The role allowed her some compelling moments opposite George C. Scott, but for the most part, all acting took a back seat to the airborne spectacle and the imminent conflagration at Lakehurst, New Jersey. Though the film was a latecomer to the disaster-movie trend, it abided by the generic habit of relegating its players to cameos and cutouts while elevating its chosen cataclysm to the level of star.

Anne's next appearance was as a lawyer in one of the cinematic abominations of the year, *Lipstick*, the first, and presumably last, starring vehicle for professional model Margaux Hemingway. The story of rape and revenge was at once sensationalistic and sophomoric, and mostly abysmally acted. Anne's performance was really little more than a character role, which she nonetheless gave more than it or the film deserved, adding what measure of poise and professional competence she could, before it all caved in around her with the story's brutally absurd conclusion.

There was obviously little point in squandering good work on ill-conceived productions, and while Anne awaited better material, a minor offer came her way which would mean disavowing an unwritten pact she and Mel had long ago made and since maintained. It all began with a talented playwright and screenwriter named Ron Clark. Referred by Mel's old friend from Red Bank, Will Jordan, Clark arranged a lunch with Mel and proposed a comedy film whose main distinction would be silence. Mel—whose comic visual component had mostly functioned as an adjunct (or antecedent) to dialogue that at its height worked as a kind of uppercase spoken caption to the visible insanity—unsurprisingly had his doubts. However, Clark prevailed upon Mel and the two of them were joined by two television comedy writers, Rudy DeLuca and Barry Levinson, in a series of tape-recorded pitch sessions that formed the basis of a story which over twelve months found its way to script.

The outcome was *Silent Movie*, a playful bit of self-plagiarism in that it was essentially a stylized account of its own making, a kind of comedy *vérité*. It tells of a downtrodden ex-alcoholic director who hits upon the idea of making a silent movie and thus rescuing from possible ruin Big Pictures Studio, which is on the verge of being swallowed up by the villainous conglomerate Engulf and Devour. The studio head at first refuses but finally acquiesces, provided the director (Mel Funn) can recruit enough "stars" to guarantee the project's success. The balance of the plot concerns that star-by-star recruitment by Mel and his two sidekicks, Marty Eggs and Dom Bell, as Mr. Engulf and Mr. Devour do everything in their power to thwart the plan.

Meanwhile, the trio pursues its luminaries—Burt Reynolds, James Caan, Paul Newman, Marcel Marceau, Liza Minnelli, and *Anne Bancroft*—most of whom put up a mild resistance before succumbing to the persistent offers. In the end, Engulf and Devour nearly succeed in pirating and destroying the lone completed print, but are foiled as the film is previewed to thunderous applause and jubilation.

It was a risky project, despite the Mel Brooks imprint and the stellar cast. It was to be a completely silent movie, except for a musical soundtrack, sound effects, and a single uttered work of dialogue (logically enough, Marceau, who replies to requests to appear in the fictional movie with a curt "no!"). The film was well cast; in addition to those stars literally playing themselves, were Mel, Marty Feldman, and Dom DeLuise essentially playing themselves, with Harry Gould and Ron Carey as the conglomerate ne'er-do-wells, Harry Ritz and Henny Youngman in walk-ons, and Bernadette Peters in a girl friend role which Madeline Kahn declined. The part of the studio president was played by Sid Caesar.

Shooting began on January 5, 1976, and the set was declared off-limits to the press. Mel kept his co-writers close by throughout, consulting them repeatedly and paying them a retainer of sorts. If Mel seemed to be expiating past mistreatment of collaborators, he was doing so in grand style.

Principal photography was completed with comparative speed and ease without the encumbrance of sound. The film opened the following June, won warm approval, and carried at the box office as much on its own merits as on the strength of Mel's name, which adorned the film at every level. The public was charmed but among show business insiders, there was some grousing. Many viewed the film as mere conceit in that it was about itself. Others took exception to what was said to be the blatant gimmickry of a silent movie in a sound era that was already half a century old. Still others criticized Mel for casting himself in the featured role of Mel Funn, explaining that while he played the part well enough, there were easily a half-dozen other comic actors who might have played it better. And finally there were those associates and fans from the days of "Your Show of Shows" and "Caesar's Hour" who were genuinely appalled at the irony of seeing Sid Caesar play second banana to Mel, in a silent picture no less.

Whatever the validity of dissent, *Silent Movie* still had much to recommend it. The sight gags worked with astonishing consistency, helped in spots by cleverly conceived titles. The film moved briskly through its long (for the silent medium) eighty-eight minutes, sustained by a sturdily constructed script and propelled by several good-natured performances. In addition, Mel's acting, if something short of first-rate pantomime, was more than adequate to the occasion, with some touching as well as comic moments, and one hilarious dream sequence with Peters à la Astaire and Rogers.

The film's epicenter was undoubtedly the scene with Anne. It began with Mel, Marty, and Dom going busily about their star casting, catching up with Anne at a local cabaret. They are dressed as dancing caballeros and Anne is dressed to the teeth in an elegant flame-red satin gown with white feather boa. She is encircled by an entourage of dashing young men, and is no sooner seated than the floor show begins and the bungling trio whisks her out of her seat for a tricornered tango. Each dramatic pirouette sends her crashing into another object, with a cutaway reaction shot which has Anne crossing her eyes in exaggerated pain. The tango concludes with a matchless pair of takes, beginning with Marty Feldman's naturally wall-eyed gaze and ending with Anne's lovely, soulful eyes partaking in ocular acrobatics—side to side, crossed separately and simultaneously—that put Feldman to shame. It was Anne's first public display of her distinctive gift since her days at P.S. 12, and she seemed to be having the time of her life.

Silent Movie is, in the final analysis, less interesting individually for Anne and Mel, than it is for the inevitable intersection of their careers. The mutual influence of their life together is implicit, with Mel tackling a sustained if lightweight bit of acting and Anne indulging a fine antic humor that might have struck her as unconscionable years before. It is, as one friend pointed out, all the public testimony their marriage would ever require.

By 1977, Mel had become something between a popular national treasure, and an unrelieved cultural phenomenon. His popularity continued to build, through a recorded reprise of his *2000 Year Old Man* routine with Carl Reiner (*2000 and Thirteen* came about by popular demand) and easily bridged a minor setback with a failed television series (a Robin Hood spoof, "When Things Were Rotten," which misapplied the anachronistic method of *Blazing Saddles*). By the close of 1976, Mel was fifth on the list of top ten box-office attractions, behind such names as Robert Redford, Jack Nicholson, Dustin Hoffman, and Clint Eastwood, and ahead of his friend Burt Reynolds whom he was in the habit of telephoning and announcing: "Hello, Six, this is Five speaking." Mel was also starting to attract some of the more formal recognition he had coveted, including the 1977 National Association of Theatre Owners Director of the Year Award. This last occasion he used as a platform from which to take stock of his film work, adopting an almost supercilious posture as something of a dean of comedy filmmakers. As quoted in *Daily Variety*:

I was a little surprised that NATO would have the good sense. I was surprised that a comedy director was chosen as director of the year because normally we are not. Normally we are overlooked as directors, and we are considered funny men or comic personalities, but we are not considered film directors.

I'm very proud and I hope that maybe the Academy of Motion Picture Arts and Sciences will look at this, and maybe it will make some sense to them.‡ If we go back in time and talk about great motion pictures, the great golden era of silent pictures, what do you see? We talk about *Greed* and *Birth of a Nation*, they are not with us. They are in museums. But *The Gold Rush* and *The Navigator*—they are with us today. . . .

Directing a movie is a very hard job. It's the same job for me as it is for Francis Coppola—except that I, in addition to setting my life and translating my performances, and metamorphosing an actor from one character to another, I actually evoke laughter from the audience; and not many directors can do that with the consistency I can.

I feel that in recognizing me as the director of the year, NATO is in a sense not only saluting me, but saluting such directors as Charles Chaplin, Buster Keaton, Paul Mazursky, Woody Allen, Stan Laurel and great, great film directors like Ernst Lubitsch and Billy Wilder, who have worked for many years in the fields of comedy, harvesting a very important and prized possession—humor.

I feel that my work, if it's examined properly, has a serious base to it. . . . When a black sheriff walks into a white town, even though you are laughing hysterically, I am saying some-

‡ That year, Woody Allen's *Annie Hall* won four Oscars.

thing very important about human nature and the human condition. When Leo Bloom, in *The Producers,* wants to succeed from being a grubby little gray accountant into a big-spending, blooming Broadway producer, I am saying something serious and important about our hopes and aspirations. In *The Twelve Chairs,* when I tell you that love is more important than greed, I am being serious.

Ultimately the comic wanted more than anything else to be taken seriously. The actress had long ago earned that right, as well as the freedom to be taken, on occasion, less than seriously. Both had, in separate ways, come of age. Few could argue the artistry of Anne's accomplishments, few the immensity of Mel's. Anne has already given the public much that is enduring and classic, and is even trying her hand at directing. Whether Mel's work will prove more than evanescent remains to be seen, but the essential truth is that he has created laughter in his time and that is never to be underestimated. As Richard Pryor frankly attested, whatever Mel's imperfections: "I still think he's a funny motherfucker."

New York City, 1977

A mild November evening. In the wings at the Morosco Theatre, Anne Bancroft prepares to go on in *Golda*. The play has been written by William Gibson, directed by Arthur Penn, and stars Anne as Golda Meir. There is a sense of symmetry rare in the theatre, as if Gittel Mosca had grown up to become Prime Minister of Israel. Actually, there have been other though unwanted parallels to *Two for the Seesaw*. The out-of-town tryout for *Golda* had been disheartening. In Baltimore a costly visual component was dropped from the show. In Boston the scenery and wardrobe were destroyed by fire. In New York the reviews have been better for Anne than for the play, but short of the raves necessary to recoup the $500,000 investment.

Worse yet, Anne has already begun to show the early signs of the acute bronchitis that will ultimately close the play. Still, she can take some comfort in the fine critical and popular reception accorded *The Turning Point*, a motion picture appearing across town in which she stars with Shirley MacLaine. The play will earn Anne a Tony nomination, the film an Oscar nomination.

In the orchestra section of the Morosco Theatre, Mel Brooks prepares to watch his wife take the stage. He will cry, as he has each time he's seen *Golda*. In just over a month, Mel's latest movie will open in New York on Christmas Day. It is a Hitchcock take-off with Mel as producer, director, co-writer, and star. He has also written the title song, which he sings in the course of the movie. *High Anxiety* will be released in time for year-end Oscar nominations, but will receive none. It will be a financial success.

In the second row of the balcony at the Morosco Theatre, a man sits leafing through his *Playbill*. He turns to his wife and whispers: "Did you know Anne Bancroft is married to Mel Brooks?"

She didn't. "I consider her a serious person."

He ponders: "How could anyone be married to him? He could drive you nuts."

She pauses, then answers: "They must laugh a lot."

At that, the house lights dim, then fade to black. The stage lights come up, the play is on.

ACKNOWLEDGMENTS

This book was conceived in good faith out of admiration for the subjects. It was written with their prior knowledge, but, regrettably, without their co-operation or blessing. Research and writing were therefore more difficult, though infinitely more rewarding as journalistic portraiture and critical biography. What was lost in subjectivity was, I believe, made up for in balance, perspective, fairness, and objectivity.

There were many people who made the task less arduous by generously contributing reminiscences, observations, and insights. They know who they are and know I am profoundly grateful for their time and help.

I am indebted to Sam Vaughan, who is a gentleman, a diplomat, and a firm friend of the First Amendment, and whose fondness for the long shot gave a young writer his legs.

I especially want to thank my editor, Lisa Drew, who is an unfaltering friend and ally. Her support and faith are only surpassed by her threshold for bad jokes. All authors should be blessed with such editors.

Heather Kilpatrick and Jerry Toner were most instructive, Lisa Healy and Mary Trone persevering and patient.

Contrary to popular belief, some institutions have feelings, too. My appreciation to the Theatre Research Collection of the Lincoln Center Library, the Motion Picture Section of the Library of Congress, the Museum of Broadcasting, and the Research Library of the Academy of Motion Picture Arts and Sciences.

My gratitude to my contacts at CBS, Kathy Sulkes, Nina Weinstein, and Betsy Broesamle.

I want very much to thank my mentors, Richard Slotkin and

especially Jeanine Basinger, without whose friendship, guidance, and active encouragement I'd still be moving Steinways in the Back Bay.

For their kind assistance, thanks also to Ted Sennett, Rhonda Bloom, and Dr. D. M. Kirschenbaum.

Max Liebman was in many ways the linchpin of this book. His knowledge of show business is encyclopedic, his taste impeccable, his wisdom boundless, his zest for life inspirational. Above all, he has paid me the high compliment of his friendship. This is the redemption of writing.

I come from a family of writers—some of them talking writers, some of them writing writers. I owe everything to them. My love to my parents Don and Ev, my sister Linda, and my brother Gene. Bobby Kligman is like family, and though he is not here to see this book, he is somewhere somehow at this very moment smiling and saying "shmuck."

Sylvia Shepard, my wife, lover, friend, and critic, has been a marvel throughout. The book simply could not have been written without her.

Thanks also to my fair-haired mishpocheh: Tad and Jane, Chuck and Jo, Tim, Jules, Bill, Buzz, Charlie, and Carey, Shepards all, and to Andra Georges, like me the spice of the strain.

And finally, thanks to my associates and especially my friends who make it all worthwhile: Orren Alperstein, Dana Asbury, Arthur Axelman, Louise Beach, Hilda Bijur, Victoria Bijur, Leo Bookman, Dale Brodsky, Cappy Cappalupo, Randy and Joan Covitz, Monica Davies, Abner Dean, Brian Firestone, Mark Frost, Susan Gage, Seth Gelblum, Steve Greenhouse, Robin Groves, Richard Hunt, Genevieve Kerr, Barb and Ron Kohn, Ed Levine, Biff Liff, Anne Meara, Bill Pearson, Nate and Pat Pearson, Buddy and Helen Pennington, Barbara Petersen, John Pitcher, Maizie Ragan, Pushka Shenker, Larry Siegel, Betsy Simpson, Brian Skarstad, Mary and David Stifler, Jerry Stiller, Kathy Toomey, Frank Trechsel, Scott Volk, Bill Watts, Michael Wilson, and, of course, Pearl.

Willy Holtzman
Wilton, Connecticut
January 1979

Index

Goldsmith, Oliver, 259
Goldwyn, Sam, 51
Good and Naughty, 2
Goode, Peter, 79–80
Good Housekeeping (magazine), 73
Goodman, Hal, 114
Gordon, Bruce, 203
Gorilla at Large, 100–1
Gotham Health Club, 59
Gottlieb, Morton, 122
Gould, Harry, 277
Gould, Jack, 121
Graduate, The, 234, 235–38,
    244–45, 250, 253, 274
Graham, Ronny, 84
Granger, Farley, 103
Granger, Stewart, 104
Grant, Cary, 202
Graves, Peter, 103
Greed, 280
Green, Janet, 220
Greenberg, Henry, 1
Greene, Herbert, 203
Greenwich Village, 55–56, 135–36,
    155, 159, 170, 183, 195, 199, 204
Gregory, Frank, 48
Grimes, Burleigh, 2
Grossinger's (resort), 9, 34
Group Theatre, 85
Guilt of Janet Ames, The, 36
Gunty, Morty, 158

Hackman, Gene, 270, 271
Hadassah, 183
Halofcenter, Larry, 63
Hamilton, Murray, 235
Hamlet, 63
Hanley, William, 235
Harburg, Yip, 53
Hardwicke, Cedric, 213
Hardy, Thomas, 20
Harnick, Sheldon, 84
Harris, Barbara, 206
Harris, Bentley M., 106
Harris, Joey, 137–38
Harris, Julie, 182
Hart, Moss, 54, 158
Hartman, Don, 54
Hayes, Bill, 63, 65
Hayes, Helen, 2
"Head of the Family," 158

Heath, Bob, 211
Heflin, Van, 110
Heim, Alan, 257
Heller, Joseph, 204
Hellman, Lillian, 253
Hemingway, Margaux, 276
Hennesy, Dale, 272
Henry, Buck, 215–16, 217, 223, 235,
    237, 244, 251, 273
Hepburn, Audrey, 196
Hepburn, Katharine, 206, 250–51
Herbert Berghof (HB) Studio, 132,
    136, 144, 169, 170
Herlie, Eileen, 189, 194
Herman, Babe, 2
Hertzberg, Michael, 233, 255, 266
Heston, Charlton, 43
Hewett, Christopher, 234, 249
Hewitt, Tarzan, 25
Hickey, Neil, 202
High Noon, 92
Hiken, Nat, 123
Hindenburg, The, 276
Hitchcock, Alfred, 6, 106
Hitler, Adolf, 12
Hoffman, Dustin, 234, 235, 236–38,
    245, 279
"Holiday on Wheels," 157
Hollywood Reporter, The, 251
Hope, Bob, 88
"Hope for the Best, Expect the
    Worst," 257
Hopper, Hedda, 220
Horner, Harry, 102
Huddleston, David, 261
Hughes, Tresa, 183
Hull, Henry, 45
Hurok, Sol, 74, 75
Hussman, Ron, 189
Huston, John, 80
Huxley, Aldous, 225
Hyman, Jo, 37

I Can Get It for You Wholesale, 205
"I Don't Know," 65
"I Get a Kick Out of You," 263
I'm Getting Married, 234
Impossible Years, The, 241
"I'm Tired," 265
Inge, William, 181

Washington *Evening Star*, 143
Washington *Post*, 143
Watts, Richard, Jr., 127, 151–52,
   181, 194, 208, 227
Wayne, David, 122
Wayne, John, 221
Weaver, Fritz, 189
Weaver, Pat, 56, 57, 61, 98, 111
Webb, Charles, 228, 235
Webster, Tony, 87, 123
Welk, Lawrence, 127
Welles, Orson, 122
Welsh, Cecil and Milton, 1
West, Mae, 2
Whale, James, 269
*What Ever Happened to Baby
   Jane?*, 206, 207
What Every Woman Knows (Bar-
   rie), 2
What Makes Sammy Run? (Schul-
   berg), 29
What's Up, Tiger Lily?, 233
"When Things Were Rotten," 279
"Whiffenpoof Song, The," 56, 65
Whiting, John, 225
Widener, Don, 275
Widmark, Richard, 73
Wilbur Theatre, 179
Wilde, Cornel, 75
Wilder, Billy, 270, 280
Wilder, Gene, 206, 233–34, 239,
   249–50, 251, 261, 267–68, 272
Wilk, Max, 113
William Morris Agency, 56, 114,
   115, 169, 188
Williams, Billy, 63
Williams, Tennessee, 181
Williams, William B., 165, 224
Willingham, Calder, 235
Wilson, Earl, 204, 251
Wilson, Elizabeth, 235, 236
Wilson and Rich (vaudeville team),
   7
Windsor, Marie, 106

Winter Garden Theatre, 193, 195,
   203–4
Wintertime (Valtin), 44
Wishy, Joe, 191
Women's Wear Daily, 127
Wonderful Town, 111
Works Progress Administration
   (WPA), 15, 17
World Pacific Records, 161, 164,
   165
World War II, 12, 27–28
Wright, Teresa, 172
Writers Guild, 61, 235, 272

Yiddish language, 2, 3, 8, 11, 64
Yonkers High School, 34
York, Jeremy, 108
Young and Rubicam Advertising
   Agency, 56, 224
Young Frankenstein, 268–73
Youngman, Henny, 277
Young Winston, 273–74
"Your Show of Shows," 27, 38–39,
   51–52, 62–70, 85, 86, 87–98, 111,
   112, 113, 115, 116, 118, 120, 121,
   128, 155, 157, 158, 185, 217, 225,
   226, 278; awards, 86; broadcast
   première of, 64–65; "cliché"
   sketches, 88–90; compared to
   "Caesar's Hour," 121; end of,
   98; foreign parodies, 95–96;
   hiatus, 80–81; *High Noon* parody,
   92–93; musical spoofs, 91–92;
   ratings (1953 season), 97; *Shane*
   parody, 93–94; spy movie
   parodies, 94–95

Zanuck, Darryl F., 72, 73
Zelinka, Sidney, 157
Ziegfeld, Florenz, 138, 243
Ziegfeld Follies, 62
Ziegfeld Theatre, 188
Zinnemann, Fred, 47